IN PRAISE OF

THE FORGOTTEN HISTORY OF AFRICAN AMERICAN BASEBALL

"Larry Hogan's *The Forgotten History of African American Baseball* is a compelling eye-opener of a narrative that anyone hoping to get the full story of baseball in America should read. It is a story in which truly heroic individuals overcome evil—personified by Jim Crow and Judge Lynch—and prevail. Hogan brings those heroes back to life in a most readable book."

Paul Dickson, author of *Bill Veeck: Baseball's Greatest Maverick* and a 2013 Chadwick Award recipient

"*The Forgotten History of African American Baseball* is an important addition to the chronicles of baseball. It brings alive a forgotten era in our social history, by bringing alive the remarkable men whose passion and pride knew no bounds."

Dave Kaplan, Director, Yogi Berra Museum & Learning Center

"Historian Larry Hogan basks in baseball's shadowed fields. He is a national treasure, and with *The Forgotten History of African American Baseball* he culminates decades of inspired investigation and—best of all for readers—great tales too long untold. My cap is off to him."

John Thorn, Official Historian of Major League Baseball

"Professor Hogan is a dedicated historian, passionate about casting a light on the people and the sport of baseball in eras that were marked by the segregation and injustice that prevailed across America. Yet, if you know him like I do, I see he's connected the dots, not only through research but by immersing himself in the people, places, and times to clearly represent these fascinating and almost bygone times. He's woven the fabric of this historical quilt together from both research and relationships with those players and individuals who lived through those times.

Whether those referenced here are little known or prominent, because of them all I've been able to build a great life through the game of baseball. I respect and honor those people and their contributions. So, thank you Dr. Larry Hogan for this latest reflection and tribute to the Negro Leagues. To me, the institution, the teams, and the people involved are national treasures."

Dave Winfield, National Baseball Hall of Fame 2001, developer of the 2008 MLB Negro League Draft and Tribute to the Negro Leagues

"Larry Hogan's *The Forgotten History of African American Baseball* stands firmly on the formidable shoulders of earlier historical studies on the life and times of modern black Americans under pressure, those who created a veritable world within a world. Their now nearly vanished world of baseball was at once a metaphor for talent and achievement, rituals, and black identity during the Jim Crow era. It was also a world that far too many Americans know little of. Hogan sheds a brilliant light on what is now known about black baseball, now ennobled as an enduring contribution to American culture, memory, and the national pastime."

Clement Alexander Price, Board of Governors Distinguished Service Professor of History, Rutgers University, Newark Campus

The Forgotten History of African American Baseball

Lawrence D. Hogan

 PRAEGER

AN IMPRINT OF ABC-CLIO, LLC
Santa Barbara, California • Denver, Colorado • Oxford, England

Library of Congress Cataloging-in-Publication Data

Hogan, Lawrence D., 1944–
   The forgotten history of African American baseball / Lawrence D. Hogan.
      pages cm
   Includes index.
   ISBN 978-0-313-37984-0 (hardback) — ISBN 978-0-313-37985-7 (ebook)
1. Negro leagues—History.   2. African American baseball players—History.
3. Baseball—United States—History.   I. Title.
   GV875.N35H64   2014
   796.357—dc23   2013034015

ISBN: 978-0-313-37984-0
EISBN: 978-0-313-37985-7

18 17 16 15 14   1 2 3 4 5

This book is also available on the World Wide Web as an eBook.
Visit www.abc-clio.com for details.

Praeger
An Imprint of ABC-CLIO, LLC

ABC-CLIO, LLC
130 Cremona Drive, P.O. Box 1911
Santa Barbara, California 93116-1911

This book is printed on acid-free paper ∞

Manufactured in the United States of America

"The more I met Alexander Crummell, the more I felt how much that world was losing which knew so little of him. In another age he might have sat among the elders of the land in purple bordered toga; in another country mothers might have sung him to the cradles.

He did his work—he did it nobly and well; and yet I sorrow that here he worked alone, with so little human sympathy. His name today, in this broad land, means little, and comes to fifty million ears laden with no incense of memory nor emulation. And herein lies the tragedy of the age; not that men are poor, all men know something of poverty; not that men are wicked, who is good? Not that men are ignorant, what is Truth? Nay, but that men know so little of men."

W. E. B. Du Bois, "Of Alexander Crummell"
From *The Souls of Black Folk*, 1903

"The legacy left by the enslaved ancestors of blues-oriented contemporary U.S. Negroes includes a disposition to confront the most unpromising circumstances and make the most of what there is to go on, regardless of the odds—and not without finding delight in the process or forgetting mortality at the height of ecstasy."

Albert Murray
From *Stomping the Blues*

To the extraordinary men and women of the black press for the legacy of grace and dignity you have left us in your record of great deeds and hard struggles.

To the extraordinary men and women of black baseball for the legacy of grace and dignity you have left us in your record of great deeds and hard struggles.

Contents

Acknowledgments

Inspiration for this book comes from those who have made me who I am, and for whom I owe a debt of gratitude and love that is incalculable—family and friends too numerous to acknowledge individually, except for those who count the most. Sally, Rebecca, Matthew, Elizabeth, our grand grands, mom and dad, Helen, Mary Elizabeth, Dan, and mom and dad again in Kate and Bob.

The writing of this book owes a considerable debt of gratitude to a team of authors who I worked with on *Shades of Glory.* As I was educated by them, and shaped and edited with them their contribution to that work, and researched into the areas about which they wrote, I found myself time and again connected in enriching and novel ways to the character and characters of the history of black baseball. And their own work, outside the confines of *Shades of Glory,* was and remains today, as they advance that work, a considerable part of the inspiration for what I am able to do here and elsewhere with this history of black baseball. A special bow in the direction of James Overmyer, Michael Lomax, Neil Lanctot, Rob Ruck, the late Robert Peterson, Adrian Burgos, Leslie Heaphy, and codirectors for the Baseball Hall of Fame's "Out of the Shadows" project Dick Clark and Larry Lester. So often through these pages, I find myself writing about people, places, and events that their own work has illuminated and added a depth of substance to that goes well beyond where I take this story of the extraordinary men and women of black baseball. Any mistakes here are of course my own responsibility. Corrections for those mistakes will, I suspect, often be found in the pages of these scholars' own works penned by our team of *Shades of Glory* friends and colleagues.

A special singling out is called for of scholar, colleague, and friend, Jules Tygiel, who was an inspiration in the work that he did and in the way that he lived a life that in its last stages was extraordinarily difficult to live with the grace and dignity he was able to show us.

A second special singling out is for filmmaker Thomas C. Guy Jr., who we lost much too early. Rest in Peace my friend.

For someone who has been at work in this subject matter for as long as I have, it is extraordinary to see the attention accorded in print today to the deeds and derring-dos of the men and women of black baseball. Much of that work I hope is appropriately acknowledged in the Bibliography section of this book. Here I would like to acknowledge and bow in the direction of the scholarship in this area of three individuals who I think must be called the founding fathers: again the late Bob Peterson, John Holway, and Jim Riley. Each, in his own distinctive way, with a respect and love for the men and women about whom they wrote, have paved a road that everyone who follows in their wake must acknowledge as the path that anyone who comes to this wonderful history tale must be influenced and directed by. Thank you Bob, John, and Jim.

Everyone who researches and writes should be blessed with a research library, archives, and tenders to the history they work with as are found in Cooperstown, New York, at the National Baseball Hall of Fame. A special acknowledgment goes forth to my friends Pat Kelly, keeper of the photos, and Jim Gates, keeper of the record.

Several special friends and colleagues working in wonderful ways in the area of public history and public education warrant acknowledgment for the good work they do, and the influence they have had on your author. First and foremost my Pop Lloyd Project stalwarts, Michael Everett and his wife, Kathy Whitmore in Atlantic City, along with our dear Belinda Manning who carries forward in her person and life the wonderfulness of her father Max, and her mother Dorothy. The indefatigable Frank Ceresi in Washington, D.C. At Harpers Ferry, West Virginia, national park ranger in charge of education, Todd Bolton. In Houston, my good friend Michael Berberich. And in very special ways in Rhode Island where public history work and solid, path-breaking research and writing are combined in the person of Dr. Robert Cvornyek, professor of history at Rhode Island College.

At Union County College, my work has been considerably aided by research librarian Sean Chen, acquisitions librarian Susan Bissett, and by my two "computer doctors" Beth Sutherland and Vince Tanzi, who have offered on countless occasions technical expertise, while always showing considerable patience in dealing with an "old-fashioned" fellow who has "sometimes" needed the experts to aid and abet.

Thanks go out to the two editors I have worked with at ABC-CLIO/ Praeger: Dan Harmon, who first saw in this manuscript the promise of a fine book, and Beth Ptalis, who picked up where Dan left off in the editing process and has contributed significantly in a professional way to making this work considerably better than it was when she first came to it.

Introduction: Baseball, and Something More Besides

O n display in these pages is the grace of field and at bat, and the baseball smarts and experiences of those who played their ball across more than 100 years of Jim Crow "Sundown" baseball. While *The Forgotten History of African American Baseball* is sharply and emphatically focused on the history of African American professional baseball, it is also about the heart and soul of the black experience in America during the era of our nation's color line.

In his dissent in the infamous *Plessy v. Ferguson* Supreme Court decision (1896), Supreme Court Justice John M. Harlan stated best the way it should have been for a nation founded on the proposition that "all men are created equal and endowed by their Creator with certain inalienable rights":

> In view of the constitution, in the eye of the law, there is in this country no superior, dominant, ruling class of citizens. There is no caste here. Our constitution is color-blind, and neither knows nor tolerates classes among citizens. In respect of civil rights, all citizens are equal before the law. The humblest is the peer of the most powerful. The law regards man as man, and takes no account of his surroundings or of his color when his civil rights as guaranteed by the supreme law of the land are involved. It is therefore to be regretted that this high tribunal, the final expositor of the fundamental law of the land, has reached the conclusion that it is competent for a state to regulate the

enjoyment by citizens of their civil rights solely upon the basis of race. In my opinion, the judgment this day rendered will, in time, prove to be quite as pernicious as the decision made by this tribunal in the Dred Scott Case.[1]

Justice Harlan's was a lone voice on a court that ruled 8 to 1 that his notion of who we were supposed to be would not be affirmed in the highest law of the land. The opposite notion of separation based on segregation was present in the earliest moments of American baseball when slaves in the pre–Civil War American South played a new game called "town ball," and free blacks in northern cities began to form teams that played largely against other black clubs. Reflecting the segregated order that *Plessy* had codified, two distinct versions of America's national pastime existed until April 18, 1946, when Jack Roosevelt Robinson took the field for the Montreal Royals of the International League of Baseball Clubs to integrate what was known as organized professional baseball.

One notable black journalist, R. Rollo Wilson, called the black version of that separate game "Sundown" baseball.[2] Sundown baseball's most famous modern chronicler, Robert Peterson, memorably wrote about largely forgotten teams and great players that played America's national pastime on fields where "only the ball was white."[3] Another notable journalist, Art Rust, recollecting what that separate era was like, characterized it as a baseball time defined by the cry, "Get that nigger off the field."[4]

The Forgotten History of African American Baseball is aimed at giving readers the opportunity to observe the experiences of those who played their ball across America's 100 years of Jim Crow baseball. Theirs were fields where either explicitly or implicitly strictures were in place that kept many black players off the playing surfaces of organized professional and amateur baseball. If you were a "Negro" in Jim Crow America, you might secure access to our nation's playing fields as a clown and entertainer for white audiences who expected stereotypical buffoonery from someone of your skin tone. If you were good enough to be a professional at your game, you could play against other all-black clubs on those same playing fields—as long as you adhered in your demeanor to what was expected of a "Negro." And you could even play against white professional teams in exhibition, postseason, and barnstorming contests galore—as long as your presence could make the turnstiles click sufficiently to swell the bank accounts of your white hosts. But in all these instances, these African American baseball men offered a quality of play and a quality of character that was second to none in the history of our national pastime. It is that play and that character that we seek out and showcase on these pages. Their stories are manifold and numerous, but in sum, they worked toward a better life, and a better world.

The Forgotten History of African American Baseball will also bring to the fore those who owned black teams, the sportswriters who wrote about black baseball, special fans of the game, such as the great comedian Bert Williams, and special moments in the black version of America's national pastime. As far as possible, these sketches are based on sources that were contemporary to the people and events about which we write.

Much of the focus will be celebratory, for "Sundown" baseball was a game that the men and women who played it relished with a glee and possessiveness that only those who have had the doors of life's opportunity closed in their face can experience. "There is nothing like getting your body to do all it has to do on a baseball field," Buck O'Neil tells us in remembering his days as a Kansas City Monarch in the Negro American League. "It is as good as sex. It is as good as music. It fills you up. Waste no tears on me. I didn't come along too early. I was right on time."[5]

But celebration is by no means what all of this story is about. As we follow the experiences of our sports heroes, we will also regularly glimpse the closing of doors—athletic and otherwise—that the players who occupy these pages, and the fans who followed their feats, experienced as a given in a world where racism ruled. And of course we will also see protests against those door closings—some direct in what they were demanding, others subtle in simply refuting racist stereotyping with counter examples. By such protest and by example, our nation could be pointed toward that hoped for day when Americans would judge their fellow citizens not by "the color of their skin but by the quality of their character."

From this peculiar American mix of opportunity denied, opportunity made, and opportunity seized comes a picture of a world that was about much more than the day's final tally of runs, hits, and errors. The historian Clement Price notes what that "much more" entailed:

We talk a lot about the Civil Rights Movement and who starts it. It may be that the Civil Rights Movement had many beginnings. Some of those beginnings are found on buses and at lunch counters and on dusky roads in the South, and on the playing fields of Negro baseball teams. It seems to me these guys must have known they were involved in the most American of all pursuits, competition. But they weren't recognized, they weren't lionized in the larger American society. They were only recognized, appreciated if you will by their own people. So I think they must have looked forward to the day when perhaps on their own terms they would be recognized as great athletes, great American athletes. It seems to me those sentiments, that vision is one of the beginnings, one of the seeds of the Civil Rights Movement.[6]

What the renowned historian and social critic Jacques Barzun has said about America in *God's Country and Mine* certainly fits that part of our nation's history on which we focus our attention: "Whoever wants to know the heart and mind of America had better learn baseball, the rules and realities of the game, and do it first by watching some high school or small town teams." One could follow far less fruitful paths in seeking "the heart and mind" of the American people than the path offered by the history of our nation's national pastime, the American game of baseball—especially, as we shall see, the "Sundown" version of that game.[7]

Just ask Max Manning about that game in 1937 in Pleasantville, New Jersey, when he proved he belonged on his high school varsity team.

The new varsity member was brought in with the bases loaded and no outs in late innings with the game on the line. He was wearing a junior varsity jersey. His father heard a fan next to him say, "Why are they bringing him in. Everyone knows his kind can't think." The untested youngster proceeded to pick a runner off third, and then strike out the next two batters. The fans erupted in cheers, with the "his kind can't think" commentator first on his feet with shouts of "give him a first team jersey."

In the fall of 1937, in his senior year in high school, Max Manning received a letter from former major leaguer Max Bishop: "I am scouting for the Detroit baseball Club and your name was sent to me. Would appreciate you filling out the enclosed player information blank and if you are not obligated to any club in organized ball would like to see you in action early next spring. Hoping to hear from you soon, and with kind regards."[8]

Manning did not reply to the letter from the white scout who thought he was writing to a white recruit. Two years later, after one year at Lincoln University, Max Manning would be in the starting rotation for the Newark Eagles of the Negro National League. After a three-year stint in the armed forces during World War II, he led the Eagles to the Negro League World Championship in 1946. A sore arm would take him out of professional baseball after 1949. His BA in education from Glassboro State College led to a 27-year career as an elementary teacher in his hometown of Pleasantville, New Jersey. In all the years of his teaching, he never once mentioned to students that he was a pitcher of major league caliber who in his youth was "mistakenly" offered a tryout by a major league scout.

The Pleasantville, New Jersey, Varsity High School baseball squad in 1937. Max Manning appears in the second row, to the far right. (Personal collection of Lawrence Hogan)

A UNIQUE VOICE—ALVIN E. WHITE

While Max Manning was doing his pitching in high school and in the Negro Leagues, Alvin White was doing his "hurling" in black newspapers across our nation. When it comes to Al White, I am reminded of what the critic Stanley Kaufman said about the acting of the ageing Fredric March in *The Iceman Cometh:* "He didn't trade on the fact of his age; he acted in a good role for which he was now the right age."[9] Across the last 10 years of a "good role" that filled 90 summers, Alvin E. White—a unique voice from the ranks of black journalism—shared with me experiences that stretched from his growing up in the 1890s in a Richmond, Virginia, where one could almost still smell the smoke of Civil War cannon and musketry, to a nursing home in Atlanta of the 1980s, where he spent his last years physically infirm but with no loss of mental and spiritual faculties.

From the spring of 1975 to his death in December 1985, I came to know Alvin White as a historical resource, mentor, and friend. Those were the last 10 years of a life he had filled with the observation, reporting, and writing of a news record that some of us are fortunate to know now as an enriching history. That sharing included several hundred pages of correspondence and several personal visits often stretching across several days each, first in his residency in Worcester, Massachusetts, where he was living with his daughter, son-in-law, and cherished granddaughter, and then in Atlanta where declining health required nursing home care. It is not possible for me to think of my friend Al White in terms other than gratitude for the history he gave me, and for gracing my life with his presence. His memory for me is one of deep affection for someone who will always be a treasured part of who I am.

Al would shake his head and I suspect have a good laugh at the use he is being put to in this book. In need of a narrative voice to comment on times far removed in their texture and substance from our own times, I considered a series of such voices, each apropos to the years being focused on. Among them were black luminaries such as James Weldon Johnson, Frederick Douglass, and W.E.B. Du Bois. Instead, I have opted to use the words of

Reporters for *Our World Magazine* working from the Brooklyn Dodgers Dugout in the early 1950s. Left to right, Alvin White, Roy Campanella, Norman Chief Cobb, Don Newcombe. (Personal collection of Lawrence Hogan)

Al White in sidebars throughout this narrative, offering accounts and assessments from someone who was there to witness the story we are telling. If Al were here to be asked about this role to which he is assigned, I suspect he would be more than a bit incredulous and more than a bit protesting. I leave it to readers to decide whether his assumed protest should have been heeded. For myself, there is no question about the propriety of this choice, for it has been a great joy to reconnect with him here, and as it were bring into this old conversation my old historical resource, mentor, and dear friend: Alvin Ellsworth White.

Al White witnessed, lived, and wrote about the history we journey into, and in his declining years, he reflected in his own inimitable way on the characters and circumstances that we try here to experience and understand. He is for us here as he was for me in so personal a fashion, chronicler, bard, and eyewitness as we move through a world that seemed set in place in its defining prejudice, but on reflection turned out to be a world under attack in direct and subtle ways by the example and feats of the players of black baseball.

While it might not have seemed so, it was a world in motion, a world undergoing change that at the time it was happening was difficult to perceive. We have in Al White someone who as eyewitness and chronicler will open our eyes in special ways to the entirety of this baseball and larger than baseball world that was separated into white and black by the veil of race. This was a world that seemed to have locked in place a set of restrictions and a way of perceiving our country's African American citizens that appeared so often through the years of this narrative, which are of course the years of Alvin E. White, to be the way things would always be. It is to our baseball players, and our Alvin Whites, who we look to in order to locate a presence and force that would help make that "would always be" into a "not always be."

CHAPTER 1

Coming to Bat in Sundown Baseball

SETTING THE SCENE—REFLECTING ON A PECULIAR HISTORY

So it is a peculiar history we are entering into, where a fine young high school pitching prospect like Max Manning has to ignore the importuning of a major league scout not because he lacks confidence that he can play the game, but because of the color of his skin. Where does the story of such an inverted world begin? In our case, with a baseball-loving poet who tells us to

> Sing a song full of the faith that the dark past has taught us,
> Sing a song full of the hope that the present has brought us
> Facing the rising sun of our new day begun
> Let us march on till victory is won.[1]

We first meet this poet on a sandlot in the mid-1880s in Jacksonville, Florida. He is just a kid that day when he takes the pitcher's mound with quiet but noticeable aplomb. "No medicine man," as he put it, "ever appeared before the tribe with more confidence in his magic than I had in mine when I faced the crowd."[2]

Quiet confidence is a quality that will characterize the significant public career of this young hurler when he comes into his maturity. This day in the 1880s, he is a mere teenager, a youth with obvious athletic promise. Our young pitcher is reported to have a "beaut" of a curveball, a pitch no one else on the teams he plays for or against can match from the mound or hit from the batter's box.

Listen to him explain how he mastered one of the most difficult pitches to deliver at such a young age:

> Before I left Stanton to go to Atlanta University, one of the pitchers on the "Cuban Giants," the crack Negro professional team of New York, imparted to me the secrets of the art of curve pitching. Under my instructor, who had taken a liking to me because he thought I showed the makings of a real player, I gained control of a wide out-curve, a sharp in-shoot, a slow, tantalizing "drop" and a deceptive "rise." I was at the time the only colored boy who could do the trick. I practiced by the hour with my friend Sam Grant as a catcher. We were the battery of our nine, "The Domestics," a club made up of boys ranging from fourteen to sixteen years of age. Our fame as a battery began to spread. My first taste of athletic glory came when Sam and I were called on to serve as a battery for "The Roman Cities," the leading colored club of Jacksonville and, thereby, the best club in the whole city, in a big game with a formidable team from Savannah.[3]

Our young hurler's confidence in his ability was well placed. His team, the Roman Cities, won the day's contest by a one-sided score while their ringer "struck out sixteen batters and held the rest to ineffectiveness."[4]

This teenager's pitching prowess should come as no surprise, for he could have had no better teacher than a certain moundsman from the first professional Negro baseball club, the soon-to-be legendary Cuban Giants. Organized in Babylon Long Island in 1885, the Cubans quickly established a reputation in the North for fine baseball while playing in the mid to late 1880s out of Trenton, New Jersey. In their inaugural season, they began a tradition of winter ball at Florida resort hotels where at the Ponce de Leon in St. Augustine, as fortune would have it, the young James Weldon Johnson had his fateful encounter with his Cuban Giants' pitching mentor.

Just who is this James Weldon Johnson who was present at the creation of Negro professional baseball as he learned his youthful pitching prowess from one of the first Negro professional players? The fact that he is more or less unknown today is a confirmation of what W.E.B. Du Bois tells us about his hero Alexander Crummell—for Crummell and Johnson come to us from the American age where "(white) men knew so little of (black) men."

Among the Negro professional baseball contemporaries of Johnson's age, we find unrecognized names like Bud Fowler and Sottswood Poles whose visages, based on their baseball ability, could well grace the walls of the shrine room at the National Baseball Hall of Fame. Perhaps, our young phenom's youthful pitching abilities might have matured into a baseball

ALVIN WHITE: "YOU DIDN'T HAVE A TEAM WITHOUT MILTON DABNEY"

Like James Weldon Johnson, Al White remembers a link to the Cubans that began in his growing-up years in Richmond, Virginia. As a young-ster growing up at the turn into the 20th century in what is known today as the Jackson Ward section of Richmond, Al White was good friends with the son of a member of the Original Cuban Giants. He was reminded of that in April 1981 when he read something sent to him by his friend and archivist at the Schomburg Center for Research in Black Culture Ernest Kaiser:

Here is a xerox Ernest Kaiser sent me a couple of weeks ago on the only black baseball guide published. It imitated the white baseball guide put out by A. J. Reach or the Spalding Company. Its author, Sol White, a Harlemite I met, was an ardent sports-man. So he published this guide. You may copy and return. It so happens he told the story of the Argyle Hotel, a resort in Babylon, Long Island, having a baseball team in 1884. A youngster from Richmond—good family friend—Milton Dabney, following tradition, went away for the summer to work as a waiter or bellman at some northern resort to earn college tuition. Milton was also a good ball player, and was on that first team. Years later he became a postal employee. His son and I were neighborhood playmates and friends. Milton Sr. retired and moved to New Jersey after his wife's death to be near his son, then a prominent undertaker in Newark. Milton Sr. and I ran into each other when we both were visiting Richmond. He felt duty bound to drop by and see my cousin whom I was visiting. I wrote him asking him about his playing baseball, and I have that letter which I value highly written when he was 98, a year before his death.

My beef is the arbitrary date Monte Irvin and others in his generation establish as baseball's limits. Players have to fall within those years—and then only certain players. Some of the truly greats are more or less ignored—like the consensus great-est of all—John Henry "Pop" Lloyd who gave me his personal pick of his idea of the greatest black players for a tale in *Our World*. Pitchers like Cannonball Dick Redding and Smokey Joe Williams who defeated all star major league teams in post-season games, or colorful Double Duty Radcliffe who started a game as the catcher, taking over the pitching if his pitcher went bad. Lloyd had an athletic field named after him in Atlantic City where he lived after retiring from active playing working with amateurs and supporting his wife and himself on a meager salary as janitor of the colored school where I went one Sunday to talk with him.

By the way, Milton Dabney played baseball on local amateur teams for years. In fact, you didn't have a team unless Milton Dabney played first base.

Source: Alvin White to Lawrence Hogan, April 7, 1981.

fame that would have put him beside the Bud Fowler and Spotswood Poles of Negro baseball lore. But James Weldon Johnson's claim to fame is found on other playing fields than those of Negro professional baseball. When he came of age, he wrote wonderful music for the Broadway stage, and represented himself with distinction in the highest political forums of his nation. In the late 1910s and early 1920s, he fought the lynchers as the point man for the infant National Association for the Advancement of Colored People (NAACP) in its unsuccessful attempt to reclaim the national congress as a forum for justice for blacks through the passage of national antilynching legislation. In 1925, he won the most prestigious award then given to an African American—the NAACP's Spingarn Medal. And perhaps most memorably he told us in the first year of the 20th century in his immortal "Black National Anthem," *Lift Every Voice and Sing,* to make ours a song "about the faith that the dark past has taught us." James Weldon Johnson's faith would carry him through difficult times, and serve both him and his people well. Black baseball and black life as a whole marched down similar paths.

BLACK BASEBALL'S FOURTH ESTATE

To march along those paths, one must enter the world of the black press to find a history that is told "only in our own newspapers." In revolutionary France, the First Estate was the king and nobles, the Second the Church, and the Third was the common folk. But it was the Fourth Estate—the press—that would have in its purview all of the other three, and all else besides. And so it would be with black journalism in the age of black baseball.

The best place—in fact today the *only* substantial place—to begin to know the Du Boisian "so little knowns" of black baseball's history, as well as the "unknowns" who lived their lives behind America's veil of race prejudice, is on the pages of the Fourth Estate. There was for black Americans of American segregation no better vehicle for separation from and at the same time immersion in the sea of American prejudice than the weekly black newspaper that brought to its readers news of their own baseball world. Week after week from the 1890s beginnings of the "Golden Age" of black baseball, one had, and still has today, no problem in locating and experiencing the evidence of that pervasive immersion in prejudice side by side with wonderful baseball separation from that prejudice.

The press that brought these contrasting sides of black identity to its readers was, as Langston Hughes memorably tells us, "unique, intriguing, exciting, low-down, and terrific."[5] And it was a press that in its extent and scope reached more black Americans in more arresting and attention getting ways than any other black institution. Starting around the turn of the century with the founding of papers like the *Afro-American* in Baltimore in 1893 and the *Defender* in Chicago in 1905, the age of the great black national weekly newspapers circulating widely through regions of the country where blacks lived in significant numbers saw the growth of papers whose readership reached into the millions. By World War II, this Fourth Estate was characterized by Gunnar Myrdal, in his epic study *The American Dilemma,* as "the single greatest power in the Negro race."[6]

It is to be expected that the play of great black baseball teams would be given significant attention on the sports pages of great black weekly newspapers. And while at times critical of their own sports heroes, much of the reportage that found its way onto those pages was of course of the celebratory sort. What could be more worthy of celebration than wonderful players playing their wonderful game in wonderful ways—or the willingness in pre- and postseason play of a white team of major league stars to square off on a baseball diamond as the purported better of a black team, and then frequently oblige the appetite of the black baseball fan by losing the contest?

But "sports" reportage on the "Sports" pages of black newspapers involved much more than celebration—and often much more than sport. A case in point that has something important to say about the way the black newspaper of America's Golden Age of Sport presented itself to its readership came in February 1922 when the *Kansas City Call* took note of the death of the black trainer of the Pittsburgh Pirates, Ed LaForce. The LaForce story is featured on a sports page that is worth our careful perusal as not at all untypical of the sports sections of papers that were the principal source of news, baseball and otherwise, for the black reading public.[7]

On the same *Call* sports page as the report of the trainer's death, we find, not unexpectedly, a story about an AAU championship track meet in Buffalo. But also appearing is a report from Texarkana, Texas, that a mob of masked men had lynched H.P. Norman the week before. It turns out Mr. Norman was confused with another suspect who had in fact committed a murder, but the mob, "saying that he was a black man anyway," refused to heed the word of the sheriff who proclaimed Norman's innocence.[8]

On the same page, next to advertisements for Ferguson & Smith Undertakers and Rajah Cleaners & Tailors, we find an *Associated Negro Press* byline sharing with sports readers an advertisement presented to a local paper in Wilmington, Delaware, by one Edward Frazier who is portrayed as an industrious, willing, punctual, and sober employee. "**Wanted**," his ad reads, "a **Master**—An able bodied colored man, good references, willing worker, will sell himself into slavery for his and his mother's sake. We have got to eat." And finally, an upbeat piece from New York City where Harriet Ida Pickens, with a 141 score, stood highest in the intelligence test of three classes in School 119.[9]

In the editor's work that shaped the content of this "Sports" page, we see something much worth noting. Black baseball as it came to the black reading public—a public expanding in record numbers through these years—was not isolated off into its own world. Baseball reporting did not occupy a niche that separated it from the reportage of the rest of black life. Even in the unlikelihood that a black baseball fan could ignore the screaming headlines of lynching, discrimination, injustice, soaring achievement, and pure outright craziness that week after week shouted at them on the front pages of papers that were their major source for black baseball news, one could not escape that front page reality by turning to the sports section. The black press—in sports coverage that often reported directly on the pervasive fact of discrimination, in front page headline stories that juxtaposed the worst of American prejudice alongside the best of black baseball, and in "extra" news coverage that found its way frequently into sports sections—would not permit that luxury.

Nor will we allow ourselves that luxury as we follow the stories that bring to us the characters and character of black baseball. Interspersed in our narrative, as they would have been in the black newspapers that reported our baseball scene, will be accounts of "America's one constant"—the prejudice that baseball fans would have encountered as they perused their papers for the baseball news they were eager to read. This was the "stuff" that they constantly faced as they lived out their daily lives as citizens of a decidedly prejudiced land of the free and home of the brave. And following the direction set for us by the papers that took their readers into this schizophrenic world where joy and awfulness existed side by side, appearing in our telling of this story alongside those constant prejudiced moments outside of baseball will be recurrent narrative visits to places where young men, and sometimes old ones as well, were simply "having fun playing our game."

As we enter the world of these "constant" items, where in baseball parks fun was the order of the day, we recognize that these are places we cannot fully understand today. How could they be as they were? How could race prejudice have been so sharp and pervasive, and how could joy have been found so often in the facing up to that prejudice?

FIRST ACCOUNTS

We begin our first visit to this world of finding joy in the face of race prejudice at a time when the game of baseball was being played and watched by freedmen who had only moments ago been slaves. Where better to first see young black men playing a game they loved to play than in a locality that had only a few years earlier been a way station on the Underground Railroad. We turn to historian of the early game James Overmyer for a telling account of the Washington Mutuals, a black squad from the nation's capital who were composed primarily of government employees.

> Charles Douglass, who worked first at the Freedmen's Bureau, the agency created to help former slaves in the South make their transition to free citizenry, had been playing with the Alerts, the first of the strong Washington teams, but had gone over to the Mutuals in 1869. He was a regular for the team, sometimes its pitcher, and later president of the Mutual Club, the social organization from which the team sprang.
>
> In August 1870, Douglass and the rest of the Mutuals went on a road trip that was remarkable in its length and intensity for that period in black baseball development. After an August 16 game in Baltimore, where the Mutuals cowed the black Enterprise team by a 51–26 score, the team departed immediately for upstate New York. They played

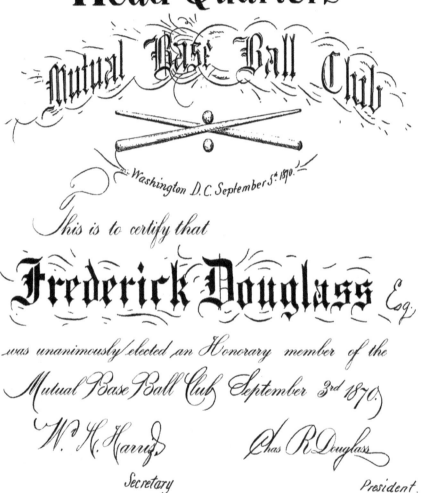

Head Quarters

Mutual Base Ball Club

Washington D.C. September 5ᵗʰ 1870.

This is to certify that

Frederick Douglass Esq.

was unanimously elected an Honorary member of the Mutual Base Ball Club September 3rd 1870.

W. H. Harris
Secretary

Chas R. Douglass
President.

Frederick Douglass, as an honorary member of the Washington Mutuals. (Courtesy of Frank Ceresi) seven games in a little more than a week along a 300-mile stretch roughly following the Erie Canal. Starting in the western part of the state, they overwhelmed six black clubs by mostly lopsided scores, and edged a "picked nine" players from the various white teams in Rochester, by four runs. Then, it was east to Rochester, where the visitors had a special experience. Frederick Douglass, Charles' famous father, was living there on a farm just outside the city. He and his wife Anna played host to the ballplayers at a house that had been the last stop in the United States during the Civil War for slaves escaping to Canada via the Underground Railroad. It was likely at this historic house where the great Douglass became a ball player of sorts.[10]

The sportswriter Ric Roberts would characterize the black world that gives us Frederick and Charles Douglass and their Mutuals as a place unconcerned with the white world that had created the conditions that made that other world necessary. For Roberts, the world of black professional baseball was a place where

We were not even aware of the white world in the sense that it meant anything of consequence to the world in which we lived. . . . Our heaven and our glory was in Harlem; not at Harvard, but at Howard and Lincoln; and it motivated south where Morehouse and Atlanta University and finally Florida A & M, and other schools west of the Mississippi, Wiley and Grambling, all joined in possession of the black world. Nobody worried about Georgia Tech, nobody worried about Auburn. Nobody worried about even Notre Dame. We had our own. We had our Howard Bisons. We had our Golden Tuskegee Tigers, and those were the things the black press wrote about. Those were the things that were celebrated and that marked the headlines that made the black press important. And of course the beautiful verses and beautiful lines of men like Langston Hughes and Countee Cullen.[11]

Echoing Roberts's encomium is a question from the great novelist and essayist Ralph Ellison: "Can a people live and develop over 300 years simply by reacting? Are American Negroes simply the creation of white men, or have they at least helped to create themselves out of what they have found around them?"[12]

In black newspapers, as in the world on which they reported, baseball could never be just baseball. But at the same time, baseball *was* just baseball. For the blacks who built their own teams and leagues, baseball separated them in important and identity-building ways from the world of prejudice in which they were immersed. Out on their "fields of dreams," they would embrace Ralph Ellison's idea of "creating our own selves from the stuff that is around us." But those institutions, such as blackball, still existed in the way they did because of the pervasiveness of the prejudice that was Jim Crow America. While they might offer relief, they could never offer escape.

CHAPTER 2

The Beginnings: 19th-Century Blackball

SETTING THE SCENE—FROM SLAVERY TO JIM CROW

Recollecting the beginnings of "sundown baseball" takes us into a pre–Civil War 19th-century America where the black press that would become our principal source for the telling of the story of blackball appeared as early as 1827 in John Russwurm's and Samuel Cornish's New York–based *Freedom's Journal*. Of course something else was present in the America of that time that made necessary the presence of black newspapers. With the invention of the cotton gin, slavery and the profits it produced had become king. The cash crop of cotton, and the labor system that produced it, had come to dominate the economic, political, and cultural life of the Southern part of the nation, while sending its tentacles into large parts of the North as it grew dramatically in historically unparalleled ways. By the mid-1830s, cotton production had reached 460 million pounds annually, accompanied of course by a growth in the numbers who planted and harvested so that a slave population numbering 700,000 in the first federal census had reached 3,953,760 by the seventh.[1]

By the 1850s, slavery and cotton had become a force that was dividing the nation into two increasingly contentious camps. After the passage of the fiercely contested Fugitive Slave Law of 1850 that brought the full force of the law to the return of runaway chattel, Negro abolitionist Martin Delaney would say

> If any man approaches my house in search of a slave, I care not who he may be, whether constable, or sheriff, magistrate or even judge

of the Supreme Court, nay, let it be he who sanctioned this act to
become a law, surrounded by his cabinet as his bodyguard, with the
Declaration of Independence waving above his head as his banner,
and the Constitution of his country upon his breast as his shield. If
he crosses the threshold of my door, and I do not lay him a lifeless
corpse at my feet, I hope the grave may refuse my body a resting
place, and righteous Heaven my spirit a home. Oh, no! He cannot
enter that house and we both live.[2]

America was now a place where the century's most important political
figure, a would be president from Illinois, presciently declared in 1855 that
his country could no longer exist permanently as it did then, half slave and
half free. By 1857, Charles Sumner would be beaten to an inch of his death
on the floor of the U.S. Senate by a member of the House of Representatives for having insulted Southern honor by speaking too strongly in opposition to slavery. And it was a place where Frederick Douglass, reacting to
the awful misinterpretation of the Constitution made by Chief Justice Roger
Taney's Supreme Court in the Dred Scott decision, would assert that "not
what Moses allowed for the hardness of heart, but what God requires, ought
to be the rule." With a searing eloquence that was his unique gift to his nation, the great orator argued that

> The Constitution knows all the human inhabitants of this country as
> "the people." It makes no discrimination in favor of, or against, any class
> of people, but is fitted to protect and preserve the rights of all, without
> reference to color, size, or any physical peculiarities. When this is done,
> the glorious birthright of our common humanity will become the in-
> heritance of all the inhabitants of this highly favored country.[3]

Such an inheritance was seemingly realized in the years of Reconstruction as the nation that ripped itself apart in the awful reality of the Civil
War found in the Thirteenth, Fourteenth and Fifteenth Amendments to the
Constitution, along with accompanying legislation, new heights of inclusive-
ness, nobleness of purpose, and hopefulness of fulfilling America's promise
of equality for all its citizens. All that promise began to be undone when in a
series of decisions beginning in the early 1880s, the Supreme Court, following the lead of society as a whole, drew back from any notion that America
was to be a country where its citizens were to be judged by the quality of
their character, not by the color of their skin.

Society's desires and the highest law of the land were brought into tan-
dem when *Plessy v. Ferguson* in 1896 confirmed as the American way what

John Marshall Harlan accurately termed a society where castes would now be acknowledged in the highest law of the land, where a constitution would be color conscious rather than color blind, where all citizens would not be equal before the law, and where the humblest would no longer be recognized as the peer of the most powerful. Regret he might that the court on which he sat had handed down a decision that he feared would be as pernicious in it consequences as the Dred Scott decision. But so it would be as Americans, black and white, watched the great 19th-century end of slavery turn into the 20th century of Jim Crow segregation.

In his tour de force *The Omni American,* the always challenging Albert Murray tells us something that it is important we understand about how we view—actually too frequently misview—the history of slavery:

> The term stigma can hardly do justice to the complex heritage of the experience of slavery in the United States. Much is forever being made of the deleterious effects of slavery on the generations of black Americans that followed. But for some curious reason, nothing at all is ever

---

ALVIN WHITE: OF CONSIDERABLE PEDIGREE

Segregation's pernicious tentacles worked their way into so many parts of American life. Interracial sexual relations, termed miscegenation in the law and outlawed throughout the entire slave South—and held to be illegal long after the end of slavery—was of course quite common. Otherwise, why have laws prohibiting and punishing it? Still the news of it in specific situations can catch the historian off guard. Such was the case during an afternoon conversation in Al White's room in his nursing home in Atlanta when he began a story that I for one had not anticipated hearing. Alvin Ellsworth White was born in Richmond, Virginia, in 1890 to William T. White. Fathers and mothers have a way of keeping family secrets from their children for their own good. And inquisitive youngsters have a way of putting one and one together, and getting two.

Or, as Alvin summarized: "When I was a youngster I sometimes asked questions I wasn't supposed to ask. And sometimes it would take time for me to put one and one together to get whatever that might add up to. That was the way that I figured out that my father's father, my grandfather, was John Tyler, 10th president of the United States."

made of the possibility that the legacy left by the enslaved ancestors of blues-oriented contemporary U.S. Negroes includes a disposition to confront the most unpromising circumstances and make the most of what little there is to go on, regardless of the odds—and not without finding delight in the process or forgetting mortality at the height of ecstasy. Still there is a lot of admittedly infectious exuberance, elegance and nonsense to be accounted for.[4]

GENESIS

Part of that "accounting" goes back to baseball fields occupied by black players who were present during the creation moments of our national pastime. Our national pastime was an evolution, not an invention. In the time of its origins, baseball's various versions were all subsumed under the name "town ball." From the 1810s through the 1860s, the game called town ball, the anticipator of the game of baseball as we know it today, became the nation's game as America readied herself for the post–Civil War professional national pastime baseball that Mark Twain would call "the very symbol, the outward and visible expression of the drive and push and rush and struggle of the raging, tearing, booming nineteenth century."[5] This town ball was played in places where most would not expect to find it. In 1938, Henry Baker, age 83, took interviewer Thomas Campbell to one of those unexpected places. It was the Ben Martin plantation in Alabama in the 1850s and 1860s where as a slave lad Baker played baseball with his black and white companions.

> At dat time we played what we called "Town Ball." De way we played "Town Ball" wuz, we had bases en we run from one base tuh de udder 'coase if de runner was hit wid de ball he was out. We allus made de ball outa cotton en rags. We played with de "niggers" on de plantation. 'Coase de white boys played wid us too. De white boys would come frum one plan'ation tuh anudder tuh play wid de "niggers" too. En slav'ry time grown white boys would come to play en wrassle wid de "niggers." Sho' would. Cause white folks den wuz mo' close to de "Nigger" den he is now.[6]

References from across so wide a swath of Southern slavery territory— Alabama, Arkansas, Georgia, Texas, Florida, and South Carolina—in the approximately 2,000 slave interviews conducted between 1936 and 1938 by interviewers from the federal government Works Progress Administration Federal Writers Project that are housed in the American Memory Collection of the Library of Congress indicate that the playing of baseball of the town ball variety was widespread among the slaves. Among the many recollections can be found

- John Cole of Athens, Georgia, recalled life on a plantation with relatively relaxed work rules where "always on Saturday afternoon you would have 'till 'first dark' for base-ball, and from first dark 'till Sunday-go-to-meeting for drinking and dancing."
- Joe Barnes, who grew up on the plantation of Jim Sapp in Tyler County, Texas, remembered that "when I's a chile us play marbles and run rabbits and ride de stick hoss and de like. When I gits more bigger, us play ball, sort of like baseball."
- Ed Allen of Des, Arkansas, reminisced that white and Negro boys played ball together. White and black interplay was not unusual in the slavery South, although societal mores changed that as the youths got older. Several of the old slaves' accounts told of the use of makeshift balls and bats. But Allen recalled to Works Progress Administration researcher Irene Robinson that "we never had to buy a ball or bat. Always had em. The white boys bought em."
- From an interview with the Reverend Squires Johnson born September 14, 1842, in a weather beaten shanty in Madison, Florida, we learn that "on Sundays the boys on the plantation would play home ball and shoot marbles until church time."

Most of the slave recollections we have are direct and to the point of baseball being present—but skimpy in their detail. But then there is Ben Leitner, 85 years of age when he was interviewed in 1936:

Member dat day baseball furst come out and they got up a team, not a team then; they called it a "Nine," when de game fust come to Woodward section. If you ketch a ball on de furst bounce, dat was a "out." No such thing as a mask for de face, gloves for de hands, and mats to protect your belly. No curves was allowed, or swift balls throwed by a pitcher. Him have to pitch a slow drop ball. De aim then was to see how far a batter could knock de ball, how fast a fellow could run, how many tallies a side could make. Mighty poor game if de game didn't last half a day and one side or de other make forty tallies.

Marse Bill Litchen was workin' in de store of his brudder-in-law, Marse John A. Brice. Him was called out to make one of de "Nines." Him went to de bat, and de very fust like, him knock de ball way ove center field. Everybody holler: "Run Kitchen! Run Kitchen! Run Kitchen!" Marse Bill stand right dere with de bat, shake his head and long black wiskers and say: "Why should I run? I got two more licks at dat ball!" They git de ball, tech him and de umpire say: "Out." Marse Hill throw de ball down and say: "Damn sich a game!" Folks laugh 'bout dat 'til dis day.[7]

If the Antebellum period, with its moments for baseball alongside the hardships of slavery, was one of those deep rivers that flowed through the experience of African Americans, so too was life in America's premier cities. Historian Jim Overmyer identifies what may have been the first black baseball game to be reported in the white press. It occurred in a premier American city on October 16, 1862, when "a sporting correspondent for the *Brooklyn Eagle,* discovering the game between two white teams that he was supposed to cover had been canceled, stumbled instead on the Weeksville Unknowns playing Brooklyn's Monitor team."[8]

Playing baseball among your own was one thing. Securing the vote would prove to be another. Sometimes life in urban free America could be as difficult and as dangerous as living in the rural, slaveholding South had been. On October 10, 1871, in Philadelphia, during the first general election in the city in which African American residents were entitled to vote, Overmyer explains that

Black voters were being attacked to keep them away from the polls, and the local police were not up to the tasks of either guaranteeing their voting rights or quelling the fighting. Octavius Cato, a young,

---

ALVIN WHITE: WITH GOD'S HELP
WE WILL KEEP THE NEGRO IN HIS PLACE

Al White was born in Richmond, Virginia, in 1890. While his childhood city was two decades and 700 miles removed from the Philadelphia of 1871 that we visit next, he remembers well a world not too different from that of Octavius Cato and his Pythians. He recalls distinctly something that caught his attention as a teenage reader of his hometown newspaper: "I recall a speech Governor Swanson made at the Southern Governor's Conference held in Richmond around 1906 as reported in the papers where I read it. 'With God's help, and our own right hand, we will keep him (the Negro) where he is today.' So help me."

fiery black teacher at a segregated school, who was also an officer in a segregated National Guard unit, dismissed his students so they could get home safely. Then he left for his own home to retrieve his uniform and military equipment, since there was a chance the black unit would be called to duty to help restore order. He was nearly home when he walked past a small group of whites, one of whom accosted and shot him at point blank range. Ironically enough, he was carried into a neighboring police station where he died. Thus expired not only a leading civil rights figure in Philadelphia, but the captain of the city's crack black baseball club, the Pythians.[9]

As the 19th century drew to a close, from Al White's Richmond in the South to Octavius Cato's Philadelphia in the North, indeed everywhere black Americans turned, they found themselves in an increasingly divided world. Politics illustrated this separation well. From the election of Hiram Revels to the Senate, and Joseph Rainey to the House of Representatives in 1870, to the departure from the Congress in 1901 of George White from North Carolina, 20 African Americans served in the House and two in the Senate. White, as the last of those to serve, in his parting address to his colleagues termed his leaving to be a temporary farewell for American Negroes from representation in his nation's congress. "For, but let me say," he intoned, "Phoenix-like he will rise up some day and come again. These parting words are in behalf of an outraged, heart-broken, bruised and bleeding, but God-fearing people, faithful, industrious, local people—rising people, full of potential force."[10]

Congressman White was the last of the breed of black federal office-holders who were the product of a Reconstruction era filled with hope for an integrated America. The Congress did not see his kind again until the election of Chicago's Oscar DePriest in 1929. In the arena of America's national pastime, it would be 44 long years before a Phoenix named Jackie Robinson would rise up to give life on America's baseball diamonds to Congressman White's powerful sentiments. We did not see in national politics White's kind in fair numbers until the Voting Rights Act of 1965 finally began to secure for black Americans a franchise that had been promised in the Fourteenth and Fifteenth Amendments to the Constitution. Coincidentally, it was in those same mid-1960s that major league baseball finally began—a decade and more after the Phoenix-like entry into its ranks of Jackie Robinson—to reflect in its on-the-field composition a fair percentage of African Americans.

SANDLOTS AND HOTELS

If baseball was played extensively by blacks in 19th-century American cities like Octavius Cato's Philadelphia, the Brooklyn of the Unknowns and the Monitors, Al White's Richmond, Virginia, and the Rochester of Frederick Douglass, it was also found on back lots in ordinary neighborhoods and at luxury hotels and resorts up and down the East Coast. As the trend in politics, on baseball fields, and everywhere else moved the nation toward the separation of the races, the nation's game remained very much a part of the formative years of black youth. J.A. Harrison was a fine turn of the 19th-century player for numerous hotel and semiprofessional black teams. A personal baseball highlight came when one of his clubs "beat the famous Cuban X Giants, with such great colored stars as Frank Grant, Clarence Williams, Sol White, the Jackson brothers and Selden." In the 1920s, he recalled what it was like as a youngster to play the game of baseball in his native Norfolk, Virginia.[11]

The baseball rivalries of his youth were fierce ones against teams like the Red Stockings, St. Clairs, and the Lancasters, facing off against the Stonewalls, Huntersville Tappers, Virginia Batters, and Quebecs. After the games were the inevitable fights: "The Bute Street boys had as their natural enemies the Cumberland Street boys, and those living in one section would have chips on their shoulders for those of the other sections. There was a team down town known as the Athletics, and to go in their territory was the occasion for disorderly retreats. A team from Norfolk playing Portsmouth usually broke the speed laws returning home."

But boys of his youth fought differently than those of his adult years. He could not recall weapons such as guns and knives being brought into play. "Boys then fought fairly and loved a fight. Today a boy will use a gun or a knife on the slightest provocation, many times with fatal results." The cop on the beat was an active presence who at curfew would chase the youngsters home at the sound of the nine-o'clock whistle.

As for equipment, you made do with what was at hand. Harrison and his fellow baseballers played with a ball called the "Rocket." It cost 20 cents, but no team was affluent enough to boast of more than one. "Duck" Davis could smite one a mile. Outfits consisted of mother's stockings and gloves. "Envied indeed was he who had a cotton flannel home-made suit. He was a star and a hero. Every vacant lot was an improvised ball ground and over the fence was out." Harrison recalled having knocked a liner through one of the new stained glass windows at St. John's A.M.E. Church. "That game broke up immediately, eighteen boys leaving at once on other business. Dr. Edward E. Field, for whom I drove a buggy, paid for the glass out of my wages."

Sometimes you went against parents' wishes because playing ball was more important than adult approval:

> If daily lickings and perseverance counted, I would be one of the greatest baseball players in the world. For some reason my father was bitterly opposed to me playing the game, but I saw no harm in it then, and have found none since. Each day I would get my gang together and play, and each night when I returned home he inquired whether I had indulged in the great pastime. I would not deny it and the lickings would follow. Being the oldest of five boys, I had to assist in doing part of the domestic work. To keep me indoors mother put me in a "Mother Hubbard" dress. I heard the boys whistling, yelling, and playing. Not to be out done I got over the back fence and took my accustomed place among the gang. I recall sliding into second, and my dress came off, but I kept playing and finished the game. Of course I got my "tanning" that night.[12]

Harrison's lickings finally ceased when his dad was bitten by the baseball bug. It happened in a big tree at the corner of Wide Street and Princess Anne Avenue. Norfolk was playing a series of games with a Baltimore club and one of its members was reported to be a colored man:

> The colored population was agog with excitement, and I had a "reserved seat" in one of the highest braches of that tree. During one of the exciting moments of that game, I heard a familiar voice rooting. Looking below me on a lower limb, I discovered my father. Whether he was ashamed to mention it that night I do not know, but I know my lickings ceased from that day. Perhaps my father caught the contagion.[13]

When he came of age, a black youth like J. M. Harrison found opportunity to participate in competitive baseball on a high level of play most often on crack resort hotel teams that proliferated throughout the upper South and Northeast. Certainly, by the early 1890s, many of the major Eastern resorts in places like the Delaware Water Gap; Bryn Mawr, Pennsylvania; Lenox, Massachusetts; Wildwood and Atlantic City, New Jersey; and up into the Catskills in hotels like the Champlain could boast of fine teams. Harrison's own semipro baseball career cut a wide swath across prime resort and hotel semiprofessional territory from Lyons, Palmyra, and the Catskill Mountains in New York; to Philadelphia, Lansford, the Delaware Water Gap, Easton, Stroudsburg, and Haverford in Pennsylvania; over to Pleasantville, Atlantic City, Egg Harbor, Camden, and Wildwood in New Jersey; to Charleston in

West Virginia; to Richmond, Roanoke, Lynchburg, and Petersburg in his home state of Virginia; and to Baltimore and Washington, not to mention extensive play in his home town and its vicinity.

It was with the crack Shelbourne Hotel team in Atlantic City that Harrison took the better of the "famous Cuban X Giants with Clarence Williams, Rube Foster, Buckner, Pete and John Hill, 'Indian' Charlie Grant, 'Kid' Carter (who struck out Buck Freeman five times in one game), Ray Wilson, Dan McClellan, Monroe and others."

While working the resort circuit at Bryn Mawr, Harrison realized one of his most satisfying hotel baseball moments. Of the many teams his club played, all of them white, the Pennsylvania Railroad nine from Philadelphia trimmed them every time. A double header between the Railroaders and Bryn Mawr's waiter staff was scheduled for July 4. Harrison assured headwaiter C.A. Burnett that his friend "Ham" Williams could deliver the pitching goods needed to serve up a victory over their hated rivals. He was given authorization to wire "Ham" his fare requesting him to report at once while apprising him of the two games. Anticipation built to a high pitch as Harrison regaled his fellow waiters with tales of his friend's prowess as a moundsman.

> Just after breakfast was over in the dinning room, I was informed that a man wished to see me. With a bat bag and valise, in the pantry stood "Ham." I ordered breakfast for him and we went to quarters, where he immediately became a favorite with his good humor and stories. Some of the waiters and bellmen looked a little suspicious as "Ham" would be taken for anything else save a ball player. I shall never forget when Burnett saw him. "Harrison," he asked, "can he wait in the dinning room?" I told him I thought he could wait on the hotel officers' table. "You say he is a pitcher?" I replied in the affirmative, but he questioned my judgment.
>
> The first game was called at ten thirty, and a great crowd witnessed it. When my "find" stepped in the pitcher's box, all eyes were on him. With a broad grin he began manipulating the ball with his long fingers, and having everything, besides being a left hander, he easily defeated the team that had been our jinx the whole season.
>
> When the team went on the field in the afternoon "Ham" faced the white boys again, and took them into camp. It is needless for me to say that he "owned" Bryn Mawr afterwards. Burnett advanced him into the main dinning room where he made good. Like Damon and Pythias, when "Ham" was at the bat, "Piggy" (Harrison's nickname) was on deck.[14]

The next team that turns up on our black baseball stage had its origins in that same hotel circuit of Ham's and Piggy's exploits. The Cuban Giants, formed in 1885, was the first black team to get paid on a regular schedule and not subsist on a share of fluctuating gate receipts as they barnstormed around. James Overmyer tabs them as "black baseball's version of the Cincinnati Red Stockings of 1869. Both clubs mark the respective points at which astute entrepreneurs made the crucial decision to forgo 'wink and a nod' secret payments, and become unabashed professionals."[15]

The Cubans would, in various versions of the original team, across a 15-year or so period of baseball ups and baseball downs, leave their special mark on the history of the game. Arguably, they are an answer to the oft-asked question of why so many of the early black professional teams bore the moniker of Giants, for in the days of early black baseball, there were black Giants by the score. Why, people often ask, were there so many early Negro professional teams named the Giants? In Brooklyn, early in the 20th century, there were the Royal ones. Some of the best early clashes in blackball had those Brooklyn Giants of saloon owner John Connors facing off against their counterpart

The Spartans of Tappin, Virginia, comprised one of numerous semiprofessional teams of the late 19th century. John Milton Dabney, a member of the Original Cuban Giants, is seated second from the left in first row. (National Baseball Hall of Fame Library, Cooperstown, NY)

Giants from the City of Brotherly Love. Out in Chicago, the franchise of black baseball's founding father, the redoubtable Rube Foster's American Giants, often brought comparisons between their skills on a baseball diamond and that of their white major league counterpart of the same name—as did the managerial smarts of their respective managers, Foster and John McGraw.

It is often said that several episodes involving John McGraw's willingness to publically admire the skills of black players, and in at least two instances seeming to try to sneak onto his major league roster light skinned players of that hue, made the name of his team a favorite of black owners. From the records we have it is easy to assemble a formidable all-time all-star team of black players about whom John McGraw is purported to have said, "if we could calcimine him, it would be $50,000 well spent to sign him for the Giants." Others have said that the dominating popularity of the New York Giants from so early a moment in the history of professional baseball made it just natural that blacks would adopt the name for their teams. But then there is the curious fact that just about the same time that the New York white club was becoming the Giants, but not yet the dominant presence they would be in the popular baseball imagination, the first of the great black professional clubs—playing out of Babylon, New York; Jacksonville, Florida; and Trenton, New Jersey—established an originating and long-remembered place within the ranks of black baseball. It may well be that those Cuban Giants—later to be called the Original Cuban Giants to distinguish them from a rival Cuban X Giants team—are, rather than the white version of John McGraw, the inspirational source for all those Giants who played their wonderful brand of professional baseball on teams and in leagues where only the ball and not the team name was white.

THE WORLD'S GREATEST SCOUT

Off the ranks of that Original Cuban Giants team came a player who would be dubbed toward the end of his long career in colored baseball as "the greatest baseball scout in the world." He was someone who Harry Hairstone recalled as having "the fight" in him, and one of a "game lot."

Hairstone's recollection came from his breaking-in-years, well before he became a mainstay with the original Baltimore Black Sox. He was playing for a white club, the Rochester Big Horns. The Horns were locked in a contentious game with a black squad anchored by John "Pop" Watkins at first base. In his first time at bat, the young Hairstone hit a sharp line drive down the first baseline headed for two base territory. The ball never reached the outfield as old Pop made a one hand stab while falling over the bag.

"Gee old man, you're lucky" yelled the disappointed Hairstone.

"Hit them right son" Pop yelled back, "and if I get a mile of them they're in the well."

Pop Watkins's Negro baseball "well" was deep and wide—so wide and deep that he came to be called the "greatest baseball scout" in the world. That judgment was based on a definition of the term "baseball scout" by the sports editor of the *Baltimore Afro-American* that is well worth hearing:

> A scout is a man, usually an old baseball player engaged by the manager of a team to go out through the country and look over the work of the young amateurs in what is known in baseball parlance as the "bush leagues" or sometimes dubbed "the sandlotters."
>
> The qualifications of a scout include a high degree of baseball knowledge, a more than ordinary ability to read character, and something of the gift of prophecy.
>
> That is to say he must be able to size up a candidate to the extent of judging whether he has the intelligence to submit to the discipline of organized baseball management, and at the same time be amenable to instruction so that the manager will be able to bring out the best that is in him. And above all this, is the scout's ability to see whether there is anything to be brought out.[16]

If the testimony found in the report of his death in 1924 can be taken at face, Pop Watkins clearly qualified as scout extraordinaire when it came to judging Negro baseball talent in the bud. The roster of his "discoveries" who he managed reads like a who's who of early 20th-century Negro professional baseball. Among them were "Duncan, Wallace, Forrest, McDonald, Lander, Scotland, Walters, Richardson, Miller, and many others." No less a testifier than Sol White in 1919 called Watkins the "dean of the Colored baseball profession" and acknowledged his role in the development of the fine pitchers Dixon of the American Giants and Phil Cockrell of Hilldale.

But it would be more than playing against and shaping top black professional baseball talent for the Brooklyn bred lad when he came into his athletic maturity. While restricted to membership on black teams, he would face some of the top white talent of his day. The *Afro* story of 1923 has him carrying the scars of a collision at first base with the great Honus Wagner of the Pittsburgh Pirates who crashed into him while he was taking a throw from short. That incident left him with three broken ribs. Another injury souvenir was a scarred lip reportedly split by a pitched ball delivered by none other than the famous Christy Mathewson.

There would be another white baseball connection for this black pioneer, one that it is difficult to credit without expressing a touch of incredulity. The title bestowed on him by the *Afro-American* scribe was not "World's Greatest 'Black' Base Ball Scout" but simply "World's Greatest

Base Ball Scout." That might seem to smack of the hyperbole that a black journalist writing about a great black baseball man would be prone to resort to. But playing against the likes of Wagner and Mathewson, we are told, led to Pop's ability as a player becoming "common knowledge to the managers of big league clubs, and in course of time he was sought to take the position of scout and coach for young players. Among the many stars he 'discovered' back in those days who later became the greatest stars of the game were John McGraw, the famous pilot of the world champion Giants, Hughie Jennings, who won fame with the Detroit Tigers, John Hummel, Al Schacht, and others. Jack Dunn of the Baltimore Orioles once used to toss them into the mitt of the famous colored scout." So we have an unknown and unrecognized black baseball pioneer as "discoverer"—whatever that might mean—of two future Hall of Famers and of a host of other major league greats.

General knowledge has it that the line separating black from white was rigid and firm in the Jim Crow decades of Pop Watkins's baseball manhood. As rigid and firm as that line might have been, it appears not to have prevented Pop's scouting and coaching on the white major league side of that segregation imposed barrier. "Pop the Crossover" crossed in another baseball place as well. It is not hard to imagine this smart baseball man as a coach/manager for a black college like North Carolina College for Negroes. He filled that role admirably for several years in the 1910s and 1920s for the spring college season while organizing and managing the top-level professional black touring Havana Red Sox out of Watertown, New York. What is hard to imagine is a black man coaching a Manhattan College team in New York City in 1904 that "sent 13 youngsters up to the big leagues in one season, a record."

But for all of what Pop Watkins may or may not have been as a baseball man, there can be no gainsaying his record on the field of play. His many seasons campaigning as a key member of arguably the best Colored professional club of his era, the Cuban Giants is testimony enough to that credit. He was first and foremost a baseball player who had "the fight in him," one of a "game lot." Let Harry Hairstone have the last word on John "Pop" Watkins:

My second trip to the bat I singled a long drive to left center, good for two bases any time, but "Pop" hooked my foot as I turned first and down I went on my face and was lucky to scramble to the bag before the ball.

I popped to left field on my third try and on the fourth attempt I drove out a sharp liner down the field for two bases. When I turned first "Pop" made a try to repeat his same trick but I was wise this time and aimed for his foot and sliced the shoe so neatly that it fell off. He came at me fighting mad, but being a swift runner I was almost to second leaving him on first hurling maledictions to the wind.

"Baseball is too much of a business now-a-days and all of the kick has been taken out of it" said the former old Sox player.[17]

THE BLACK KING OF SWAT

If Pop Watkins being dubbed "the world's greatest scout" has the touch of the hyperbolic about it, it is hard to attach hyperbole to the feats of the 19th-century black King of Swat. His obituary in his hometown paper in Findley, Ohio, tells us that he was a man of music known in the city of Buffalo where he resided in the later years of his life for his musical ability as a member of the Bethel Baptist Church where presumably his fine voice gave him a prominent place in the choir. Unfortunately, his last years were spent in the Erie Home for the Blind.[18]

Blind was something he could never be accused of on the many baseball diamonds on which he appeared as a star player for most of the great black clubs of the turn of century. The beauty of his singing voice was matched by his ability to hit a baseball. A reported 60 home runs in his rookie season for the strong semipro Findlay Sluggers earned him the sobriquet he would carry for the rest of his baseball career—even when for many seasons in the dead ball era he averaged only 10. His stats are nothing short of remarkable. Probably most eye catching came in Cuba in 1910 for the Havana Reds when his .412 out hit Sam Crawford and Ty Cobb of the touring Detroit Tigers. Cuba was a favorite hunting ground where, historian James Riley tells us, "he captained the Reds to a winter league championship and became the first American to win a batting title on the island." We have him as early as 1907 on a fearsome Cuban Fe team that had garnered in him and his teammates, Pete Hill, Rube Foster, Charlie Grant, and Bill Monroe, "the cream of American black baseball." That Fe team, to which he contributed significantly, would continue to show itself in subsequent seasons when he combined with the likes of Bruce Petway, Smokey Joe Williams, John Lloyd, and Louis Santop to bring to the island the best of America's black game.[19]

Looking at him in his most famous photo from Sol White's *Official Base Ball Guide* with bat cocked high, loose of limb, poised, and focused, it is easy to see why historian Riley would characterize Johnson as of the sturdy, raw-boned type whom the newspapers, by the second decade of the 20th century, were referencing as "a high class ball player not showing his age." Called "Dad" by other players, he was "a favorite with the crowds with his witty sayings, good playing and good conduct winning him many friends."

He was a student of the game, framing his thoughts carefully when he put his long experience at bat into words in *The Art and Science of Hitting* in Sol White's *Guide* while identifying what was most essential to being a good batsman. According to the creed of "Home Run" Johnson, there were two requisites to being a first-class hitter—confidence and fearlessness. Johnson's hitting lessons have the ring of familiarity about them—tried and true things we have heard from our youth from those who know best how to play the game. Best known as a home run hitter he may have been, he had early on learned not to swing for the fences. It was a natural mistake he said for a batter to try to become a home run hitter by hitting the ball "with all the force at his command at all times with a full swing of the bat." Any pitcher worth his salt would rather, with the game on the line, "face the mighty swinger to the cool steady batter who tries to meet the ball and place it to the best advantage." Most of the time, he cautioned, let the first ball go past to get a line on the speed or curve of the pitcher. To improve the batting eye bunting should be practiced before every game. Besides, "a player who can both hit and bunt is a very valuable man to any team."[20]

In his day, what our black home run king advised others to do was never more adeptly put into practice than when Grant "Home Run" Johnson stepped to the plate.

AMERICA'S ONE CONSTANT

But for all his stepping to the plate and swatting round trippers, Grant Johnson was still a black man living in a world of constant prejudice. Witness for that is the story of our "last black congressman" from America's Reconstruction Era, George Henry White, whose two terms in office from 1896 to 1900. overlap several of Johnson's best baseball seasons in the sun. While the Original Cubans were making their name playing their game, while Pop Watkins was well into a career that would make him a premier figure within the ranks of black baseball, and Grant Johnson was hitting those round trippers that earned him his "Home Run" title, George Henry White from North Carolina was experiencing America's constant dance with race prejudice as he became the last black congressman of the post–Civil War era. Elected from a predominately black district in 1896 and 1898, he declined to run for re-election in the fall of 1900 after his state's voters, aided by "creative" vote counting among white election officials, passed an amendment to the state constitution that required voters to be able to read and write.

The amendment contained a "grandfather clause" that, on its face, seemed not to disenfranchise existing registered voters. It specified that if a potential voter's ancestor could vote in 1867, the literacy test would not apply. The trick, though, was that blacks, deprived of the vote in North Carolina in 1835, had not had it restored until 1868. So all of them were subject to the new test,

UNCLE SAMMY, FATHER ABRAHAM, MASSA ROBERT, AND BASEBALL

A quintessential American quartet of Uncle Sammy, Father Abraham, Massa Robert, and our national pastime, speaks in moving poetic words to the defining reality of segregation and exclusion that came to inform the history of baseball from the late 1880s of George White through the coming in 1945 of Jackie. The poem's author, George Moriarty, had a long career as a major league player and umpire.

Sammy Lincoln Lee in Baseball

Little Sammy Lincoln Lee is jest as black as he can be,
an he is pitchin fer our nine' cause we don't draw no color line.
Sam's got de coives; he's got de speed dat always keeps us in de lead,
so we don't mind if he is black an' lives down by det railroad track.
Las week he strikes out fifteen guys, an make the rest hit-pop up flies.
He's got a shine ball dat's immense,
an' when he t'rows dere ain't no dents put in it when dey swings dere clubs;
Sam makes dem look like busher-dubs.
But dere's de pity of it all
w'en Sammy grows up big an' tall,
he won't be on no big league club,
not even on de bench as sub, 'cause big league players must be white, an Sammy Lee is black as night.
Las' Sunday, me an' Sammy seen a big league battle played between de Panthers an' de Kangaroos, an' Sammy got de blues,
fer as we watched it from a tree, he's puzzled an' he says ter me,
"where is de colored players at?
I ain't seen one go up ter bat!"
So Billy Briggs an' me jest dream an' wonder if dere ain't some scheme to change Sam's color, black as tar, an' make him white like us kids are.

Source: This poem, from George Moriarty's *Ballads of Baseball,* is found in the *Baltimore Afro-American,* March 31, 1922.

while few whites would be disqualified by it. Since many African Americans in the South, only recently freed from slavery, would likely be illiterate or made to appear so by white registrars, the result was to drastically tip the voting balance in North Carolina toward whites.

In the face of all of this truly foolish racial prejudice, a different and more joyful foolishness would be seen on baseball diamonds where players were just having fun playing the game they loved. From the *Cleveland Leader* of May 10, 1883, comes the following account:

> The colored boys of Cleveland yesterday met with the dusky blonds of St. Louis in the ball field, and the enemy captured the Cleveland lads in a manner that was remarkably wonderful to see. . . . There were many handsome black eyes watching the home team from the grand stand, and it is quite probable that our boys wanted to appear so fine before their fair admirers that in trying to outdo themselves they made some very grave errors, so the girls should let the boys down as light as possible in getting defeated, for they were slightly responsible for it. . . . Milligan came up, looked at the ladies in the stands, and smiled a smile that seemed to say "Watch me bring those two fellows in on my three-base hit." He fanned the air with his timber three times in the most desperate manner and took his seat on the players' bench. Trip gave Milligan the laugh, and then stepped up to the bat and did the same thing, much to the astonishment of a maiden who was hoping to see him pound the sphere out of sight. Everybody had just what they went out for, lots of fun, and the boys ought to have had a much larger attendance.[21]

CHAPTER 3

The Age of Great Players Playing for Great Independent Teams, 1900–1920

SETTING THE SCENE—THE NADIR

In the early 20th century, politically, socially, and economically blacks began to dig themselves slowly out of the pit that the betrayal of the hopes of Reconstruction era had plunged them into. On the baseball side, all-time greats like John Henry "Pop" Lloyd, Louis Santop, Cannonball Dick Redding, and Smokey Joe Williams emerged among a people who were beginning a migration from the South to the North that would transform forever America's racial scene.[1]

Henry McNeal Turner, a bishop in the African Methodist Episcopal Church (AME) who had been the first black army chaplain for the Union during the Civil War, had served as a legislator in Georgia's short-lived Reconstruction era–integrated legislature. But he had grown disillusioned over the years. In 1889, he would comment acerbically about the Supreme Court that had declared unconstitutional the Sumner Civil Rights Act of 1875 with its provisions guaranteeing equal accommodations in public facilities of the United States:

God may forgive this corps of unjust judges, but I never can. Their very memories will also be detested by my children's children. Nor am I alone in this detestation. The eight million of my race and their posterity will stand horror frozen at the very mention of their names. . . . But we will wait and pray, and look for a better day, for God still lives and the LORD OF HOSTS REIGNS.[2]

By 1893, the bishop's store of patience was exhausted. He was no longer willing to wait and pray in the land of his birth and rearing:

> I do not believe that there is any manhood future in this country for the Negro, and that his future existence, to say nothing of his future happiness, will depend upon his nationalization. . . . The Negro cannot remain here in his present condition and be a man, nor will it be possible to remain here a great while, for at the present rate his extermination is only a question of time.[3]

The impractical championing of a "Back to Africa" movement became Turner's work for the rest of his life.

The black major league baseball player, Moses Walker, who in the heady days of the 1880s came closer than any other African American ballplayer to achieving parity with whites, but had been "segregated out" as Jim Crow became the American norm, became in his middle age a strong advocate of voluntary separation of the races. In 1908, he wrote a pamphlet, *Our Home Colony: A Treatise on the Past, Present, and Future of the Negro Race in America,* which set forth in 48 well-written pages the case for African Americans giving up on the long denied vision of equality in America. The opportunity for advancement did not exist for Negroes, he wrote. "We see no possible hope that the Negro will ever secure the enjoyment of this social freedom or equality. Without it, he can never expect full and complete development."[4] Assisted by his baseball playing brother, Welday, Moses Walker opened an office in Steubenville, Ohio, to promote resettlement to Africa and lectured on the subject until his retirement in 1922, two years before his death.[5]

It is a remarkable commentary on the status of African Americans that as blackball moved from the 19th into the 20th century in the midst of sea changes for the nation's black population, Moses and Welday Walker, thoughtful and articulate professional baseball players, and Henry McNeal Turner, thoughtful and eloquent AME bishop, would make common cause in an impractical movement to remove blacks from America en masse and return them, so many generations removed, to their native continent. "One three centuries removed from the scenes his father loved, Spicy grove, cinnamon tree, What is Africa to me?" the black poet Countee Cullen wondered in the 1920s.[6] Well might Cullen wonder. An impractical dream-laden road back to the homeland was not a path to follow for the vast majority of African Americans. "We live here—have lived here—have a right to live here—and mean to live here" Frederick Douglass said in response to the circulation in the mid-19th century of Back to Africa notions.[7] For most African Americans at the turn into the 20th century, the sentiments of the great Douglass rang truer than those of Moses Fleetwood Walker and Henry McNeal Turner. And yet, when one looks around at the signs of the time when black baseball prepared to and then in fact entered the 20th century, one can understand the despair in their native land that must have gnawed at the spirit of ballplayer and bishop.

To understand the despair felt by the many who were attracted to the appeal of a Back to Africa call, one needs to see the reality of that apparent permanent American racism constant as it infected the nation's scene at the turn into the 20th century. That seeing can be done by visiting several places on what we will call, to use a baseball metaphor, a "spring training road." While none of the places to be visited will seem at first glance to be connected to the black version of America's national pastime, one finds time and again on this baseball journey we are taking that anything connected to the "Race" is connected to everything connected to the "Race."

This turn into the 20th century in America's baseball story occurs at the point that the historian Rayford Logan, in his monumental work aptly titled *The Betrayal of the Negro,* called "the nadir" in the history of African Americans. Logan tells us blacks had clearly been assigned to their "ugly" place in the American polity, "a terminal that seemed indestructible. On the pediment of the separate wing reserved for Negroes were carved Exploitation, Segregation, Disfranchisement, Lynching, Contempt."[8]

Of the hundreds, indeed thousands of places, peoples, and moments, one can visit to see what Logan meant by his characterization, as well as the despair felt by Bishop Turner and the Walker brothers. Brownsville, Texas, in the summer of 1906 is as good a place as any to start. Witness there in late July a "race riot" involving three companies of the black 25th regiment who it was said had "shot up the town" and murdered and maimed the citizens of Brownsville. On the basis of one report from one inspector, and apparently with no effort to distinguish participants from those who didn't join the fray, President Theodore Roosevelt dismissed the entire battalion without honor and disqualified its members for service in either the military or civil service of the United States. Even the racist senator from South Carolina, "Pitchfork" Ben Tillman, termed it an executive lynching. Senator Foraker from Ohio and John Milholland from Boston, one of the leading lawyers in the nation, carried on a long fight to win justice for the innocent. Blacks, who held their soldiers in considerable pride at a time when they had few heroes to so hold—14 Medal of Honor winners among them—were outraged and wounded by the president's judgment. Teddy Roosevelt was, after all, the first "real" friend they had had in the White House since Lincoln.[9]

Springfield, Illinois, is our next "spring training" stop. It is the summer of 1908 as the town, and indeed the nation, was preparing for the centennial of the birth of the greatest citizen that Illinois had given to her country. It was from that Springfield state capitol in 1861, with the America he would soon lead disintegrating around him, that President-elect Abraham Lincoln bade farewell to his fellow citizens. It was there that he returned four years later to be buried in arguably the nation's most sacred tomb. And it was there more than anywhere else in 1908 that his countrymen were busy preparing to commemorate most appropriately in public ceremony the upcoming centennial of his birth.

That preparation was interrupted by the unthinkable in August when interested citizens learned that George Richardson, Negro, accused of having raped the white wife of a white streetcar conductor, had been removed by train to safekeeping in Bloomington. Furious at being deprived of access to this "fiend"—who incidentally had by then been completely exonerated of the charges—these "fine" citizens turned into a mob bent on wrecking "justice" on their fellow Springfield Negro citizens. An accounting taken several days later, after more than 5,000 state militia had restored order, reported among the dead a Negro barber lynched behind his shop and an 84-year-old Negro, married to a white woman for over 30 years, who was lynched within a block of the state house. One of these lynchings occurred within a half mile of the only home that Abraham Lincoln ever owned. The other happened within two miles of his final resting place. Historian John Hope Franklin tells us that the news of this riot was almost more than Negroes could bear: "It seemed to them a perverse manner in which to approach the centennial of the birth of their Great Emancipator. Their cup was filled. They hardly had the voice to cry out against this outrage."[10]

"Spring training" stop number three is 1600 Pennsylvania Avenue. It is early November 1914. The president in residence at the White House, Woodrow Wilson, has been "swept" into office by the narrowest of margins in a three-way race that has made him a minority popular vote chief executive. Arguably, an important part of his victory margin had come from a black Northern electorate who were moved by Woodrow Wilson's campaign promise to their leaders that if he should become president of the United States they could count upon him for "absolute fair dealing, for everything for which I could assist in advancing the interest of their race in the United States."[11] Based on his promise, they cast their ballots for Wilson in several key states that gave him his electoral victory. When one of their most eloquent spokesmen, William Monroe Trotter, met with his president in the oval office and argued too passionately for Woodrow

Wilson's taste that his people deserved justice, he was told never to come again. The president had already acknowledged his debt to those blacks who voted for him, and to all those Americans who believed in justice for their nation's "Negro" citizens, by introducing formal segregation into the administration of their government in their nation's capital. So much for absolute fair dealing.[12]

One more "nadir" place to go before our "spring training" journey ends on a note of hopefulness. When we see what we find here, we will wish we hadn't come to such an awful place. It is mid-May 1918 in Brooks and Lowndes Counties, Georgia. Earlier that year, the NAACP had issued a study titled *Thirty Years of Lynching in the United States, 1889–1919*. During that period, "Judge Lynch" had taken a toll of 3,224 unfortunate souls. The "Judge" was about to take one more. Actually two. Number one was Mary Turner. She was eight months pregnant. Number two would not be given the chance to be named. An account follows:

> Her ankles were tied together and she was hung to the tree, head downward. Gasoline and oil from automobiles were thrown on her clothing and while she writhed in agony and the mob howled in glee a match was applied and her clothes were burned from her person. When this had been done and while she was yet alive, a knife, evidently one used in splitting hogs, was taken and the woman's abdomen was cut open, the unborn baby falling from her womb to the ground. The infant, prematurely born, gave two feeble cries and then its head was crushed by a member of the mob with his heel. Hundreds of bullets were then fired into the body of the woman, now mercifully dead, and the work was over.[13]

As Mary Turner met her brutal end, black soldiers, some of them professional baseball players "on leave" from their game, were preparing to acquit themselves in heroic service to their country in the final battles of a war to "make the world safe for democracy." In their own country that was presumably already safe for democracy, a half dozen people were lynched in Brooks and Lowndes Counties in the state of Georgia, from May 17 to 24, 1918.

These early decades of the 20th century must be seen for the awful times they were. They were years that were filled with events and personages that make understandable the anger and despair of Moses and Welday Walker and Henry M. Turner. But they were also times when seeds were being planted that would bear great and positive fruit. Certainly, those seeds and the hope they engendered can be found in the reminiscences of Walter White.

Atlanta born and reared, Walter White came North in the 1910s to assume a leadership position in the NAACP that across the four following decades made him one of the most eminent and productive black leaders in American history. As executive director of the NAACP from the mid-1930s through the mid-1950s, he was one of the shapers of the strategy that culminated in *Brown v. Board of Education*'s dismantling of the edifice of segregation of America's educational sector that had been supported in the highest law of the land since the "separate but equal" *Plessy v. Ferguson* decision in 1896.

In his memoirs, *A Man Called White,* Walter White recollected how close he came to losing his life at an early age when he and his father faced down a mob bent on killing his kind of people. And how close too that mob came to making him into an embittered hater.

> In the quiet that followed I put my gun aside and tried to relax. But a tension different from anything I had ever known possessed me. I was gripped by the knowledge of my identity, and in the depths of my soul I was vaguely aware that I was glad of it. I was sick with loathing for the hatred which had flared before me that night and come so close to making me a killer; but I was glad I was not one of those who hated; I was glad I was not one of those made sick and murderous by pride. I was glad I was not one of those whose story is in the history of the world, a record of bloodshed, rapine and pillage. I was glad my mind and spirit were part of the races that had not fully awakened, and who therefore still had before them the opportunity to write a record of virtue as a memorandum to Armageddon. It was all just a feeling then, inarticulate and melancholy, yet reassuring in the way that death and sleep are reassuring, and I have clung to it now for nearly half a century.[14]

We have heard Albert Murray tell us that more needs to be made of the legacy that comes to "Blues-oriented contemporary U.S. Negroes" that urges them, as their slave ancestors did, "to confront the most unpromising circumstances and make the most of what little there is to go on, regardless of the odds." In so doing, they may well find what he startlingly claims their ancestors did—"delight in the process" while "forgetting mortality at the height of ecstasy."[15] Is there not, in Walter White's refusal to allow those who hated to turn him into a hater, a considerable piece of joy, elegance, strength, and exuberance that Murray sees as an often-overlooked legacy from slavery times? Should we be surprised to find similar qualities in the black men who as heirs of slaves played and ran baseball in the early years of the 20th century?

Left to right: Roy Wilkins, Assistant National Secretary, Walter White, National Secretary, and Thurgood Marshall, Chief Counsel, National Association for the Advancement of Colored People. (Library of Congress)

SPECTACULAR BLACK BASEBALL

And could they ever play baseball! Witness the "Windy City v the City of Brotherly Love" headline in the dog days of the summer of 1909 reporting on a black professional baseball series between the American Giants from Chicago and their counterparts from Philadelphia. The lineups for these games read like a Who's Who of turn of the century Negro professional baseball. Philadelphia could boast of John Henry Lloyd, Dan McClellan, Bruce Petway, and Spotwood Poles. Chicago responded with the likes of Pete Booker, Chappie Johnson, Pete Hill, and George Wright.[16]

Spectacular fielding marked these contests. In the first game in Detroit on August 9, Chicago's George Wright "drove a shot labeled home run to the center field flag pole." The fleet-footed Spotwood Poles, sprinting from his center field position "at a 90 degree angle to the ball, leapt at the last second and pulled it down." "A more spectacular bit of fielding was never seen on the lot," wrote the *Detroit Free Press* covering the game. "There are few outfielders in the game who could have speared it."[17]

Managerial "genius" was on display as well. In the eighth inning of Poles's great catch game, "big side-wheeler Pat Dougherty throwing from the left side gave up two straight hits to open the inning. With two dangerous right-handers coming up Rube Foster sent Dougherty to the outfield and waved righty Walter Ball in from the field. Without warming up, Ball got two outs, then Dougherty returned and got a left-hander out."[18]

Outstanding pitching determined the outcome. Tied in games 1–1, Bugs Hayman took the mound for the third contest. He had also taken the mound for the second, holding Chicago to four hits in a 6–1 victory. With no days rest between starts, and with the aid of a triple play, Lloyd to Francis to James, Hayman notched another one run victory while his teammates supported him with nine runs of their own.

The series came to a close in Chicago on August 17, when Rube Foster, not yet recovered from his broken leg of early July, was bombed in a 12–2 shellacking. Series to Philadelphia, 3 games to 1. In blackball, it was indeed an era of great independents leaving their mark on the national pastime—as the likes of Mary Turner left a decidedly different mark on those best of times and worst of times.[19]

BLACK BASEBALL'S GREATEST PLAYER

Of all the baseball talent that was on display in this series, none turns out to be more outstanding than the man they called "Pop." Christened John Henry Lloyd, it seems apropos that we reference the story in song of his famous namesake as we go backward in time to the beginnings of this special player by listening to the testimony of the baseball men who knew him best.

> De man dat invented de steam drill thought he was mighty fine
> John Henry drove his fifteen feet an' de steam drill only made nine
> Lawd, Lawd, an' de steam drill only made nine.[20]

In the summer of 1985, Pop's old friend Henry "Whitey" Gruhler, former sports editor of the *Atlantic City Press,* nearing the end of his own time, recalled with considerable emotion the wonderful baseball memories of a wonderful man of long gone summer days. "You can see by the tears how much I loved him," Whitey would say.[21]

Since 1977, when his plaque went up on the wall in the shrine room at the Hall of Fame in Cooperstown, visitors to those hallowed halls on the site where baseball purportedly had its beginnings learn about the baseball feats of the man his friend and pupil Max Manning referred to as a "gentle giant." The inscription on his plaque tells us that he was "regarded as the finest shortstop to play in Negro baseball," and that among his many accomplishments, he was "instrumental in opening Yankee Stadium to Negro professional baseball in 1930."[22]

In October 1949 when the city fathers in John Lloyd's hometown of Atlantic City dedicated a park to their gentle giant, his soft-spoken almost reverent words rang strong while tears of emotion welled in his eyes: "I gave my best when I was playing ball, and today I mean to give the best that I have in expressing appreciation of the honor that has been given to me this day. I hope the young men, not only of Atlantic City but of the entire nation, will benefit from what I have tried to give the youth of America. And I promise that this day, more than anything else, inspires me to continue to live righteously, so that I may justify the confidence you folks have shown in me."[23]

> White man told John Henry,
> "Nigger damn yo' soul,
> You might beat this steam an drill of mine
> When de rocks in dis mountain tuns to gol"
> Lawd, Lawd, when de rocks in dis mountain tuns to gol[24]

It was November 1929, when decked in overalls with a dust rag in one hand and broom in the other, a reporter "recognized him in disguise" as a member of Postmaster Al Perkins crew at the main post office in Atlantic City. Perkins, a dyed-in-the-wool baseball fan, was pleased to act favorably on "Pop" Lloyd's application for off-season employment. His new hire "went about his business as though he hadn't been cheered all over the land by thousands, or that he hadn't been the greatest colored ball player." At the time, he had just passed his 45th milestone. When asked about retirement, John Lloyd quipped, with his inimitable chuckle, "I am just getting old enough to play baseball. I feel as young as I did 20 years ago."[25]

In 1928, "Pop" was welcomed back to New York with a joyous headline announcing that he was "Back in Town looking the picture of health and carrying the same winning disposition which has made him beloved in and outside the United States." While noting his "two score and four years," he is, the story tells us, "but a husky example of what the clean life can do for an athlete. . . . Fans, players and an army of other friends bid him welcome to the old town, hoping that this will be one of his most successful years in the game in Greater New York."[26]

> John Henry tol' his cap'n,
> Lightin' was in his eye,
> "Cap'n, bet yo' last red cent on me,
> Fo' I'll beat it to the bottom or I'll die,"
> Lawd, Lawd, I'll beat it to the de bottom or I'll die.[27]

Speaking from Cuba in 1927, Rafe Conte, "the dean of sports chroniclers in Cuba," said about the man they had long called "Pop," and now were referring to as the "Ancient Mariner" and "Old Warrior," that "this athlete will pass into history as the greatest player of all time to be produced by the national game."[28]

The *New York World* had singled out the "Ancient Mariner" as one of the big guns in semipro baseball. Commenting on that white paper's praise for this old black player, Romeo Dougherty of the *Amsterdam News* recollected how many times back in the early 1910s the old Lincoln Giants anchored at shortstop by the then young "Pop" had beaten the best white teams to be secured. "Big League players," the black scribe recollected, "used to come to Olympic Field between 136th and 137th to learn the finer points of the game from John Henry and his associates on the old Lincolns."[29]

> Oh, de Captain said to John Henry.
> "I b'lieve this mountain's sinkin in"
> John Henry said to the captin
> "Oh my, ain nohtin but my hammer suckin' win,
> Lawd, Lawd, ain nothin but my hammer suckin win."[30]

In October 1924, Ed Lamar, one of those present at the creation of black professional baseball, told columnist Rollo Wilson that he was especially happy when he found the reporter writing about his friend "the Kid." "I was the first white man he [John Henry Lloyd] played ball for in the North about 1905 or 1906. I wish I had a team composed of nine of his kind. I look upon him as being the greatest asset to a club of any player in the game today."[31] The "Kid" had given his old friend much to be happy about earlier that year when "he tied Tris Speaker's, Lamb's and Chas Dressen's record for most consecutive base hits"[32] and established another by getting the most bases out of his 11 in a row during a stretch of 3 games.

In April 1923, we find John Lloyd in Baltimore recently returned from the Cuba that was his second baseball home during winters in the prime of his career. He was residing at 1028 North Eutaw Street with his very charming and comely wife in a nicely appointed apartment. As a member that winter of the Havana Reds of the Cuban League, his team had finished in second place and he finished second in the batting race to the great Cristobal Torriente. Cuban fans idolized him. To show their appreciation for his fine play, they took up a public collection and presented him a diamond-studded watch fob.

This diamond-studded watch fob of a man was just

a gawky kid from Jacksonville, Florida in 1906 when he came north to play for Ed Lamar's Cuban X Giants in Philadelphia. This 16 year old had impressed the players who had gone south each winter to be waiters and to double in brass as players in the "Hotel League." After seeing him in action for several years they decided he was ready and Lamar paid his railroad fare north. His first game was against the Wilmington Giants at the old Phillies ball park. His double in the 10th inning off the famous Kid Carter won the game for the Cubans, who were not Cubans at all.[33]

A year prior to his coming North, we see our "Pop" to be as the subject of a cartoonist. The cartoon has a player on his backside, stars circling his head, with a dazed look mumbling, "Verdun had nothing on this."[34] The scene was Augusta, Georgia, 1905 with the famous twirler "Georgia Rabbit" on the slab. Our famous to be shortstop was at the time a catcher catching without a mask. "In the third inning a foul tip pounced on his left lamp; the lid closed. He moistened his finger, rubbed the bruised member, and carried on. In the seventh another foul pounced on his right lamp; it sought redress in darkness. Our young player, like a good sport, exclaimed: 'Gentlemen, I guess I'll have to quit. I can't see the ball.'"[35] Next day, he purchased a wire paper basket, enclosed his mug, and finished the series, some would say, as the inventor of the catcher's mask.[36]

John Henry Lloyd was born in Palatka, Florida, in 1884. He passed to his reward in Atlantic City, New Jersey, in 1965. He was, baseball historian Jim Riley tells us, "a complete player who could hit, run, field, throw and hit with power, especially in the clutch. He was a superlative fielder who studied batters and positioned himself wisely, got a good jump on the ball, and possessed exceptional range and sure hands with which he dug balls out of the dirt like a shovel."[37]

John Lloyd began his "big league" black professional baseball career in 1906 when Ed Lamar brought him to the Cuban X Giants. The next year, he jumped to Sol White's champion Philadelphia Giants. After playing the 1910 season in Chicago with the Leland Giants, he came east to New York with the Lincoln Giants of Jess McMahon. Back to Chicago in 1914, his four-year tenure with Rube Foster's American Giants saw the Giants claiming three Western championships with victories over the Eastern champions in 1914 and 1917. From 1918 to 1920, he was in New York with the Brooklyn Royal Giants and the New York Bacharach Giants.

"Wherever the money was, that's where I was," Lloyd said later in life.[38] In 1921, the money brought him to Columbus, Ohio, to manage and play for that city's Buckeyes entrant in the Negro National League. The year 1922 had him with the Atlantic City Bacharach Giants in a community where he would take up residence in his retirement years. In 1923, he moved a bit north and west to Philadelphia to play for: Hilldale Daisies. The years 1924 and 1925 had him back in Atlantic City with the Bacharachs as player/manager. He played out his remaining years at the top rung of Negro professional baseball as manager and first baseman for the New York Lincoln Giants and New York Stars.

In his retirement years in his adopted Atlantic City where he became a much-beloved community personage, he would manage two local semiprofessional clubs, the Johnson Stars and Farley Stars, both taking their name from political bosses in the area.[39]

When asked in 1949 at the dedication of the stadium named in his honor if he regretted that his playing days were long past before the color line in baseball was erased, John Henry "Pop" Lloyd, "this athlete who will pass into history as the greatest player of all time to be produced by the national game," replied: "I do not consider that I was born at the wrong time. I felt it was the right time, for I had the chance to prove the ability of our race in this sport, and because many of us did our very best to uphold the traditions of the game and of the world of sport, we have given the Negro a greater opportunity now to be accepted in the major leagues with other Americans."[40]

> Dey took John Henry to de graveyard,
> An dey bired him in de sand,
> And every locomotive come roaring by says
> Dere lays a steel-drivin man, Lawd, Lawd
> Dere lays a steel-drivin man![41]

ALVIN WHITE—WITNESS AND TESTIFIER: "ASK RIC ROBERTS ABOUT JOHN LLOYD"

In September 1981, when I asked Al White about the black sportswriter, Ric Roberts, I got a typically succinct comment, and something more as well.

As for Ric Roberts, he will speak—and how—for himself. If you can recall it ask him about ball player John Henry Lloyd whom

I blasphemously say outranks Josh Gibson. Lloyd was a great infielder, short, second, first in that order as he grew older. He was one of the greatest right handed batters of all time, as Babe Ruth once said. Lloyd played long before Gibson arrived. All the Gibson addicts were contemporary. You realize, knowing a player who is concurrent establishes him with that generation. Tradition keeps some players great. Do you know that Hub "Shucks" Pruett, a lefty with the old St. Louis Browns, fanned Babe nine times in succession but was not able to beat any other teams?

Source: Alvin White to Lawrence Hogan, September 9, 1981.

BERT WILLIAMS AS A BASEBALL MAN

If we can dub Pop Lloyd as the "Somebody Man," next comes the "Nobody Man." If Pop was best at shortstop, Bert Williams was definitely the best front and center stage making us laugh. There was simply no one like him back then, before him, and apparently since. Interestingly, as we shall see, the same might be said for him as a baseball guy.

As with anyone who was privileged to see Bert Williams perform, Al White remembered him well. My old friend writes in a letter dated February 27, 1977, that

> I am looking forward to this Minstrel thing touted for TV next week. Sometime ago I contacted all three major networks. You know the old routine, fill out this and sign it, etc—suggesting a program marking the 100th birthday of Bert Williams, the greatest black comedian ever. He was starred ten years in the Ziegfeld Follies. I was fortunate enough to see him in Washington just before he died. Ben Vereen does what he calls a Bert Williams thing, signing his favorite song, "Nobody." Let me tell you emphatically, Ben Vereen, talent and all, is no more Bert Williams than I am Caruso—and I don't know one damned note from another.[42]

His biographer, Ann Charters, tells us that Bert Williams was "the first Negro entertainer in America to win the wholehearted admiration of white audiences, and in a *Variety* poll of 1953 which selected the names of the ten most important comedians in the history of the American popular theater, he was high on the list."[43] This comedic genius is not normally associated with America's national pastime, but belong there he does. While it is doubtful that Ernest Thayer had Bert Williams in mind when he penned his immortal opening verses of the most memorable of all baseball poems, as we shall see, well he might have:

> The outlook wasn't brilliant for the Mudville nine that day
> The score stood 4–2 with but an inning left to play,
> And then when Cooney died at first, and Barrows did the same
> A sickly silence fell upon the patrons of the game.
>
> They thought if only Casey could but get a wack at that,
> They'd put up even money now with Casey at the bat,
> But Flynn preceded Casey
> And so did Jimmy Blake
> And the later was a lulu, and the former was a cake.[44]

As we all know, that mighty Casey "did strike out." But why? Might it have been a hole in his bat? And what kind of fielder was the mighty one?

The newspaper report for a game early in June 1908 has it that as captain and first baseman of the Williams and Walker team facing off against the Colored Vaudeville Artists, Bert Williams distinguished himself in several ways. "In the first place he brought with him a bat with a hole in it that caused him on more than one occasion to do what Casey did at the bat—strike out."[45]

We have no account of how the Mighty Casey did in the field. His erstwhile imitator appears to have performed there in a fashion similar to what he and his "mentor" did at bat when it came to clutch hitting. It was said that one time in Boston, a nine of burlesque comedians undertook to annihilate Bert Williams's team and that Williams contributed to an inglorious defeat by muffing a ball at a critical point and stopping it with his teeth instead of his hands.

One baseball commentator was bold enough to suggest that Bert Williams had elected himself captain of the Williams and Walker ball team by virtue of his prominence as a star of the stage, and that this same spirit of bravado had prompted him to challenge the whole theatrical world. Another critic characterized him as being as incompetent a player as he was expert a comedian. If that characterization is at all close to the mark, given how good he was as a comedian he may well have been the world's worst amateur baseball player.

If the June 1908 contest is any fair test, these critics could well have been on the mark. Our reporter for that game tells us that Williams participated in two plays

> that assisted in making history for the Williams and Walker team. In the last half of the ninth inning with the vaudeville players at bat, "Bass" Foster hit the ball near second which should have been Shipp's, but the comedian went after the ball, leaving no one on first to put the runner out. Shortly afterwards a ball was knocked over first which made the first baseman and his teammates "feel so sick and so forlorn." He saw the ball coming toward him, but it looked like about the size of a marble, hence it made its way into the field uncaptured and the bases were cleared.[46]

Nobody left on base—nobody to blame but himself.

> When life seems full of clouds and rain
> And I am filled with nothing and pain
> Who soothes my thumping, bumping brain?
> He paused and shrugged with a sigh
> **Nobody!**[47]

Bert Williams first sang "Nobody" in 1905. It is the song he is most remembered for. Audiences responded so enthusiastically that he was forced to include it for the next 17 years in nearly every stage performance. It became his trademark, the statement of a hard-luck character who had done "nothin' to nobody, no time."[48]

In the bible of early black baseball, *Sol White's Official Base Ball Guide*, our "Nobody Man" comedic genius is captioned under his photo as "Manager and First Baseman of the W. and W. B.B.C., and all around fan." It might well be that he was more than just an amateur player of baseball and an "all-around fan" of the Negro professional version of our national pastime. Bill Yancy, who starred for many years on the highest levels of Negro professional baseball, tells us that the Philadelphia Giants who gave him his first professional try out in 1923 had been owned by our Edgbert "who had broken the Broadway color line with the Ziegfeld Follies."[49]

> When summer comes all cool and clear.
> And my friends see me drawing near,
> Who says come in and have some beer?
> A note of surprise in his voice,
> **Hum—Nobody!**[50]

Apparently Williams was something of a boxer as well who gained his skill in that sport from "no less a sparring instructor than Joe Gans, once champion lightweight of the world."[51] In a trade-off that gave Gans access to a comely beauty featured in the Williams and Walker theatricals, our erstwhile Casey learned to box with a fair degree of skill. But in spite of his apparent inability to play it as well as his teammates may have wished he could, baseball seems to have been his favorite sport. We have no reports, however, of protests by his players of his captaincy, nor of their being especially upset with him for his performance at bat or in the field. It would indeed have been hard to be upset with the likes of this particular Casey. Listen to the sentiments he merited on the occasion of his death in a piece by Roger Didier, Percival Prattis's nom de plume, that bears the title

Thousands Kneel at Bier of Williams

Artists, Producers, Stars, Chorus—
Millionaire and Ragamuffin Rub
Elbows over Remains of Peerless
Comedian
There's strangeness all around us
now,
How come it strange? we wonder
how
Each sunbeam has a brighter hue?
Each raindrop is a crystal blue;
And clouds, those dull, gray globes of
mist
With drops and sunbeams hold a
tryst
The March winds e'en don't blow so
cold,

And there's a dancing in the snow.
If I beyond the skies could see
The hands that send the things to
free
Old Earth of sorrow and of pain,
That baffles all our might and main;
Of hungry hearts and stomachs, too,
Of mean men who our hopes subdue,
And all those crushing, blighting
things

> That kill us with their hurts and
> stings.
>
> I'd see an angel in that isle,
> With shambling gait and quick'ning
> smile,
> Who'd tell the Hands that set us
> free,
> Just what it takes for you and me;
> For Bert's up there, explaining how,
> That's why it's strange. No wonder
> now
> Each sunbeam has a brighter hue,
> Each raindrop is a crystal blue.[52]

So who was this Bert Williams whose baseball playing finds it ways onto the sports pages of the *New York Age,* whose photo adorns the premier guide to black baseball, and who may have been an owner of a Negro professional team? From his own day, testifiers abound. Their commentary echoes the mores of a time very different racially speaking than ours, and perhaps impossible for us to fully understand. But what there can be no doubt about is the character and talent of the man to whom they testify. On the occasion of his too early death, words of praise rang strong.

The *Chicago Defender* called him the world's greatest comedian, terming his death an "international calamity. It is not only a serious loss to the Race or group with which he was identified, but to the human race."[53] W. C. Fields said he was the "funniest man he ever saw, and the saddest man he ever knew."[54]

> When winter comes with snow and sleet,
> And me with hunger and cold feet,
> Who says, Here's twenty-five cents,
> go ahead and get something to eat?
> He shook his head sadly
> **Nobody!**[55]

From theatrical impresario George M. Cohan, who knew the theater profession inside and out, came the encomium that he knew no man in the profession "who was more highly respected or better liked. I never heard Bert say an unkind word about any man or woman, and by the same token I never heard any man or woman say an unkind word about him."[56]

The great comedian and actor Eddie Cantor was particularly thoughtful in his assessment of the work of his friend:

> Those who have followed his work in detail will agree with me that very frequently during moments in odd scenes Bert Williams dipped into the great realm of the fundamental art of acting and gave us emotion or comedy which was as universal in its appeal as the very writings of Shakespeare himself. Bert Williams had a natural aptitude for acting which was born with him, and which he cultivated industriously during all the years of his career. But he also had a great affection for human nature. So his analysis of his fellow man was never cold, and consequently his reproduction of it in his acting was human and compelling.[57]

But not all were so praiseworthy as his fellow white stage greats. The radical black monthly, the *Messenger,* saw his career differently than did the likes of Fields, Cohan, and Cantor:

> As we see it, Bert Williams, as he was, rendered a disservice to black people. He was heralded throughout the country as a great comedian; but he left in his train the fallen gods of Negro culture-urgings. He played in theaters that either barred or Jim Crowed Negroes—a policy born of the conception that all men of color are inherently inferior to white men. And by a strange irony of fate Bert Williams himself was a facile instrument of this insidious cult. At the end, he lamented his failure to be considered and acclaimed as a whole, full-orbed man on the American stage and yet his life's work rendered it possible for the Negro actor to be received as a half-man only.[58]

The *Messenger*'s cannot be the last word. Give that to the man, Dr. W.E.B. Du Bois, who is, often as not, the right last word source to turn to:

> When in the calm afterday of thought and struggle to racial peace we look back to pay tribute to those who helped the most, we shall single out for highest praise those who made the world laugh; Bob Cole, Ernest Hogan, George Walker, and above all, Bert Williams.
>
> For this was no mere laughing; it was the smile that hovered above blood and tragedy; the light mask of happiness that hid breaking hearts and bitter souls. This is the top of bravery; the finest thing in service.
>
> May the world long honor the undying fame of Bert Williams as a great comedian, a great Negro, and a great man.[59]

And we would add a great all-around fan of the game. But as to whether our Casey could play it well, that is another matter all together.

ANOTHER BLACK CASEY?

In the same *Sol White's Official Base Ball Guide* where Bert Williams makes a baseball appearance, there appears a poem by a Nat Wright titled "When Casey Slugged the Ball." Up to the debut at the 2013 Cooperstown Symposium on Baseball and American Culture of Kevin Kane's wonderful "Breaking the Line with the Mudville Nine," this could well have been "the official," and certainly the first, "Black Casey." The poem was originally published in *Sporting Life* in 1895. Its author, Mr. Wright, was apparently white.

> Oh, you all have heard of Mudville,
> Heard of Mighty Casey too;
> Of the groans amid the bleachers
> As the ball thrice past him flew;
> But you haven't heard the story.
> The best story of them all,
> On the day in happy Mudville,
> When great Casey slugged the ball.
>
> Twas the day they played "the Giants,"
> And the score stood ten to eight;
> Two men were on the bases,
> And great Casey at the plate.
> "Swipe her, Casey" yelled the rooters,
> And the hero doffed his cap;
> Three to win and two to tie,
> And Casey at the bat.
>
> Mid a hush of expectation,
> Now the ball flies past his head;
> Great Casey grins a sickly grin;
> "Strike one," the umpire said.
> Again the pitcher raised his arm,
> Again the horse-hide flew;
> Great Casey spat upon the ground,
> And the umpire said, "strike two."
>
> "It's a roast," came from the grandstand,
> "He is bought without a doubt!"
> He is rotten roared the bleachers,
> "Throw the daylight robber out!"

"I'll break yer face," says Casey,
"That one went below my knee";
"If I miss the next, ye blackguard"
"Ye won't live long to see."

The next one came like lightening,
And the umpire held his breath,
For well he knew if Casey missed
T'would surely mean his death!
But Casey swung to meet it.
Backed by all his nerve and gall;
Oh, if you had but heard the tell,
As Casey smashed the ball!

He caught the pigskin on the nose,
It cleared the big town lot,
It sailed above the high church tower,
In vain the fielders sought;
And Casey didn't even run,
He stopped a while to talk,
And then amid the deafening cheers
He came round in a walk.

And now he keeps a beer saloon;
He is Mayor of the town.
The people flock to see him
From all the country round;
And you need not look for Mudville
On the map upon the wall,
Because the town is called Caseyville
Since Casey slugged the ball.

Source: Sol White's Official Base Ball Guide.

THE CLAN DARBY SEIGE GUN

Black baseball during Bert Williams's time was many things, as it is of course today. It was and is fans, and executives, and owners, and umpires, and league organization, and on and on. But what it is always in its essence is the player out on the field. Rube Foster and Tenny Bount went to the mat in the winter

One of the best independent, nonleague teams of the 1910s and 1920s was the Mohawk Giants. The Giants played out of Schenectady, New York. (National Baseball Hall of Fame Library, Cooperstown, NY)

of 1924 over the way the Negro National League was being run. "The fan," Ira Lewis intoned in a 1925 column on the Foster/Blount rhubarb, "is not very much interested over who owns the club or where the money goes. All he wants for his coin is an honest to goodness game on the level all the way with evenly matched teams that can play ball up to the handle, and the politics of the game can go hang."[60] One of those players who always gave to fans "an honest to goodness game on the level all the way" is the man they called "The Lone Star Ranger" and the "Clan Darby Siege Gun," Louis Napoleon Santop, often simply called "Top."

In the East, during the first two Eastern Colored League seasons of 1923 and 1924, for at least one more afterward, and for so many seasons before the league's founding that only old-time fans could recollect with any precision exactly how many, there was "Top," a standout catcher playing Negro professional baseball, swinging a bat he named "Big Bertha." You rooted strongly for Top—or strongly against him—but you could never ignore the "Seige Gun."

Sportswriter Bart Giblin was a youngster when he saw him in Montclair, New Jersey, in the early 1920s. He was then a catcher well past his prime. For 20 minutes during pregame warm-ups, he fired the baseball accurately around the horn from the crouch position—first base! shortstop! third base! back to first—with the infielders never sure where his hard throws would come next. On that Hilldale team, "Top" was passing his skills and baseball smartness along to "Biz" (Hall of Famer Raleigh "Biz" Mackey), and "Biz" in turn would pass them to "Campy" (Hall of Famer Roy Campanella).[61]

Henry "Whitey" Gruhler, longtime sports editor of the *Atlantic City Press*, remembered a game in Atlantic City, New Jersey, probably about the same time that Bart Giblin marveled over the great catcher's rifle of an arm, when "a little colored woman who couldn't have weighed 90 pounds was ragging 'Top' from behind a chicken wire screen in back of home plate." She wanted him to "bring her some wood"—baseball terminology for a strike out. With his "Big Bertha" in hand, he went over to his manager, borrowed a dollar, came over to her, got her dollar in return, stuck both through the fence, and said, you hold the stakes. He went back up to the plate, pointed Bertha toward the outfield fence like the great Babe purportedly did in the 1932 World Series, hit the next pitch for a home run, trotted around the bases, and came over to pick up his winnings. In all his years of watching baseball, Gruhler said he never saw a fan happier to lose a wager than that chicken fence lady.[62]

Rollo Wilson gives him to us in the spring of 1926 preparing for his 19th season in professional baseball. Over that winter, he had stayed in shape working at a quarry in the Broad Street subway in Philadelphia. The normal hard rock man would use a sledge and drill or an air hammer to make holes for dynamite shots. But with tongue only slightly in check, scribe Wilson tells us that our friend Top, who hails from Tyler, Texas, on the Rio Pecos, did his drilling in anything but a normal fashion. "He stands in front of particularly obstreperous mounds of rock and CUSSES holes into them and then they are ready for the shots." This, Top would tell Wilson, is the first time in his history that he has received money "for exercising his inherent talent as a blasphemer of parts."[63]

Louis Santop came to the Philadelphia Giants and their manager Home Run Johnson in 1911. His teammates included several greats of that era, among them the fine backstop "Doc" Wiley and the great "Cannonball" Dick Redding. When he left the Giants, Top went to Jess McMahon's Lincolns in New York where he remained through 1916 playing with the likes of John Henry Lloyd, Pete Booker, Judy Gans, Spot Poles, and Tom Johnson. He joined the Hilldale Daisies for the 1917 season and played for Uncle Sam's Navy in 1918. In 1919, he managed the Brooklyn Royal Giants, and came back to the Daisies in 1920 to anchor clubs that would win championships in the Eastern Colored League and a Negro World Series title in 1925.

As Top's time left in the game grew short, it was not hard for veteran writer Wilson to conjure up vivid baseball images of this great player:

- Santop and his arrogant swagger towards the plate when a hit means a run and mayhap the old ball game.
- Santop tramping the turf of the batter's box.
- Santop meeting a fast one on the inside.
- The only pitchers who do not respect his prowess when the going is rough are those who have had no previous experience with the Disappearing Gun.
- He retains his edge even at his advanced baseball age. His joints may be creaky, his eyes may be rheumy, but his educated bat can always pick out the good ones and ride them to and over the outfield barriers.[64]

And then the most notable context of all. When we get around to naming that all-time, all-star team, and "someone-for instance, Rube Foster-with an intimate knowledge of Negro baseball and its players, writes a history of the game, his All-Time team will have as its first-string catcher our boy friend of the Rio Pecos, Louis Napoleon Santop."[65]

THE CANNON

One of the pitchers that the "Siege Gun" would have caught on that imaginary Fosterian all-time, all-star team, as well as on all-time, all-star squads actually picked by Al White and "Pop" Lloyd, would be Dick Redding, the man they called the "Cannonball." As the 1924 season approached, *Pittsburgh Courier* columnist Rollo Wilson shared a communication with his readers from one of his favorite ballplayers: "Bunnie Downs and the rest of the gang are back from the Florida season. The fellows are all tanned and healthy. They are rarin' to go in the Eastern League. Wooden Shoes Richard (Dick Redding) avers and affirms that he has found out how to add an extra mile a second to his cannonball. Which makes us glad that we shall be writing and not playing ball on the Eastern circuit this summer."[66]

He was called "Grenade" after his exploits in World War I. His better-known nickname tells you all you need to know about his pitching prowess. "Cannonball" indeed! From his era, there is no finer judge of talent than the first baseman and manager, Ben Taylor, who tells us that the Cannon had more speed on his fastball than probably any man in the world. Weighing in at 225 pounds on a compact 6-foot frame, you see in his photos the build of a great speedballer. Taylor, one of the best hitters of his era, faced "Grenade" often. In 1925, he would testify to the futility of that experience: "From 1911 when he broke into fast company, until a few years ago he used nothing but his 'smoke ball.' And it was impossible to hit it. I know, because I have tried."[67]

In May 1919, he lost a no-hit no-run contest to the other great pitcher of his era, Smokey Joe Williams. Our scribe tells us that Dick Redding, always a good loser, remarked after the game, "You have to take your hat off to Joe."[68] Most of the time the hats were taken off to the "Cannonball." Incomplete as our records are for the prime of his era, it is clear that few, if any, equaled Dick Redding when it came to winning big games against major league competition. A year after he came up to the big black leagues in 1911, he recorded exhibition game victories over the New York Giants, the Boston Braves, and the Jersey City team of the International League. In the later tilt, the sepia moundsman fanned 24 batters. Carl Mays, the great submarine ball pitcher of New York Yankee fame, went down to defeat by our black hurler in 1921 in a 15-inning contest by a score of 2–1. In that same year, by that same score, he bested Jack Scott's All-America club comprised mostly of major leaguers. The young Bambino, Babe Ruth, coming off of a 59–home run season, went down on strikes three times in 1922 against our old baseball hero as he neared the end of his career. Against Negro professional competition, the Redding record is equally outstanding. In his rookie season, he won 29 straight games against some of the best colored teams in the country, including four victories over Rube Foster and one over the great Mendez. He once struck out, in 1912, 25 men in a nine-inning game, facing that day a minimum of 27. In that same year, he bested the Cuban Stars without a hit or run. Across his black baseball career, he is credited with 12 no-hit games.[69]

With an approaching old-timer contest in 1939, the *Amsterdam News* columnist St. Claire Bourne was moved to write that

> It is too bad that the campaign now going on to win Negro players an opportunity in the white major leagues wasn't being waged two or three decades ago. One of my most esteemed contemporaries recently opined that one of the many ills now afflicting Negro baseball is unfamiliarity of the public with any of its stars or their records. Your correspondent, motivated by the announcement of the old timers game this Sunday at Randalls' Island, dug up some old stuff and found snatches of the record of "Cannonball" Dick Redding, and "Pardners," with his record, it should have taken very little pushing to have him snapped up by any of the ofay magnates.[70]

In other words, the Cannonball was Big League star material.

In that same year, organized white professional baseball marked the 100th anniversary of its purported founding in 1839 by Cooperstown's Abner Doubleday. Ceremonies across that summer were highlighted with the induction of an outstanding first class of baseball greats into the newly opened National Baseball Hall of Fame. Among them was the pitcher Grover Cleveland Alexander. There was a time in Dick Reading's career when he crossed the color line and hitched up with an Eastern League All-Star aggregation, teaming up with such men as Larry McLeon, catcher; Mike Dolan, first base; Paul Dietz, shortstop; Chief Bender; Andy Coakley; and Matty Sheridan. Playing the regular Boston Braves with the addition of Ty Cobb in right field, Redding scored a 1–0 shutout in 10 innings. In a second game, he and Grover Cleveland battled to a 14-inning 2–2 tie. Redding carried off major honors by winning a third contest, 3–1 beating Dick Rudolph.

When Dick Redding was pitching his old timers' game at Randall's Island, Grover Cleveland was going into the Hall of Fame. As of this writing, more than 70 years later, we are still waiting for the Cannonball to join the great Alex in Cooperstown's shrine room.

Let his friend, contemporary, and frequent opponent Ben Taylor's be the last word on Cannonball Dick Redding:

> He has truly been an iron man. Many times pitching doubleheaders and two or three days straight without any rest. His name should go down in history as one of the greatest pitchers of all time.[71]

In other words, Dick Redding is a baseball immortal and worthy of Hall of Fame induction.

ALVIN WHITE—WITNESS AND TESTIFIER: SINNERS GOING TO SUNDAY BASEBALL

An April 20, 1981, letter from Al White takes us back to a time when the likes of the Cannonball and his contemporary, Smokey Joe, couldn't pitch on Sundays.

> Blacks were the Guinea Pigs in busting the law against Sunday baseball. Now this was way back yonder around 1914, before Irvin and Leonard, in the heyday of Joe Williams and Dick Redding. Spectators had only Sundays off to see games. Baseball was played at Olympia Oval where the Riverton apartment stands, only a few blocks from the Schomburg. Players hit balls eastward to the Harlem River. Every Sunday the police would arrest the pitcher, catcher and umpire for violating the law. They would be fined, but these were only ruses so the real game could get underway. I did the story on how they broke the barrier when Jimmy Walker, then a state senator, introduced legislation outlawing barring Sunday sports. He provided a concession of course to the church groups opposing him. No game could start until 2:05 PM which gave church folk time to switch from saints going to church to sinners going to baseball.

Source: Alvin White to Lawrence Hogan, April 20, 1981.

THE BIGGEST DADDY OF THEM ALL

If the Cannonball was something else, then his sometimes teammate and oftentimes rival Smokey Joe Williams was something else plus. In 1926, Jim Keenan, involved in amateur and semiprofessional baseball for more than 25 years, 15 as owner of the Lincoln Giants, would say that the greatest pitching duel he ever witnessed was when the "Big Train," Walter Johnson, bested Smokey Joe by a score of 1–0.

Smokey Joe Williams was the object of considerable pride, and could be the object of considerable argument whenever black fans gathered to talk baseball. You could expect a "h of an argument" when arguably the premier orator of his day, Colonel Roscoe Conkling Simmons, and FAY Young, arguably the premier sportswriter of that same day, got to talking whether Walter Johnson or Joe Williams was the greatest American pitcher. FAY claimed that in making the case for Smokey Joe over the Big Train, he won all the time because "he didn't let the Colonel get a word in edgewise."[72]

Young had considerable ammunition at his call. Perhaps, he used as arguing points Joe Williams's lifetime record of 20–7 in exhibitions against major league competition. Or perhaps, more specifically, his 6–0 besting of the world champion New York Giants in 1912. Or perhaps, the time in 1915 when he struck out 10 batters while throwing a 3-hit shutout at Grover Cleveland Alexander and the Philadelphia Phillies. Or perhaps, his extraordinary performance in 1917 when he lost a 1–0 tussle to the New York Giants while striking out 20 and giving up no hits.

His mere physical presence on a baseball diamond even when he wasn't pitching was such as to rally his troops and inspire comparisons to great characters from literature. In a Bacharachs versus Lincoln Giants battle in late July 1923 at the Protectory Oval in the Bronx, the Atlantic City squad pushed 2 runs across the plate in the top of the 7th for a seemingly insurmountable 4–1 lead.

> But in the bottom of the 8th the Oval band struck up "Tell Her I Stutter" followed by the sweet strains of "Dixie," and the redoubtable Joe Williams took the coaching lines for Lincoln. He posed upon the diamond this time hurling, rather than fast pitches, quick advice coupled with defiance born of studied resistance.
>
> Joe stood for a moment and appeared as Milton described the warrior: "Like Tenerife or Atlas unremoved," or "Expert when to advance, to stand or retreat."
>
> Such was Joe's insight into the game that it seemed to act like an inspiration for his players, and they pounded the sphere and sprinted

around the bases, Poles, Perry and Marcell scoring and tying the score. Marcell's hit was one of the greatest line drives of the season and the spectators showed their appreciation, as did good natured Jim Keenan in a substantial way.

Smokey Joe's inspiration continued into the ninth when, with the score tied, "High Pocket" Hudsfeth [*sic*] faced the Bacharachs Arthur "Rats" Henderson. Hudsfeth sent a whizzing single to left field. Perry forced him out at second by a close margin. Poles went out to left field. Pierce drove a grounder between Francis and Lundy, and Perry scampered over the rubber with the winning run amid vociferous cheers and general, intense excitement. Score 5–4 in favor of the (Joe Williams inspired) Lincoln Giants.[73]

By 1924, reports had it that he had "gone back so far" that he had lost his speed. But apparently, he had more than most to lose. One report early that year had it that "players of the Eastern Circuit were claiming that if Joe hits you on the arm or leg with a ball now it will only break the arm or leg."[74] One might wonder what it would have done when he was in his prime. Word was that the 47-year-old hurler's best days were behind him. The astute Cumberland Posey thought otherwise when he signed the aged veteran to a Homestead Grays contract. Rollo Wilson agreed with Posey:

> In snaring Joe Williams, my playfellow of the Monon Valley has made a ten-strike. Cum has gathered in one of the real pitchers of baseball and one of the great drawing cards off all time. Cyclone Joe is one of the immortals, one of the old guard who die but never surrender. Truly independent clubs of the Pittsburgh district are in for hard sledding when they face the G.A.R. vet. Back of the ball wizardry which he summons with his supple fingers and steel muscles is an agile brain and a clean life. In any battle where brain and skill are pitted against brawn and dumb luck, I'll bet the B.R. ride on the intelligentsia entry.[75]

Williams's Lincoln Giants would rue the day that their great Smokey went West to Pittsburgh. In early June, with all the cunning that a veteran hurler can bring to the mound, he defeated his former teammates 9–0, making them "do everything but walk on a tight rope" and sending them into a spin that saw them drop 2 out of 3 to the Bacharachs and a key Saturday game to Hilldale.[76]

Three years later and still with the Grays, the "50 year old wonder, the great veteran, the daddy of them all"[77] scored two successive shutout victories over a team of major league all stars in what was becoming an annual and profitable postseason exhibition series for his Homestead team. These major league contingents had the likes of Heine Manush, Harry Heilman, and Jimmy Foxx in their lineups.

Watching someone pitch a great game or two is one thing. Watching someone pitch great games across a 25-year career is quite another. John Condon was a white man who did that 25-year kind of watching. Condon just loved to watch Negro baseball. One of his favorite spots to watch it was Protectory Oval in the Bronx where he regularly held forth with cigars and a cherry word for players and scribes while his favorite among favorites held forth on the pitcher's mound for the Lincoln Giants. The redoubtable Rollo Wilson tagged Condon as one of the most ardent followers of Negro baseball in the world. A good part of that enthusiasm was produced by his all-time favorite, Joe Williams.

> During 25 years of experience of the writer, no pitcher has ever had his poise, speed and equipoise during trying times, and his manly bearing has won for him the respect, admiration and well deserved praise of all the baseball customers, friends and foe alike.
>
>   His pitching with curves, speed, deception and change of pace show great possibilities, regardless of color, and he is an example of patience, loyalty and firm determination, which is a good talisman for many white pitchers in the "big show" to follow.[78]

There must have been many memorable Joe Williams gems for John Condon during the many seasons he cheered for the great hurler. But none was likely more remembered than the early season tilt against a strong Bushwick club in 1924. Pitching on this occasion for the Brooklyn Royal Giants, Williams, in mid-season form from his Florida winter season, relieved Flourney in the first inning after four men had come to bat. One run was over the plate and the bases were full. An error permitted another run to score, and then Williams started his strikeouts. He fanned 3 in the 1st, 2 in the 2nd, 3 in the 3rd, 3 in the 4th, 2 each in the 5th and 6th, 3 in the 7th, 1 in the 8th, 2 in the 9th, 1 in the 10th, 2 in the 11th, and 1 in the 12th. When the Royals of Brooklyn pushed across a go-ahead run in the top of the 12th and Williams retired the first 2 Bushwicks in the bottom half of the inning, victory seem secure enough to send fans toward the exits. But his 25 total strikeouts would go for naught when a 2 out rally ending with an error in center gave the contest to the Bushwicks by a score of 4–3.

SMOKEY JOE AT HIS BEST

A great Joe Williams pitching performance moved the ardent John Condon to poetic praise in

> "Cyclone Joe"
> (A Tribute to Joe Williams)
> All baseball players, listen!
> I'll tell you what I know,
> Of that great Negro pitcher,
> That's known as Cyclone Joe.
>
> He faces the batters, one and all,
> He hears the umpire shout,
> "Just take that bat, take him away,
> That makes three strikes; you're out."
>
> Record strikeouts have been made
> As sure as you're alive,
> But Cyclone Joe has distanced them
> With his great twenty-five.
>
> When Joe just gets a-going
> The sphere just seems to fly.
> No batter gets a safe one,
> The champions are his pie.
>
> He journeyed on to Brooklyn
> In nineteen-twenty-four.
> He startled all the Bushwicks,
> Who thought his work was o'er
> He bowled these star performers;
> The ball just seemed to dive
> Of twenty seven batters,
> He fanned just twenty-five.

And in closing verses reminiscent of *Macaulay's* "Horatius at the Bridge," our baseball poet looks forward to a time

> When future baseball writers
> Give honor men a crown,
> The palm will go to Cyclone Joe,
> He'll wear the laurel crown

When kiddies hug the wintry fire
And Northern breezes blow,
They'll sound his praise with one accord,
They'll cheer for Cyclone Joe.

Source: New York Amsterdam News, July 7, 1923.

Joe Williams: the "Smokey" one. (National Baseball Hall of Fame Library, Cooperstown, NY)

Let John Condon have the last word on the pitcher who in a poll of knowledgeable black baseball men conducted by the Pittsburgh *Courier* in 1952 beat out Satchel Paige 20–19 for all-time best Negro pitcher honors.

"Yes, the 'Texas Wonder,' Cyclone Joe Williams, is a credit to his state, his colleagues in the American Negro League, and to the colored people at large."

"The great veteran, the daddy of them all" indeed![79]

SOUTHWARD BOUND

That "Daddy of Them All," as did all the other star "Daddys" of North American black baseball, found year-round employment in Caribbean climes doing what they loved to do best. Starting in 1906, and for every season thereafter, a substantial contingent of players from "North of the border" would take up baseball residence in the winter months to "South of the border" and leave their mark on a game they were making international in its extent and scope.

The connection here went both ways. The baseball men of the Caribbean, mostly from Cuba, came North as well. Interactions on the U.S. and Cuban playing fields produced new Latino stars for black baseball. Historian Adrian Burgo has chronicled well how their exploits facing off against North American greats like Foster, Lloyd, and "Home Run" Johnson propelled Latinos such as Jose Mendez, Cristobal Torriente, and others into black baseball's elite in the United States.

But for the baseball fans of Cuba, what mattered the most was not who went North to star before foreign crowds, but who came South to play in their winter leagues and to give them their annual winter baseball treats. Those who came from the North once would usually become repeat visitors. The list is indeed impressive with easily recognizable names like Rogan, Marcelle, Lundy, Charleston, Warfield, Holloway, Mackey, and others appearing regularly in box scores of Cuban winter league play carried in Northern black papers.

Among the repeat visitors, John Lloyd stands out. "Idol of Cuban Fans" reads the heading on an article in the *Baltimore Afro-American* reporting on "Pop" Lloyd's return to the United States after playing one winter as a member of the Havana Reds in the Cuban League.[80] He had finished second twice in that season, with his team second in the standings and himself second in hitting to the great Cristobal Torriente.

In a scene worthy of a Dickens, the *Afro-American* writer recounts the favor Lloyd earned among an unusual group of fans. The home park of the Reds was situated on a hill overlooking the Cuban penal institution.

Every day the prisoners were marched out into the yard and allowed to occupy a point of vantage where they could watch the games. When the season ended, they showed their appreciation of the famous ball player by presenting him a hand-engraved walking stick, the figures of which illustrates a bull fight, the whole colored in various tints. They tried to force from him a promise that he will return next year as early as October.[81]

Julian Rojo, generally considered to be one of the best Cuban catchers ever to play in the Negro Leagues. (National Baseball Hall of Fame Library, Cooperstown, NY)

WORLD WAR I

By 1917, black baseball was involved with things international that had far greater consequence than its Latin American connection. Spring training that year witnessed America's entry into the conflict that had been raging in Europe for close to three years. In response to the country's involvement, black leadership struggled to formulate a strategy appropriate to their people's peculiar relationship to a nation that was deeply theirs—and yet also deeply not theirs. That response would be as varied as W.E.B. Du Bois's famous line "close ranks for the duration" stance in the infant and remarkably growing *Crisis Magazine* of the infant and remarkably growing NAACP—we must support the war effort and wait till the fighting is finished to press our demands for home front justice; to a young A. Philip Randolph serving time in jail for opposing the war and what his nation had come to stand for on the racial home front; and to Harlem's soon to be famous Hellfighters Division, the 369th, on its way to France by December 1917 to compile a war record second to none.

There would be little public questioning, little ambiguity in the response that was forthcoming from the ranks of black baseball. Many of the best players traded in their bats and gloves for rifles and canteens to fight, they thought, for a better life for their people and their nation. The baseball ranks quickly began to be depleted, as all through the first wartime summer and into the next the soldiers' ranks swelled with black enlistees and draftees. Cannonball Dick Redding was dubbed "Grenade" after the war for his fighting exploits. Louis Santop traded his "Big Bertha" and his catcher's tools for the tools of war. Dicta Johnson and a host of others abandoned their baseball wars for a much more dangerous and consequential form of warfare.

World War I of course had a meaning for black Americans well beyond the toll it took from baseball clubs. They were fighting as they had since the wars of colonial times in the hope that service to their country in her time of greatest need would translate into justice from that country in more normal times. While they fought in foreign lands, their people at home witnessed a continuing incidence of lynching, had to deal with the fear of being tagged as an enemy fifth-column undermining from within, and saw the growth of a Klan emboldened by its nation's cinematic embrace of D. W. Griffith's racist classic *Birth of a Nation*. They also continued to face the inbred racism of a South that at the same time loved and hated its "negras" whose migration to the North, swelled by the labor demands of an expanding wartime economy, ironically led to increasing racial danger in the rural and small town land they were leaving as well as in the cities of their destination. And in the immediate aftermath of the war, they were assaulted by the "Red Summer" of 1919 with race riots in at least 22 U.S. cities and 74 blacks lynched in that year alone.

All this combined to make the war years and the immediate postwar scene a period of intense racial tension. Often that tension would manifest itself in the most horrible of way. Witness what we saw with Mary Turner at this chapter's opening. The direct response from black Americans generally took two forms—a questioning and wondering, and a resolve to stand and fight. In 1919, Du Bois thundered in the *Crisis:*

> This is the country to which we Soldiers of Democracy return. This is the fatherland for which we fought! But it is *our* fatherland. It was right for us to fight. The faults of our country are our faults. Under similar circumstances, we would fight again. But by the God of Heaven, we are cowards and jackasses if now that the war is over, we do not marshal every ounce of our brain and brawn to fight a sterner, longer, more unbending battle against the forces of hell in our own land.
> We return.
> We return from the fighting.
> We return fighting.
> Make way for Democracy! We saved it in France, and by the Great Jehovah, we will save it in the United States of America, or know the reason why.[82]

ALVIN WHITE—WITNESS AND TESTIFIER: A RACE RIOT IN FRANCE ON PALM SUNDAY

As Al White tells us in an April 9, 1981, letter, sometimes the saving of democracy abroad could be a messy business. What would be a lifetime friendship between Al and the distinguished historian Rayford Logan began on

> Palm Sunday, 1919 in a segregated camp of black soldiers-labor battalions just outside Bordeaux, France when Logan and two other black officers were called to action to quell a riot. It started when a newly arrived regiment of marines visiting the local bistros in the district (Bassens) found the black soldiers were more welcome and liberal than the stiff neck (white) marines. Then a fist

fight ended in a Mexican stand off, resuming when both groups were reinforced. With their fighting blood stirred up, the black soldiers continued the fray assaulting and beating up their officers all of whom were white—even the non coms above the rank of corporal. My battalion, the 701 Engineer Stevedore, and its sister 702 were the only ones with black non coms from 1st Sergeant. He ran the company, which was my rank.

The soldiers were pushed into rioting. Just outside our camp, enclosed behind a seven foot barbed wire fence, was the road to embarkation piers and a steady stream of white soldiers passing. They didn't have the inverted V gold hash mark issued for six months overseas. We called it the service stripe. Some of the labor units' men had three stripes for 18 months. The passer-byes indulged in nastiness and their remarks were outrageous. All this, plus other indignities just added fuel to the fire. You should hear Logan tell it. I do know that in three hours peace was restored and that regiment of marines, somehow I keep thinking it was the 13th, was saved being sacrificed. The blacks had machine gun nests on the top of the slight hill on which the camp was built. Streets—or so they were called—were lined with two story barracks buildings. The machine guns and ammunition had been stolen from shipments handled on the docks built by Americans when this area was assigned them as the port of entry.

Source: Alvin White to Lawrence Hogan, April 9, 1981.

Both the questioning that the Du Boisian strategy put off while the fighting was in process, along with the resolve to fight that he preached in the postwar period, are found in striking form in moving lines by the poet, entertainer, and baseball fan Andy Razaf:

In Flanders Field

(With apologies to John McCrae)

In Flanders field where poppies grow,
Beneath the crosses, row on row,
We blacks an endless vigil keep—

Yea, we, thou dead, can never sleep—
Ingratitude has made it so.

What are we here? Why did we go
From loving homes, that need us so?
Was it for naught we gave our lives,
On Flanders field?

Ye blacks who live, to you we throw
The torch; be yours to face the foe
At home; and ever hold it high,
Fight for the things for which we die,
That we may sleep, where poppies grow,
In Flanders field.[83]

THE GREAT MIGRATION

While black baseball players fought abroad to make the world safe for democracy, things between black and white were changing dramatically on the
home front. What came to be known as the Great Migration can be characterized as the most consequential event in the 20th-century history of black
Americans. This migration, first a trickle, then a flood tide, was fueled by
the labor needs of home front America during World War I to a point where
black/white relations would be altered fundamentally by the movement of
record numbers of black migrants from the South to the North. Black baseball players were increasingly now playing the game they loved anywhere and
everywhere beneath the stars and stripes. They went as best they could where
they wanted to go, and they went in the way they wanted to, sometimes even
to places where they were not wanted.

And sometimes, if stories about the "Father of Black Baseball," Rube Foster, are to be believed, it seems they went by extraordinary means. Here we
have the *Chicago Defender* on April 12, 1919, reporting that

When the American Giants go to Detroit Michigan to play the Detroit
Stars, the sporting editor of the *Chicago Defender* has advised Rube
Foster to charter an aeroplane and travel through the clouds. Foster is
elated over the suggestion, and when he gets a chance to count noses
he will ask all those who relish the thought of flying to work to step forward. Speaking about the question of traveling this summer, Mr. Foster
said: "I am convinced that the cloud boats will soon take the place of
stuffy sleeping cars."[84]

The *Defender's* Windy City competitor for a black readership, the *Whip*, has Foster one year later taking up its hometown rival's flying suggestion:

Well Rube Foster has solved the secret of transportation. The *Pittsburgh Courier* says Rube Foster's Giants lost a practice game to R. Park's team, Friday, March 16 at Jacksonville, Florida. Rube Foster, who is a general on transportation matters, knowing that he must have his team back in Chicago to open Saturday, secured two airships with Liberty motors; had the airships come to the ball park; put the street clothing of the men into the ships and immediately after the ball game, the bats and hand baggage was loaded on the ship. The players piled into the ships in uniform and dressed on their way. Rube Foster leads—others follow.[85]

With a greater number of black professional teams than ever before, individual players became travelers as well in ways that were new to the black game, and often difficult to chart. Historian Jim Riley tags one of those increasingly typical peripatetic travelers, the Bill Pettus who came to the top ranks of black ball in 1910 when he joined Frank Leland's Chicago Giants,

---

RUBE IN THE AIR

If Rube in fact went by air, sometimes it seems Rube himself would be in the air.

During the time when Christy Mathewson, John McGraw and "Doc" White were taking to the stage, "Uncle Rube" hit it from the Southside. It was the first night in Columbus, Ohio on the Klein circuit (vaudeville), when "Rube" came before the footlights. As he approached the middle of the stage a voice rang out from the audience, "Take Him out!" "Uncle Rube" mistook this occasion and thought he was on the ball field. He forgot the footlights and approached the audience in a manner similar to one when he was managing the Giants. He forthwith stepped directly into the band pit, plunged through the bass drum, doing $200 damage to the drummer's outfit. "Rube" returned to Chicago the next morning.

Source: Chicago Defender, April 12, 1919.

as "one of the most underrated players from black baseball." Underrated he may be, he was certainly not under traveled. Let us follow Riley as he follows Pettus.

> After two seasons with Leland's team he jumped East to New York, playing first base and catching with Jess McMahon's Lincoln Giants. In 1913 he jumped to the Brooklyn Royal Giants as their first baseman and cleanup hitter, leaving after a year to reunite with the McMahon Brother, who formed the New York Lincoln Stars. . . . In the fall of 1916 he began a series of moves that requires a road map to trace. In September, when the franchise began dissolving, he jumped back to the Lincoln Giants for the remainder of the season. Then in 1917, he played with half a dozen teams, beginning as the first baseman with the Chicago Giants. He was first sought by Jewell's ABC's in June, before serving brief stints with a trio of teams in July (the Philadelphia Giants, Hilldale, and the Bacharachs), and ending the season again with the Lincoln Giants. In 1918 the jumping between teams within the season continued, but on a lesser scale, and he left the Lincolns in August to join Hilldale, where he was called "old reliable."[86]

One might wonder about that last moniker in so far as it applied to longevity with any one club. Where of course this gifted baseball player could not travel was onto the roster of a major league club. If color was the thing that made the difference in traveling to the bigs, color would be transcended time and again by those who were black and played their own game in their own bigs. Witness Rollo Wilson's "Called Out for the Last Time":

> As we write a wire comes to our desk, brief but full of sorrow: "William Pettus dies August 22-His wife." Thus passes a staunch figure of our sporting world, one who made his mark as a pioneering figure in modern baseball; a still strong man in a blatant land. Blackmon Pettus, "the youth in life's green spring and he who goes in the full strength of years." For Sacks the last great mystery is solved.
>
> We do not know what Bill's private life was, but he must have been a prince. In the baseball world he was one of the Immortals. If a player had it in him Bill saw it and developed his talent. He was a clean athlete and insisted that those under him be clean. He regulated their conduct on and off the field. He drove home the fact that only the men who keep themselves physically fit could hope to advance in the game. His creed was short: "Fair Play," and he exemplified it at all times.
>
> The Great Pitcher had him in a hole and cut a corner for the third one. He's called out for the last time.[87]

If Bill Pettus is typical of those black players who define this era in their traveling and traveling, there were those as well who traveled and stayed. One of those traveler/stayers held down the first base sack for the Atlantic City Bacharach Giants for 10 of his 13 seasons in Negro professional baseball, venturing off onto the well-traveled road only as far as nearby Pennsylvania to give three seasons to the Hilldale Daisies. Christened Napoleon, named "Chance" from being compared to the Chicago Cubs great first baseman Frank Chance, he would become for readers of Rollo Wilson, "Itchy Feet" Cummings.

Like blacks everywhere in those tough times of post–Civil War America, baseball players had to learn to be tough. Early in the 20th century Napoleon "Chance" Cummings came North with his entire Jacksonville team, the Duval Giants, to play first base for the Negro Bacharach Giants of Atlantic City, New Jersey. He recalls just how tough he and his teammates were.

> You see, in the first place, we all had guts. We all worked downtown in Jacksonville. We had a lot of experience during the Jack Johnson Jeffries fight. There were thousands of whites in our part of town. Of course, we had no chance to play with whites down there, but we worked downtown with a whole lot of white fellas.[88]

In the middle of a decade when migration of blacks from the rural South to the urban North was becoming a flood tide, it would come as no surprise if a few individual members of this team of talented Southern baseball players ended up playing professional ball in the North. But for the entire team to do so must have caught some by surprise.

> And when we came up here and started playing ball with white boys, they were more scared of us than we were scared of them. Because we had such a hell of a ball club; we had a powerful ball club! There were other colored clubs here then, but we broke 'em up, we were so strong, and everyone wanted to play the Bacharachs. We played so many ball clubs, and beat everybody, that people came all the way from Philadelphia to see who the Bacharachs were.[89]

Cummings and his teammates did more than play baseball. As he remembers it, they arrived in their New Jersey resort city home to be on May 5, 1916. On May 8, they were registered to vote in City Hall. And on May 10, Cummings and several of his teammates were on the city pay role. He would remain both an Atlantic City resident and oftentimes a government employee for the rest of a long life well lived, a good part of it devoted to playing the game of baseball.

Napoleon Cummings, along with his baseball "kith and ken," was part of a migration that by decades end had gone a long way toward turning a Southern rural people into Northern city residents. The decision of him and so many fellows like him to change their location would have consequences incalculable for black and white Americans as the decade that would come to be tagged "The Golden Age of American Sports" dawned.

NAPOLEON OF THE ITCHING FOOT

Newspaper scribe Rollo Wilson found the Napoleon of Atlantic City baseball to be a wonderful source for lively copy. The Bacharach's first baseman turns up often in colorful accounts in his Eastern Snapshots column.

> Chance Cummings of the itching foot attracted more attention than the Boardwalk Easter Sunday. Chance failed to dispose of all of his stock in trade Banyan Street haberdashery last winter so he brought the balance of his Banyan street haberdashery to the Shore with him. Following practice Mr. Cummings decided to give the natives and strangers at the gate an eyeful of Florida fashions. Willie Woods, ex president of the Eastern Shore League, and now a private under J. Hennery, (John Lloyd) reports to me that honorable Napoleon made seven complete changes in raiment and as many promenades of Arctic Avenue between four and nine o-clock that day.
>
> Cummings sent the column a box of wonder fruit from the Beach last winter and the memory lingers. He did not forget his comrades-at-arms when he entrained for the north and to each one he brought a cocoanut, a grape fruit and an orange. He claims that his gifts were symbolic, but no one knows the answer.

Wilson again, later in that season: "I Gotta Hand Cummings Another Prize. To him I present last year's Ice Bridge over Niagara Falls for having the dirtiest baseball uniform in this or any other city."

Source: The Pittsburgh Courier, March 22, 1926, and August 15, 1926.

CHAPTER 4

"New Negroes" in the Midst of American Sport's Golden Age, 1920–1930

SETTING THE SCENE—THE NEW NEGRO AND A GOLDEN AGE OF SPORT

In the 1920s, we witness for the first time an organized league structure on the diamonds of Negro professional baseball. Encountering new heights being reached by professional black ball, we enter at the same time the world of the "New Negro" of literary and artistic fame. The Howard philosophy teacher and social critic Alain Locke is generally credited with giving the term "New Negro" to the era in the black American experience that is roughly delineated from the beginnings of the Great Migration of blacks from the South to the North in the 1910s to the opening of the Great Depression. In his 1925 essay of the same name, Locke celebrated a New Negro who for him was best seen in the work of the Negro men and women of literature who make up what came to be called the Harlem Renaissance. For Locke, Negro artists were transforming the popular image of the Negro from that of ex-slave to that of culture bearer for the race. This transforming New Negro was embracing a "new psychology" and a "new spirit" that would equip him and his fellow blacks to smash all of the racial, social, and psychological impediments that had long obstructed their people's achievement.[1]

In mid-decade, the "poet laureate" of black America, Langston Hughes, captured well a mood and an attitude among the "literati" set, of which he was a member in good standing, that lent the decade of the 1920s its moniker as the time of the New Negro:

Let the blare of Negro jazz bands and the bellowing voice of Bessie Smith singing the Blues penetrate the closed ears of the colored near intellectuals until they listen and perhaps understand. Let Paul Robeson singing "Water Boy," and Rudolph Fisher writing about the streets of Harlem, and Jean Toomer holding the heart of Georgia in his hands, and Aaron Douglas drawing strange black fantasies cause the smug Negro middle class to turn from their white, respectable, ordinary books and papers to catch a glimmer of their own beauty. We younger Negro artists now intend to express our individual dark-skinned selves without fear or shame. If white people are pleased we are glad. If they are not, it doesn't matter. We know we are beautiful. And ugly too. The tom-tom cries and the tom-tom laughs. If colored people are pleased we are glad. If they are not, their displeasure doesn't matter either. We build our temples for tomorrow, strong as we know how, and we stand on top of the mountain, free within ourselves.[2]

Who was this New Negro who peopled the decade of the 1920s? In the pages of the *Independent Magazine,* he was someone who "When He's Hit, He Hits Back!" In the years immediately following World War I, tens of thousands of Southern blacks and returning soldiers flocked to the nation's Northern cities looking for good jobs and a measure of respect and security. Many white Americans, fearful of competition for scarce jobs and housing, responded by attacking black citizens in a spate of urban race riots. In urban African American enclaves, the 1920s were marked by a flowering of cultural expressions and a proliferation of black self-help organizations that accompanied the era of the New Negro. What was new in the New Negro was an aggressive willingness to defend black communities against white racist attacks and a desire to celebrate the accomplishments of African American communities in the North.[3] A white Congregational minister, Rollin Lynde Hart, the author of "When He Hits," tells us that this New Negro

was no mere fanciful bugaboo. He exists. More than once I have met him. He differs radically from the timorous, docile negro of the past. Said a new negro, "Cap'n, you mark my words; the next time white folks pick on colored folks, something's going to drop—dead white folks." Within a week came race riots in Chicago, where negroes fought back with surprising audacity.[4]

That New Negro world was also the world of the "Great Migration" of Southern and West Indian rural folks who were now beginning to be Northern urban African Americans, establishing new places for themselves politically, socially, economically, institutionally, and recreationally in an America that had not seen their like before. If largely imperceptible at the time, this was a world gradually being moved toward the destruction of Jim Crow that would finally come in the civil rights movement of mid-century.

If it was the age of the New Negro, it also came to be known as the "Golden Age of Sports." The 1920s was a decade of a great love affair with an American sporting world accorded an attention that was extraordinary. Nothing like it had been seen in American sports up to then. Arguably, nothing since has matched it for sheer excitement. By far, more Americans than ever before read about, watched, and participated in sporting contests. On the highest levels of professional and amateur competition; and indeed on the local sandlots, gridirons, municipal tennis courts, and YMCA gymnasiums; and in college competition across a wide spectrum as well, it was the golden age of American sport.

In baseball, the gold was Babe Ruth, Lou Gehrig, and the Yankees' Murderers' Row with the dark cloud of the Black Sox scandal giving way to bright sunshine as Ty Cobb and Tris Speaker played out the waning days of great careers. In tennis, it was the great "Big Bill" Tilden versus the tough Vincent Richards—and the mercurial Suzanne Lenglen versus the stoic Helen Wills. In golf, Walter Hagen and Bobby Jones announced the arrival of American dominance after long years of English and Scottish prominence. It was legendary sports writers Ring Lardner, Paul Gallico, Heywood Broun, and Grantland Rice whose names were as familiar and revered as the sports heroes about whom they wrote. In college football, the gold was Red Grange, the "Galloping Ghost" from the American heartland. It was also the immediately made legendary Stuhldreher, Miller, Crowley, and Layden of whom the legendary himself Grantland Rice wrote perhaps the most remembered opening story lines ever penned by a sports scribe. He would memorably paint with his typewriter the Four Horsemen of Notre Dame outlined against a gray blue October sky in victory over a fighting Army football team before 55,000 spectators at the Polo Grounds in 1924. On the racing turf, it was the great Man o' War at the decade's opening, and jockey Steve Donoghue winning four Kentucky Derbys from 1921 through 1925. On a different kind of track, it was Peter DePaolo, Erwin "Cannonball" Baker, and Henry Segrave reaching dizzying speeds in their auto racers. Track and field saw Harold Osborn set decathlon and high jump marks at the Paris Olympics in 1924 as Johnny Weissmuller of swimming and Tarzan fame took four medals in his competitions. And in the ring, it was the incomparable Manassa Mauler, Jack Dempsey versus the erudite and well-read Gene Tunney in two fights that would be rivaled in popularity four decades later only by Frazier and Ali and their ring wars.

Much of this stuff of the world of sports—events and names—is familiar even to many who give little attention to America's professional and amateur sporting heroes. But from over on the black side of the ledger how familiar to the most avid and knowledgeable of sports buffs is the name Harry Wills? Jack Dempsey knew Wills well, and avoided him like the plague when it came to defending his heavyweight championship:

> I can't see why Dempsey don't fight,
> If he's the champ of the world he should prove his right.
> Just to say "I'm King" certainly must be grand,
> But "talk is cheap," It takes money to buy land.
> Jack, get a new fad, quit trying to stall,
> If you're a "fighting bearcat"
> Meet Wills—Dass all![5]

How many "sports junkies" recognize the name Fritz Pollard in football, or are aware of the annual Howard Lincoln Thanksgiving Classic that in the mid-1920s regularly drew 25,000 or more football enthusiasts to American and National League Ballparks in Philadelphia and Washington, D.C. On the black side of the ledger in track, it was Eddie Tolan, the school boy wonder from Detroit; but also broad jump record holder DeHart Hubbard whose 25 feet 10 and 7/8 inches bested the race's first champion Ned Gourdin who was the first to break the 25-foot barrier. The decade saw Charlie Brookins run 23 2–5 in the low hurdles blasting a mark that had withstood all assaults for a quarter of a century. In mid-decade, Tommy Milton, "the fastest man in the world," announced his retirement from motor racing.[6] Unable to compete at Indy in the famous 500, blacks raced at the world renowned oval from 1924 through 1936 in their own 100-mile Gold and Glory Sweepstakes. Race champion Milton, Rollo Wilson proudly proclaimed, was the only man up to then to win the Indianapolis Speedway Race more than once, and the only human "who has traveled 156.04 mph on the ground."[7] While Milton's retirement may have been disappointing, black Americans could continue to call as their own Robert Wallace, "ace of the Indianapolis drivers," and Bill Carson, Bill Buckner, and Hugo Barnes were still in the motor competition ranks.[8] At the same juncture, arguably the world's greatest basketball team was shaping itself into all-time world-class competition status at the Renaissance Ballroom in Harlem in the persons of Bob Douglas's Rens led by the likes of Tarzan Cooper and Clarence "Fats" Jenkins.

Edgar Brown, Arthur Francis, Eyre Saitch, Ted Thompson, Dorothy Ewell, Miss Isadore Channels, and by the end of the decade the great Ora Washington were matching in national competitions in places like Baltimore,

Chicago, New York, and Bordentown, New Jersey—the feats of the Tildens and Lenglens on the white side of the tennis ranks. And on the golf links, the United Golfers Association of America was holding its first national tournaments at the first African American golf and country club, the famous Shady Rest in Scotch Plains, New Jersey, and staging other competitions across the nation at courses in Baltimore, Chicago, Braintree, Massachusetts, and Washington, D.C., while young up-and-comers like the Chicagoan Robert Patrick Ball challenged old veterans like John Shippen for black king of the links.

And on a different level of popularity and participation, the decade witnessed blacks competing among themselves for bowling and horseshoe championships; flying a neat little homing pigeon named Miss Pittsburgh to easy victory in tough competition; hosting before crowds of as much as 12,000 the Uruguayan soccer team with Negro stars Jose Andrade and Antonio Recoba; rooting for J.W. "Bam" Sims, colored national billiard champion, and Jimmie Evans, the world's colored champion of pocket billiards; and cheering for Sammy Bush, king of the steeplechase jockeys as he left for a competition in Paris, France, and marathoners Rufus Tankins and Ed "Shiek" Gardner as they set records in that grueling sport.[9]

The strong sense of "ours" and "theirs" that characterized the black sporting public and of the specialness of "our own" 1920s golden sports story is clearly evident in the "Ho Hum" reaction of *Afro-American* sports editor G.L. Mackey at mid-decade to the fervid commentary of Roger Pippin of the *Baltimore News*. Pippin reported being astonished by the wonderful quality of play of the Baltimore Black Sox that he had recently witnessed:

It's the same old story. The Sports Editor of the *News* was astonished at the ability of Sox players. Maybe the Baltimore scribe would be shocked if told that De Hart Hubbard, a race youth, has recently equaled two world records, the 50 and 100 yard dashes, and can do a broad jump of 25 feet or more every morning before breakfast.

And the writer on the *News* would be startled if told that a colored boy by the name of Randolph Ruff established two Maryland state records, one in the running broad jump and another in 880 yard run last week at Bel Air. And he would be very much agitated if told W.M. Clark a West Indian, had given the champion tennis player, Bill Tilden a hot time down in Jamaica. And he would be scandalized if he knew that a 17 year old Baltimore boy has beaten the *News* duck pin champion by two pins when this same boy bowled over a total of 162 pins in a single game. And last but not least the good Sports writer would throw a quick fit if told Harry Wills can lick Jack Dempsey or any other man alive that dare face him in the ring.

The daily broadcaster of news seems to be sadly behind the times. If he would ask any colored boy on the street he would be told off hand the names of nearly every player in the National, American, International, and both Colored leagues and their outstanding performances. Any Douglass school student will be able to tell the learned Editor of the *News* the names and colleges of the country's track stars White or Black.[10]

Measure then by what we find on the sports pages of America's black weeklies, the 1920s was clearly a golden decade of sports for black as well as white Americans.

BLACK BASEBALL IS EVERYWHERE

There can be little doubt that the decade's baseball opening gave off the luster of gold. The headline in the *Chicago Whip* in the spring of 1921 announces that "Baseball Now Spans Entire Hemisphere." The author's paean is to a National Association of Colored Baseball Clubs that "represents the loftiest ideals in the great national game of this continent." The tally of where blackball has been present is an impressive one, extending to "all parts of the globe." Black players serving in the armed forces have competed in the European war-theater. The Kansas City Monarchs have played in the Philippine Islands. A Negro National League lineup has just won the Pacific Coast winter championship. The past season, the Bacharach Giants of Atlantic City held up the league banner in Cuba's winter league, while the American Giants did the same in Florida. The St. Louis Giants had just won a successful tour of the American South. The Detroit Stars were fighting it out up in the Canadian league. Well, might the writer of this piece take pride in noting that the fans who will witness the opening of the official league season on May 1, 1921, will "know of what the National Association of Colored Professional Baseball Clubs stands for."[11]

In the winter of 1920, with Chicago's Rube Foster and Indianapolis's C.I. Taylor in the lead, the first real black major league was established.[12] The National League was joined in the ranks of majors in 1923 with the Eastern Colored Leagues' first season of play. Ed Bolden of the Hilldale Club took the lead in organizing this second Negro major league.

If it was a time of goldenness for black baseball and for black sports in general, it still remained in all areas of life what it seemingly always would be for black Americans: a time of pervasive prejudice, as well as a time to stand against it. That pervasiveness, as well as the standing against it, was seen in

striking ways in early April 1922 in Atlanta, Georgia, when a streetcar conductor on the Emory University line attempted to eject "a colored man who
got on at the white entrance to the train and sat in a seat for whites only."
Maintaining that he was a freeborn American, he insisted he could sit anywhere his heart desired, and Georgia law be damned. When he was told by
the conductor that he had to take a back seat, this unknown one pulled out a
revolver and ordered the conductor, the motorman, and all white passengers
off the coach. Holding possession of the car, while defying anyone to enter,
he sat alternately in every seat that had been occupied by white students of
Emory University. Having stood defiantly against Jim Crow, he slipped off
quietly presumably not to be heard from again.[13]

BLACK AMERICA'S TEAM—THE CHICAGO AMERICAN GIANTS

Slipping quietly off not to be seen again was certainly not the modus ope-
randi of a black team from Chicago, the likes of which the American sports
scene had not witnessed. By the time of the founding of the Negro National
League in 1920, for which this special squad served as anchor team and winner of the championship for the league's first two seasons, its players had traveled more miles, played in more places, entertained more fans both black and
white, commanded more newspaper space, and earned more money for its
founder than anyone would have imagined to be possible at the time of the
club taking the field in 1911 for the first time. As the famous and dominant
Chicago American Giants of its famous founder, Andrew "Rube" Foster, it
can rightly be dubbed "Black America's Team." As the golden age of sports
dawned, both black and white America were taken aback by the accomplish-
ment and exploits of this truly remarkable golden club.

First and foremost the Giants were a Midwest power. Historian Michael
Lomax notes that "by 1915, Andrew 'Rube' Foster had emerged as the dominant black baseball promoter in the Midwest. A series of astute moves spurred
his rise to the top. These included forming a partnership with a white tavern
owner, expanding his barnstorming tours during the winter, reviving the East-
West colored championship, and developing good press and community relations to burnish a public image that had been tarnished by charges that baseball
revenues were 'going over to the other race,' and that the American Giants
were not supporting race institutions in the black community."[14]

Never intending to limit himself to establishing a strong home base in
Chicago, Foster from the outset looked westward. Starting in 1912, several
winter barnstorming tours along the West Coast as well as entry into a strong

A rare team photo of Rube Foster's Chicago American Giants. (National Baseball Hall of Fame Library, Cooperstown, NY)

California winter league where they won the championship in that league's first season made them into something no black team had been—a presence to be reckoned with in the West.

The East was next, and Foster began his work in establishing a Chicago presence there when in the summer of 1913 he arranged what was billed as a championship series with the powerful Lincoln Giants of New York. Powerful, the Lincolns would prove in winning the "World's Colored Championship" nine games to four. But victory in this instance involved more than an on-the-field advantage as the Midwest baseball baron spread his barony into Eastern climes.

Having looked successfully to the East and the West from his Midwest home base, Foster and his players were ready now to be all-season baseball men, and that meant barnstorming on an unprecedented scale. Historian Lomax deems the American Giants 1915–1916 tour "undoubtedly their greatest," giving the team and their owner/manager "heightened celebrity." It took them to their second California Winter League championship in four years. They then touched base in Cuba, playing credibly in the island's Winter League. The West and Southwest were next where they won 57 and lost 15. When the local season began in May, the American Giants had traveled over 20,000 miles. During this tour, sportswriter Frank Young made the somewhat exaggerated claim that "the Rube had brought Chicago more promotion than all other city enterprises combined."[15]

Advancing his and his team's baseball presence and profits was foremost in Andrew Foster's scheme of things. Another way to do that was to rent major league ballparks from owners in Detroit and Cincinnati, staging attractive contests between his now well-known Giants and popular clubs like the Havanas and the Indianapolis ABCs. Going himself one better in Detroit, he established a second team, the Stars; installed his own man, John Tenny Blount, as business manager; stocked it with several of his own players, while holding their contracts, as well as the lease to the team's stadium. All this maneuvering and entrepreneurship saw the man who would come to be called the "Father of Black Baseball," amassing unheard of profits—reportedly as much as $15,000 in 1919.[16]

Beside the West and East and Midwest, by the opening of the decade of the 1920s, Foster's Giants had established themselves as a year-round business through a strong presence in Florida, stretching them coast to coast and border to even beyond border up into Canada. The 1921 winter season affords us an opportune time to look southward as Chicago's "Big Chief," aside from a few exceptions, had his American Giants squad, representing the Poinciana resort, intact for the season's opening tussle on January 25. His Giants were to face off against a John Lloyd-led team that represented the best of the colored players of the East. There was in the *Chicago Whip*'s account of this situation a note of speculation, indeed doubt, about how well the intact Fosterites would fare against the "cream" of the East. What was a sure thing, according to the scribe, was that if the Western team from his home city lost, "there was nothing in the make-up of the Big Chief to indicate a squeal."[17]

By the time March rolled around, Foster had little to squeal about. On March 5, his hometown paper reported another victory for the Chicago squad. Under the headline "Johnson Goose Eggs Breakers," we find an account that has to be listened to as it was reported:

> Overseas heroes, Lieut. Johnson, Malarcher and Bobby Williams were the flies that pestered the Royal ointment when the former, hurling for the Poincianas, lived up to his overseas prestige for hand-grenading the enemy, while his aids kept up a barrage lasting one hour and thirty-five minutes in which the enemy was driven back into the dense palm thickets, while Gen. Foster, Capt. DeMoss, Lieut. Johnson and fighters advanced their territorial possession by a count of five games to two. The Breakers are but a few miles removed from the ocean, and fierce and continued fighting will ensue from now on, but it is hoped that the great leader, Lloyd, and his squad will save themselves from the last resort—the Atlantic—in order to avert an overwhelming victory by the Americans.[18]

Victory in the winter series for Foster's "baseball army" would indeed come shortly thereafter—and shortly after that victory, in terms of bragging rights, its spoils as well. The winning of the Winter League championship by the American Giants was the occasion for hosannas on the home front. "Pitted against a collection of the best ball players in the world, stars picked from the Royal Giants, Lincoln Giants, Hilldale and Bacharachs, the Foster machine still reigns supreme in the baseball field of endeavor" reads the report filed to the *Whip* from Palm Beach on March 15.

Chicago and the Midwest, California, and Florida regularly scheduled swings into the Eastern bastion of black baseball, and trips north to Canada. By 1922, they were an "everywhere team," and they were clearly black America's team. Their Florida triumph in the 1922 winter season presented an opportune moment for their hometown paper to review the greatness of a team that in the past year had been counted out by many, but had gone on to defend and win six championship series: the Three Eye League, Chicago Ball League, National Negro League, Southern League, World's Championship against the Bacharach Giants, and the Florida Winter League Championship against the Royal Giants. "They were universally looked upon and conceded to be the most formidable aggregation of players on soil other than their own home that has yet been displayed before the fans of this country." It would come as no surprise then that they are "acknowledged to be the most powerful attraction in baseball for drawing and attracting the fans to the baseball parks."[19]

It is worth noting that nowhere in this encomium is the greatness judgment qualified by the designation black. But that they had become black America's team is seen in the Giants spring training trip South from Chicago to Houston, Texas, in 1924.

In a March 8 story in the team's hometown paper, the *Defender* picks the club's travels up at the 43rd Street station, boarding the 10:05 Illinois Central for Houston. Many of the players' friends were left waiting at the gate at the downtown station, where they had mistakenly gone to give their favorites a royal send off. Grant, the paper tells its readers, was the only man who was left behind. Several of those who made the train were nattily attired. Gardner was there with everything new on, even to his underwear. And so was Jim Brown, who purportedly was engaged to a rich girl who had recently discovered three more oil wells on her property in Oklahoma. Present as well were "Captain DeMoss, Tom Wilson, Treadwell, Harney and the rest." Those who were not traveling with the team from Chicago, "Torriente, Bobby Williams and Roth," would join the club when it arrived in Houston.[20] Three days of practice would make them ready to play Texas clubs in exhibition games that would lead to a return trip North where along the way they would be booked as a feature attraction against local teams eager to face these big leaguers.

A "royal reception" awaited them on their arrival in Texas. Actually, the receptions started earlier than the Houston arrival. One reported on in the *Defender* points up what made this founding club of the Negro National League so different than any white major league team. On the way South, the train made a scheduled stop in Benton, Arkansas, but apparently not for a ball game. The town's black population turned out when the Giants train rolled into the local station. Rube Foster came over from Hot Springs, Arkansas, to join his club. The townsfolk shook hands with the big fellow and with Mrs. Foster and wished them good luck on their journey. Baskets of hot biscuits and fried chicken and old-fashioned Southern corn bread were given to the players. This was clearly black America's team—arguably the first national black baseball heroes adored by black America.[21]

It would be easy to regard receptions of this sort as simply a matter of black folks finding uplift from the negatives of a white America that in so many ways was telling them they were second-rate folks. But might it not also be a matter of hospitable people, with no or little reference to white folks' ways at all, embracing their own with the special hospitality and warmth that was just part of what literary luminary Amiri Baraka tells us was a baseball that was "like a light somewhere. Back over your shoulder. As you go away. A warmth still connected to laughter and self-love. The collective Black aura that can only be duplicated with Black conversation or music."[22] And of course is an aura often accompanied by hot biscuits, fried chicken, and old-fashioned Southern corn bread. After all, sports writer Ric Roberts remembered, "we had our own. We weren't concerned even with Notre Dame."[23] "We created ourselves from what we found around us," Ralph Ellison tells us.[24] And we were, as Albert Murray so beautifully asserted, full of "elegance, exuberance, and (good old fashioned) nonsense."[25]

It was said about the extraordinary black educator, Mary McLeod Bethune, that when she traveled North as she frequently did by auto from her college in Daytona Beach, Florida, to tend to her many national duties and stayed overnight, as custom and law required, with her own folks in their own homes in their own section of town, the best chickens in the henhouse would panic and run for cover at the news that Mrs. Bethune would be dining that night in their vicinity. Might we suspect that on that March day in 1924 when news reached them that Rube and his American Giants were coming to town, the best of the resident chickens of Benton, Arkansas, experienced a similar panic?

On their arrival in Houston, the team went straight to their stopping place. That afternoon, practice began in earnest with Rube Foster taking charge of everything. The next day's practice was called off due to inclement weather. But the players insisted on practicing anyway, and their manager was forced to let them go to another park where they went through a hard workout despite the rain. The team's first spring training games were scheduled for Sunday, Monday, and Tuesday at the Scott Street grounds for 2:30 each day against the Houston Black Buffaloes. In the age of the New Negro, this black baseball business was serious stuff, being pursued by serious men, in a serious way, in a sports age that was golden.

THE MAGNIFICENT PAUL

Probably, no individual figure presents the 1920s' goldenness and its "New Negroness" better than a man who is usually remembered for his prowess in arenas other than those of athletic endeavors. Five springs into the golden decade of sports, an athletic champion returned to a field of play where he had starred as an undergraduate at Rutgers University:

The Rutgers Varsity Baseball Team featuring Paul Robeson, second to the left, middle row. (National Baseball Hall of Fame Library, Cooperstown, NY)

> The game between Rutgers alumni and the varsity baseball teams is ex-
> pected to be one of the most interesting events of the commencement
> week as it will be played on Commencement Day, June 14. Paul Robeson,
> four letter and Phi Beta Kappa alumnus, now starring in "All God's Chil-
> lun," will play with the alumni which defeated the varsity last year.[26]

Paul Robeson was a New Negro. Among the many, many other things
he would be, Robeson was also a superb athlete. In fact, his athleticism was
a part of his New Negroness. The Walter Camp 1917–1918 All-American
end for Rutgers University was a four-sport varsity letter winner at the
New Jersey school where he stood out for his academic as well as athletic
prowess—to say nothing of the color of his skin. It was not uncommon
to find accounts of his collegiate athletic feats on the pages of great black
national weeklies alongside stories about Negro professional baseball. While
best known as a gridiron star, he had a real love for and considerable skill
at the game of baseball. When his college career concluded, he continued
to pursue athletics in a serious way as a pioneering professional football and
basketball player. But for all that he did in his youth as an athlete, for all that
he came to do in his maturity as a political and cultural activist, ask those
who experienced Robeson what they remember most, and invariably they
will say the signing voice.

It is that voice we want to imaginatively listen to now as it takes us on an
incredible historical journey into the world of Alain Locke's New Negro. The
places that we go to will not seem to be baseball places. Indeed, in a direct
way, they are not. But they are places to which Robeson linked himself and
his people in claiming in startling ways for them and for himself an identity
and a history that was bigger, and larger, and far more profound than the
mean places assigned to him and them by the racism of their times. Those
people who he always acknowledged as his own were doctors, lawyers, and
school teachers; bank presidents and bank clerks; and common laborers who
were never "common" to him. And as we learn from veteran Negro leaguer
Gene Benson, who roamed the outfield in fine fashion and more than held
his own at bat with the Philadelphia Stars of the Negro National League for
many a season in the sun, they were baseball players as well. For as Benson
put it after an evening of listening to an actor dramatize the great Robeson in
a dramatic exchange with the great integrator Branch Rickey set in 1946 and
based on actual history, "Paul Robeson spoke for me. What he said, I felt and
could not say as he could."[27]

The "baseball" journey we take as we travel into the era of the New Negro
has the former Rutgers catcher seeing where the roots of the preaching that

was his father's can lead us across history. It was a preaching marked both in style and substance with wonderful cadences. It combined in distinctive ways the oral and the visual elements of delivery. It drew on a storytelling that had deep roots in the history of preacher and listener. And it touched the spirit of all who heard it. All of this, Robeson tells us, was the unique purview and possession of the "Colored Preacher," of whom his father was a fine example.

That distinct Robeson voice, with its deep bass sounds, starts us out on our journey into the roots of the Negro preacher—and into much else that was black—in the New Jersey world of his bringing up years in the 1910s. The preacher journey came to him first in a father's presence and voice that resonated in the young lad's ears from pulpits that his dad held in churches in Westfield and Princeton.

Robeson speaking: "When he was very happy he would start moving about. And from that has grown, as James Weldon Johnson tells us, much of the art of any phase of our Negro life."[28]

Next the preacher's son has us back in slavery times among those "Black and Unknown Bards," the slave composers of the spirituals, whom James Weldon Johnson celebrates as the equals—indeed, in many ways, the artistic betters of the great European masters of classical music.[29]

Robeson singing: "I want you to go down death easy, and bring my spirit home."

From the slavery times of his father, Paul Robeson sings us back to the ancestral homeland in a chanting African American style that he convinces us has its origins in West African chant. "We find the same form in African religious festivals."

Robeson singing: "Cha la pala pat ta i."[30]

And suddenly we are many centuries back into the past to ancient Ethiopia at the dawn of the Christian era where again the singer/historian finds affinities and suggests connections to the voices we hear in Africa, and subsequently among the African slaves in the Americas.

There are several more Paul Robeson stops to make in the musical and historical web he is weaving. Still none of them are seemingly connected to black baseball. But as we shall see—indeed as we know from Gene Benson—they are connected nonetheless. Startling is too weak a word to describe what we feel when we understand historically where these stops take us.

For, Paul Robeson tells us, this African and American slave chanting and preaching is connected not just to "the ancient roots of Christianity in Ethiopia and the Sudan that were part of the eastern churches of Byzantium,"[31] but also to "the development of the Czech Plain Choral that preceded the

Lutheran Choral and was part of the development of Gregorian chant in the early Church of the Middle Ages."[32]

Robeson singing: "Slati votz clave," the deep voice of this son of an African American preacher powerfully intones.

And finally Paul Robeson brings us to our intended destination—where his father's roots, his own as a black child of the early 20th century, and Gene Benson's too are found—into a kinship with the oppressed wherever they are found—through the song he then sings for us, the 18th-century Hassidic Chant of Rabbi Levi Yitzhak of Sarah of Berditchev:

> A good day to thee Lord God Almighty
> I, by Isaac, Son of Sarah of Berdechev am before
> Thee with a grave and earnest plea for this my people.
> Why hast thou so oppressed this Thy people?
> From my place I will not move
> And let there be an end to this sorrow and suffering.[33]

All this as a way of understanding who his father is—who he himself is—and who any of his fellow African Americans can be when they are exposed to and connect into the great tradition of that quintessential American character type, the "Colored Preacher," and follow out the historical journey to where it will take us if we understand what that journey, baseball and otherwise, is really all about. And when that journey, on a personal level, comes to its end, your author can testify from personal experience that it will be the likes of the Colored Preacher that Paul Robeson sang so movingly about who will send the Gene Bensons of Negro baseball lore off to the eternal reward they have so justly earned.

BLACK BASEBALL PLAYERS AS NEW NEGROES

When all is said and done, Paul Robeson's "roots of the Negro preacher's" search is the kind of journey that defined the New Negro; so too were the journeys taken by our baseball heroes of the 1920s. While not often perceived as such, it would be only a small step from the new psychology and new spirit of Alain Locke's black men of New Negro literature; from the stirring black identity claims of Langston Hughes; from the journeys across vast sweeps of history by Paul Robeson, from Rube's black America's team; to the new psychology and new spirit as seen by baseball men like Charles Starks and

Rube Currie who wrote about new doings in the New Negro black baseball of the 1920s.

"White psychology so far as applied to Negro baseball is a dead issue," sports editor Charles Starks reported on November 3, 1922, on the *Kansas City Call*'s sports page.[34] The "psychology" he referenced was one that went well beyond the baseball diamond. It was an outlook that "implies always the superiority of the whites and the inferiority of the blacks." He noted that too often this psychology had produced among his people an "acceptance of white standards of valuation instead of creating our own after our peculiar conceptions."[35] Under such conditions, the development of a sense of one's own identity was impaired in ways that were extremely harmful. "In our particular case psychology is the expression of a mental attitude of the white man influencing the mental concepts of the Negro and causing a certain moral depression on our part. The white man emphasized the thought of our terrible inferiority in the past, and we believed it because of our ignorance."[36] Yes, this is a sports writer, writing on the pages of a major Negro weekly. "White sports writers," Starks noted, "usually advance this psychology. Negroes are fair enough in the physical feature, but baseball requires quick thinking and acting, and the Negro hasn't got these qualities in the high degree the white man has."[37]

So for Starks and his kind of New Negro sports journalism, the real stakes in Negro professional baseball involved not just who won the game—who was the most exciting to watch—but who was the most skilled. On the playing fields of Negro baseball, the efficacy of white psychology and its estimate of who the Negro was, and how he defined himself, was being tested across nine innings of play every time Negro National League teams took the field. Where else in the long history of America's national game could what was at stake in the on-the-field contest be so framed?

Starks's black baseball of the 1920s showed what was wrong with the negative thinking produced by America's white psyche. "It has been recently proven too well that Negroes play the game with much more thought and snap than the average white player,"[38] our scribe confidently announced. "If you want an instance of strategy highly embodied on our part, then compare Rube Foster, our best, with John McGraw, the acknowledged white master. We dare say the Fosterian genius would tally up with the other."[39] The *Call*'s reporter concluded this accolade by holding out the tantalizing possibility that public sentiment might well crystallize to the point where "it will question the results of a world series championship between two white teams as conclusive when perhaps there are one of several colored teams in the country better than the contenders."[40] In the meantime, his prescription was "to continue to let the race hit the ball in every progressive way."[41]

Written celebrations of the achievements of black professional baseball of the early 1920s, and what this baseball meant as psychological uplift and challenge, were not limited to journalists reporting the game. Starks's claims for the black game found echo in an extraordinarily thoughtful and nuanced piece penned by the star Kansas City Monarchs moundsman, Rube Currie. Currie was responding in December 1922 to a story in the white press that intimated that recent off-season victories by black "small town" teams over white major league clubs should not be credited to the superior ability of the black players. Such victories were rather to be passed off to poor conditioning on the part of the whites.

Currie noted that in his three years with the Monarchs, he had learned that "the white man is too apt to consider us the personification of jester in respect to knowing our value of an organization. I have further concluded that he considers us baseball automatons when it comes to the playing side of the game. In fact he does not consider we have an iota of sense concerning the scientific side of baseball."[42] Currie will brook none of that foolish prejudice:

> Just like the white man studies baseball day and night, so some of us study it. I think we are just as fit mentally and physically as the whites are. Also it might settle their worried minds to know some of us study our opponent's weaknesses and are capable of making our observations mean something toward their defeat. We have pitchers who can pitch as much as some of the leading pitchers; we have hitters who stand second to none; we have wonderful fielders; and whenever you stagger upon a bunch of players of the caliber of the Monarchs of last season, you had better prepare yourself for a ball game.[43]

For the average baseball fan, these are startling claims to find on the sports pages of a major paper. How one asks could a mere sport be written about in such a way as to make it appear to be so much more than merely a game? Charles Starks wrote in July 1923 that black Kansas City was "Baseball Daffy . . . Enthusiasm, interest, pride, race glory and great strides in the development of national character" were products of the baseball madness that was gripping fans as they gloried in the on-the-field exploits of the Cubans, the ABCs, Toledo, St. Louis, Detroit, and Milwaukee.[44] "It's Monarchs this, Monarchs that, Rube Foster this, Rube Foster that," the sports scribe noted. Sportswriters frequently indulge in this kind of hyperbole. But then Starks ups the ante with the most startling claim of all. "Here in Kansas City we see baseball as a wonderful contributor to the solution of an ancient race problem."[45]

What had black baseball done to merit such a claim? Most visible was its realization of a long-held dream, the creation of the Negro National

Baseball League, founded in the winter of 1920 by Rube Foster and his cohorts in Kansas City. From its inception, the National was a Midwestern league, with two teams that first season based in Chicago, and clubs representing Dayton, Detroit, Indianapolis, Kansas City, and St. Louis. The Cuban Stars, operating out of Cincinnati, but with no specific home city affiliation, rounded out the eight-team circuit. Through its first years of operation, several teams joined, while others dropped out. Starks detailed what was at the heart of his people's approval:

> Four years ago we had no semblance of a league, therefore as players we did not know the comparative high salaries our athletes are now receiving, and the fans had no where to lay their heads. They had to camp on the burning bleachers to watch the white sons of baseball perform their skillful play. . . . Baseball is a great thing for the race in a big way. . . . There are no greater things about it . . . than the elevation of our players in the industrial and economic scale, and the redemption of our people from the humiliating necessity of viewing high class baseball wherein not only our boys were excluded from playing, but we were plainly given to understand that we were not wanted. Our league has solved this phase of life very nicely. We have tasted in a national way the meaning of league baseball, and we have approved of it and declared it all right for adult and child—we the people.[46]

The early 1920s were heady times for black baseball. While Starks was writing, a second Negro major league, the Eastern Colored League, was in its first season of play under the leadership of Ed Bolden. But what the reporter was referring to goes well beyond the joy and comfort fans were experiencing seeing the fine play of their own kind on the black diamonds of professional baseball, and well beyond the respectable salaries players were now earning. Indeed, his sentiments take us to the heart of who the New Negro was. This era of the New Negro is best seen as a time when African Americans journeyed, as we have witnessed Paul Robeson do in breathtaking ways, to new places where they laid claim to territory that had not been acknowledged as theirs, taking possession rightfully of what had been taken from them. Robeson's incredible journeying across what was now for him, and for the first time for his listeners, black history and time, echoed his contemporary Langston Hughes's claims for his people—"I've known rivers ancient as the world and older than the flow of human blood in human veins"—in his signature poem *The Negro Speaks of Rivers*.[47] And it was a journey pursued in eloquent and elegant ways by sports writer Starks and pitcher Currie as they celebrated and played "a great thing for the race in a big way," something so especially "right for adult and child—for we the people."[48]

MIGRATION IS THE HEART OF OUR STORY

At the heart of all this New Negro business was the migrant. Journeying voices like those of Hughes and Robeson, and their literary and artistic fellows in the Harlem Renaissance, had their counterparts in the masses of folk who comprised one of the most spectacular journeys in American history. That was the journeying of black Southerners from out of the rural South and into the urban North that we have come to call the Great Migration. Indeed, theirs is, alongside of the movement to the American West, the most consequential mass internal movement of Americans in the history of our nation.

ALVIN WHITE—WITNESS AND TESTIFIER: "SINGING THE STAR-SPANGLED BANNER IN DEEPEST, DARKEST DIXIE"

Al White remembers well the Roscoe Conklin Simmons who was a power, to the degree there could be such for blacks, in National Republican Party circles during the first half of the 20th century. "He was an old fashioned eloquent operator who strutted, postured, asked the audience questions—and when he turned around and said scornfully, 'Sirs, I give you this,' you were ready to stand up and sing the Star Spangled Banner in deepest and darkest Dixie, which is where I heard him in 1915 when Villa was giving the U.S. an unmitigated headache."*

What Will It Take for Us to Stay? By Roscoe Conklin Simmons—*The Chicago Defender,* Saturday, June 23, 1917

"The hand of war has led ten times ten thousand of my people to seek new homes, and tens of thousands more are eager to follow.

Their leaders make mistakes, but the people do not make mistakes. They follow an unseen hand.

We love our South, and we would stay to till and possess the soil, erect our homes, rear our children, and grow mighty in the place of our nativity, but we know that anywhere beneath the stars and stripes is 'home, sweet home' to us.

---

* Alvin White to Lawrence Hogan, January 4, 1979.

> I can say for my people that we will stay. The white race asks for terms. I will relate them.
>
> We will stay if the doors of education are thrown open to the children; If judges speak the language of law, and courthouses become temples of justice; If we are given a part in the Government we are taxed to maintain, and the ballot is put in our hands.
>
> We will stay if the true-blues will cut up the lyncher's rope and put out the torch of the mob."**
>
> ———
>
> ** Roscoe Conklin Simmons, "What Will It Take for Us to Stay?" *The Chicago Defender*, June 23, 1917.

It is not possible to understand black baseball, and a hundred other "black things" of the 1920s and beyond, without referencing into the fact and meaning of the New Negro migration. The same newspapers that give us the baseball record also recorded, explained, documented, and promoted this massive movement of America's black population from rural South to urban North. It would of course be those migrants and their children who made up the bulk of the black fandom that filled the seats of the ballparks where New Negro players, being paid by New Negro owners, cavorted on the playing fields of New Negro diamonds.

The contours of the migration itself are seen most clearly in the pages of the great weekly newspapers that were reporting on the new black baseball of that era. The most influential instrument of promotion for the migration, the *Chicago Defender*, would sing North its black Southern readers in poetic terms:

> Why should I remain longer in the South
> To be kicked and dogged around?
> Cracker to shoot me in the mouth
> And shoot my brother down.
> I would rather the cold to snatch my breath
> And die from natural cause
> Than to stay down South and be beat to death
> Under cracker law.[49]

The Great Migration possessed an inexorability that is rooted in Southern and national post-Reconstruction racial realities, but is also inextricably connected to the coming of World War I and the labor needs of an expanding American economy that had lost its supply of cheap labor from traditional immigration sources. The migration, with its beginnings in the decade 1910–1920, is the ground on which everything having to do with black 20th-century America rests. Of the 10 Northern cities with more than 25,000 Negroes in 1920, all but 2—Pittsburgh and Kansas City—registered gains of over 50 percent from the 1910 census. In Detroit, the Negro population increased 611 percent; in Cleveland, 308 percent; in Chicago, 148 percent; and in Philadelphia and Indianapolis, 59 percent. In sheer numbers, Chicago, the capital of black baseball, represents well the magnitude of this mass movement. The 1920 census placed the nation's second city Negro population at 109,458, an increase of 65,355 since 1910.[50]

This "journeying to new places" perspective found in the beautiful singing of Paul Robeson, in the poetry and prose of Langston Hughes and his fellow Renaissancers, in the musings of the likes of Charles Starks and Rube Currie, as well as in the decisions of the countless thousands of black Southerners to leave their ancestral homes and seek the promise of new opportunities in new American places offers us good vantage points from which to view the "Old" and the "New" Negro:

- The Old Negro was a rural person steeped in the folkways of an agricultural society that was defined by the order that was slavery, and in the postslavery years by sharecropping and Jim Crow. That Old Negro could not take, either in the imagination or in person, the kinds of journeys that would characterize this newly minted American type.

- This New Negro, freed in ever increasing numbers from the confines of the rural world of his slave forefathers, would be urban in large and exciting ways.

- In subject focus and outlook, the Old Negro was a literary animal only in ways that the confines of slavery permitted. The New Negro of Langston Hughes, Countee Cullen, Zora Neale Hurston, and Claude McKay was variegated in origins, in subject matter, in literary product, and in what they hoped their work might do for the sense of identity held by black Americans.

- The Old Negro's institutional world was to a considerable degree confined to the black church, and seldom if ever produced national organizations that offered the possibility of securing the affiliation of blacks of all types, backgrounds, and classes.

- The New Negro's institutional world was that of the National Association for the Advancement of Colored People, the National Urban League, a blues and jazz music idiom that would capture the soul of the world, and most emphatically for the purposes of understanding our subject, a national black press that circulated a powerful message of group identity week after week in the most attentively compelling of manners to black Americans wherever they lived in significant—indeed even in insignificant numbers. If Langston Hughes, with his poetic breakthroughs in subject focus and delivery mode, was the New Negro, so were Robert Abbott with his *Defender* in Chicago and Robert Vann with his great *Courier* in Pittsburgh.

- And so was a baseball fellow named Andrew Foster who began his life in Calvert, Texas, and came into his manhood operating a national baseball organization after 1906 out of a Chicago that was increasingly becoming through the migration of folks like him a black city in its population composition. And so too was another baseball fellow named Ed Bolden in Philadelphia who followed in the Chicago fellow's wake with a similar baseball operation. And along with these executives as New Negroes, and the New Negro fan base they cultivated, so too would be migrant players with nicknames like Pop from Palatka, Florida; Smokey Joe from out Texas way; and the Cannonball who hailed from Georgia, all of whom built baseball careers geographically across a wide swath of territory that would have been unimaginable for blacks to occupy before the advent of the era of the New Negro.

A NEW NEGRO INDEED!

So yes, there was a New Negro—and at times, he would be a poet of the likes of the Harlem Renaissance's Langston Hughes, Countee Cullen, and Claude McKay. But he was also a baseball player. And sometimes it would be the poet of baseball who would best give him to us. A New Negro game—if there ever was one, was a contest between the Hilldale Nine (the Daisies) and the New York Lincoln Giants witnessed by "8,000 Howling Fans" at the Protectory Oval in the Bronx in early August 1923—inspired John Condon to poetry:

"The Great 12-Inning Game"
by John F. Condon

All baseball fans attention! Just hear
about a game
At Vannest in Proctory grounds, recorded now in fame.

The Hilldales came in numbers to scalp
the Lincolns sure,
And what the Lincoln Giants did will
surely long endure.

Warfield, Hampton, Cockrell, Santop
very tall
Threw down the gauntlet and Jim Keenan
answered their sharp call.
The two teams met in drizzling rain but
soon it cleared away,
Just as the mist upon the deep, the
world's great water-way.

The Hilldales started off with Briggs,
the Johnsons played quite well,
But Holland twirled his zig-zag twist
and cast o'er them a spell.
Blank after blank both sides received,
or one run at a time
'Twas nip-and-tuck, yes horse and horse,
none could the steep hill climb.

But Lincolns had some up their sleeve,
young Wilson covered right,
He dove up near the scoring board and
stopped old Santop's might.
Then Jewel Thomas sprinted hard and
clasped one in his glove,
And saved a run by lightening throw,
it was a work of love.

Next came the hero, Shifty Poles,
whose noble work in France
While wounded for Old Glory's sake,
showed a desperate chance.
He ran from fence outside of short,
dove forward with a spring
And falling prone he grasped the sphere,
Just hear the welken ring.

The Hilldale team then took the lead,
It stood just six to seven.

Old Santop came to taunt the men—
The shout went up to Heaven.
Marcelle took base on balls and Thomas'
sacrifice,
Bewildered Hilldale's veterans fair,
remained like quite mice.

Singer, Rose of New Rochelle,
smashed one to center field.
The score was tied, nine innings gone,
the Lincolns never yield
Bill Pierce gave way to Wiley then,
the doctor calm and firm,
Held Hilldale runners on the bag,
he made them crawl and squirm.

Joe Williams batted then for Poles,
dear good old Cyclone Joe,
He made those Hilldale pitchers seem,
as though they were quite slow.
His coaching and his headwork,
his pitching and his bat
Proclaim star par excellence,
his rooters all stand pat.

Willett worked a double play with the
Rose of New Rochelle,
And Hudspeth stretched like elastic band,
he plays both hard and well
Streeter left the mound secured by
Williams' Texas star,
Tornado, Cyclone, Avalanche,—Joe did
the Hilldale mar.

Lloyd coached and signaled, signed and
helped his comrades all in vain,
Joe Williams twirled a wicked ball,
they never scored again.
Like Alexander, firm he stood,
unbalanced not a bit,
Mid praise or censure still he drove
the ball in Wiley's mit.

> Doc Wiley yelled "Take him away!"
> Hey! Lincoln there goes one!
> "There's two,—yes two," he shouted,
> "our task is almost done."
> Wilson, Thomas, Wiley and gallant,
> bold Marcelle,
> Highpocket, and great Singer, the
> "Rose of New Rochelle"
> Landed one more tally in that twelve-
> inning game
> That showed—the—Lincoln's—mettle
> and added to their fame.[51]

The game account in the *New York Age* reports, "local fans were filled with joy at Protectory Oval on Sunday, August 5, when the Lincoln Giants took both games of a double header from the Hilldale team of Philadelphia. The first game was won in the eighth inning when the Lincolns came from behind and scored four runs making the score 7-4. The second game lasted twelve innings and was finally won by the Lincolns 8-7, when Thomas's single scored the winning run. About eight thousand fans witnessed the games, among whom were several hundred from Philadelphia who were confident their team would win the series."[52]

CHAPTER 5

The "New Negro" as Baseball Player, 1920–1930

SETTING THE SCENE—BASEBALL PLAYERS AS WELL AS POETS, JAZZ MUSICIANS, AND INTELLECTUALS

If up to now we have largely seen this early 20th-century New Negro period as one of literary luminaries filling with wonderful poetry, novels, short stories, and musings a literature artistic pot that we call the Harlem Renaissance, perhaps we should now see it as the historian Clement Price pictures it:

> One has to have a long memory to document Negro baseball. At least into the later 19th century. Certainly in the early 20th century when Blacks are moving about this country as part of the great migration. Negro baseball surfaces as an important symbol of Black accomplishment in the cities, black accomplishment on the playing field, and black business development. The New Negro Era long known for its poets and its jazz musicians and its intellectuals must now be reconsidered for its sports figures.[1]

OSCAR THE GREAT

Poetry of the traditional sort would now be matched by poetry on the base paths. Sometimes, this matching can be found in the same person. Listen to "Gentleman" Dave Malarcher, third baseman and manager, Chicago American

Giants, do that matching in his paean to black baseball's Charlemagne, Charles the Great, the incomparable Oscar Charleston:

> Sleep, Charlie! thou, the great, the strong!
> Within the depths of mud and mire!
> While high above the diamond throng
> Thy sterling statue in retire
> Proclaims the splendor of that game
> Thy paramount, unequaled fame![2]

It is as if the reader is a pitcher staring in at a left-handed batter whose stance is relaxed but focused, poised obviously to do damage to the hurler's tosses as his bat springs forward to drive the spheroid "where they ain't." Of all the players who have played professional baseball, this batter was arguably more adept than any other at hitting them where they ain't. Below the photo that ran in black newspapers we are informed that the rumored purchase by the St. Louis Giants baseball club of this outfielder for the Indianapolis ABCs is the cause of considerable discussion among Western circuit fans. It had been recently reported that the New York National League club had offered the St. Louis Cardinals $200,000 for Rogers Hornsby, twice as much as the purchase price in 1919 of Babe Ruth. How much is this black phenom worth asks this reporter writing in the *Chicago Whip*.

How much was Oscar McKinley Charleston worth? Ask the great Ben Taylor, who swung a mean bat and played a flawless first base opposite him for many a season:

> Oscar Charleston is the greatest outfielder that ever lived, the greatest of all colors. He can cover more ground than any man I have ever seen. His judging of fly balls borders on the uncanny.[3]

How much was he worth? Ask those fans who saw him hit:

> Fans along the Seaboard recall one powerful Ruthian smash of Charleston's that traveled on a line more than 464 feet before it touched the soil. So prodigious was the clout that Wellington Jones of the *Harrisburg Telegraph* measured the distance officially and placed the hit at 465 feet. Wotta man mates.[4]

> Thou wert the best who roamed the field!
> Thy stalwart fingers never failed
> The batters' erring fate to seal,
> The pitcher's powers wrought to fail!

> Oh! would thy skill could live always
> To stir the sportsman's happy praise![5]

How much was he worth? Ask the fans of the Baltimore Black Sox. "Charleston Has a Busy Day," the *Afro-American* reports.

Oscar Charleston, playing manager of the Harrisburg Giants, had a busy day in Baltimore Sunday. In the first game with the Black Sox Charleston assumed a new role for local fans when he stepped in the box to relieve Corbett who was being badly mauled.

Fans gasped when Charleston walked into the box and began steaming them over without warming up. They didn't know that Charleston entered baseball as a pitcher and was switched to the outfield because of his hitting ability. Charleston allowed the Sox seven hits, one less than the visitors got off of Pritchard. In this game Charleston also got a base on balls and a stolen base. He failed to get a hit.

In the second game he got a single, a double, a home run, a stolen base, and had three put outs. For one of these he ran to the center field fence before he could pull down a long fly of Rojos.[6]

> Sleep, Charlie! I, who knew thee well,
> Do here declare to earth and time
> In Heaven's language, thus to tell,
> In poignant poetry divine,
> The glory of that destiny
> Thus this undying rhyme to thee![7]

How much was he worth? Ask scribe Alvin Moses:

Perhaps after sagas without number have been sung of his greatness by writers of our group and other groups, he will best be remembered because of his great hitting ability, on a par with the best the game has produced anywhere—and that goes for sandlot, semi professional variety, or the charmed circles of the Big Leagues from which he was barred because of that damnable "Unwritten Law" prohibiting members of his race. Yes "Chinks," Japs, Slavs, Poles—or any other nationality on the face of this tempestuous ball are to be found around the circuits ruled over with an iron hand by former judge Kenesaw Mountain Landis—but not a black face "In a Carload,"—and this in America, the fabled land of freedom and free speech—it is to laugh.[8]

> Sleep, Charlie, now in holy dust!
> As mighty Cobb and Petway rest
> Bearing the praise of all of us,

The diamond's greatest and the less
Here honor we on thee bestow
That ages will thy greatness know.[9]

How much was he worth? Here is Alvin Moses again:

Oscar Charleston of the Hilldale Club of the Eastern Colored Baseball League is the greatest ballplayer of Color produced in this country. Not only is he the finest player of African extraction—but in our judgment he ranks on equality with Cobb, Mathewson, Wagner, and any other American or National league maestro the national pastime has known. Charleston hits with the cunning of a Ty Cobb and the power of a Babe Ruth; runs the bases like a Bob Bescher, Max Carey, or an Eddie Collins; fields his position like only a Tris Speaker could; an arm like Bob Meusel, and the dynamic personality of Johnnie Evars, plus real baseball brains and you have met Oscar Charleston as we have known him and hundreds of thousands of colored and white diamond fans will attest.[10]

How much indeed is Oscar McKinley Charleston worth? Check what the National Baseball Hall of Fame has to say:[11]

OSCAR McKINLEY CHARLESTON NEGRO LEAGUES 1915–1944 RATED AMONG ALL-TIME GREATS OF NEGRO LEAGUES. VERSATILE STAR BATTED WELL OVER .300 MOST YEARS. SPEED, STRONG ARM AND FIELDING INSTINCTS MADE HIM STANDOUT CENTER FIELDER. LATER MOVED TO FIRST BASE. ALSO MANAGED SEVERAL TEAMS DURING 40 YEARS IN NEGRO BASEBALL.[12]

**ALVIN WHITE—WITNESS AND TESTIFIER:
"THE OLD TIMERS WERE THE BEST"**

Al White interviewed John Henry "Pop" Lloyd for a 1953 *Our World* article "Baseball's Greatest Then and Now." He subtitled the piece "Were the Old Timers Better than Today's Stars?" It seems that "Pop" certainly thought so. "Tell me today, who rates with Johnny Beckwith? The same year (1927) Babe Ruth hit 60 home turns, Johnny hit 72. And in 1915 Dick Redding won 20 straight games in two months. I could go on naming great old time ball players and still miss many. In my book, they were not only great, they were the best."

Source: Al White, *Our World,* July 1953.

A BLACK BABE RUTH?

If Oscar Charleston, and others of his baseball contemporaries, could be referred to as "the Black Babe Ruth," it seems legitimate to ask where the white version of the "King of Swat" fits into our story of black baseball. There is no one in the history of sports more gargantuan in his presence when he played his game, and more impactful on the course of that sport when measured against his predecessors, contemporaries, and successors, than George Herman "Babe" Ruth. But there were limits even to the great Bambino's reach. It would seem irrefutable that Babe Ruth was never a Negro Leaguer. As far as we know, he never took a turn at bat nor held down the mound for even an inning for a Negro professional team.

A nonplaying but more direct Ruthian connection to Negro baseball has often been speculated about. While stories have abounded across the years in rumor and folk tale about Ruth's possible Negro ancestry, none of his biographers have ever been able to find historical support to establish such speculation as more than just "stories."

But as one reads through the black press that chronicled the record of Negro professional baseball, it is an easy thing to find a considerable Ruthian presence both on the black field of play, in the consciousness of those who wrote about and read about the Negro professional game, and in the memories of those who played it. In some sense, Babe Ruth may indeed have been a Negro Leaguer.

The "Sultan of Swat's" presence on the "half black" field of play is the easiest and least surprising of all black baseball Ruthian connections to find. At least as early as 1918, and then throughout the 1920s and into the 1930s, postseason contests between Negro and white professional players often featured Babe Ruth as the featured draw. Turn to the October 8, 1920, *Baltimore Afro-American* for a typical headline and story. "Ruth Gets Home Run Off of Redding" announces the story that reports a Philadelphia October 4 game between "Babe Ruth and his so-called All-Stars losing their first attempt at postseason pastiming to the Bacharach Giants of Atlantic City by a score of 9–4 in a contest played at Shibe Park." The black paper reports with what seems to be some glee that while "Ruth fulfilled any extravagant advance notices that might have been made by walloping the leather over the right-field wall into Twentieth Street in the seventh inning, in every department of the game the shore tossers appeared superior and smashed Carl Mays's offerings for eight runs in the first six innings besides playing errorless ball afield."[13]

It was often the case in his own time, and remained such for many years after his retirement, that Ruth and his baseball achievements would be the measuring stick against which promising major league newcomers or veteran greats would be assessed. The same was true for the darker side of America's national pastime. The number of times Josh Gibson has been referred to as the black Babe Ruth is incalculable. But one did not have to wait until Gibson's heyday in the 1930s and early 1940s to find the Ruthian comparison in print in the black press. "Mackey, Former A.B.C. Star, Is 'Babe Ruth' of Eastern League" reads the headline in 1923 in the *Pittsburgh Courier* in September of the second Negro Major League's first season. At the time of this accounting, it was Hilldale catcher Raleigh "Biz" Mackey's batting average of .439 that warranted the Ruthian comparison.[14]

The Ruthian shadow stretched far. "A Colored Babe Ruth" is the title of a piece in the *Chicago Whip* of March 20, 1920, recounting "the biggest sensation in the just concluded Cuban winter season, the batting of the 'Black Babe Ruth,' Christopher (Cristobal) Torriente who has out Babed the Babe with his tremendous stickwork." Tantalizingly, the paper reports that Torriente "has won such fame that various independent teams not particular about color in the United States are bidding for the services of the colored Behemoth."[15] Given the color barrier in the North American majors, none of those clubs could have been big league teams. But the prohibition against blacks would not stop a direct match between the two Babes. In November 1920, before an eager crowd of over 10,000 Cuban spectators, the Latino Babe out homered the Yankee Babe three to none to confirm his right to be called the "Colored Babe Ruth."

Perhaps, the oddest of black Ruthian pairings in the Babe's own time was the *Chicago Whip*'s championing of a black "nemesis for the champion of champions among the sluggers." In the earliest moments of his Yankee home run career, white baseball magnates were worrying, according to this report, that "if Ruth was not stopped from losing balls by knocking them into oblivion, they won't have enough to finish the season's games, yet they cannot afford to take a drawing card such as Babe out of the national game else the gates receipts will fade into infinite nothingness." The *Whip* writer found a promising answer in an Associated Press report about a young colored southpaw holding down the mound for the Montgomery Grey Sox who "would prove Babe Ruth's master. Streeter is the name of this king pitcher. In a recent game played with some of the greatest players in the Southern League this giant struck out 27 men in succession. He did not allow a single man to knock a foul ball. It is said he has more curve and better control than any man who has tossed a ball."[16]

The *Whip*'s estimation of the pitching nemesis "King Streeter" might pose to the great Bambino would of course go untested in regular league play.

From 1920 through 1936, Sam "27 in a row no foul ball" Streeter compiled a distinguished record on the highest level of Negro League competition. He pitched solid baseball at the outset of his career in his native South for the Montogomery Gray Sox and Atlanta Black Crackers. He went on to national fame with the Chicago American Giants, Atlantic City Bacharach Giants, and New York Lincoln Giants. He was a top pitcher for the Birmingham Black Barons in 1927 when Satchel Paige was a rookie in his first full season. The waning days of Streeter's career saw him with the Homestead Grays, Baltimore Black Sox, and Cleveland Cubs, and ending with the Pittsburgh Crawfords. In 1933, he was the starting pitcher for the East squad in the first annual Negro Leagues East–West All-Star summer classic. There is nothing in the record as we have it to indicate that he had any opportunity to see if he was the one to keep the Babe in the ballpark.

In the *Baltimore Afro-American* for June 10, 1921, "Bambino Ruth" became baseball instructor for black readers. In "Home Run King Gives Pointers," the new king of swat revealed in straightforward prose several of the key points in the swing that was revolutionizing baseball. Given a lifestyle that was sometimes less than exemplary, perhaps his most attention getting revelation to his black readers was the care he claimed he took to keep fit in season and out. "Between seasons I keep fit by hunting, fishing, hiking, and keeping out in the open and getting as much exercise as I can. During the baseball season the professional player keeps in trim by just playing the game and, of course, obeying the routine rules about getting enough rest, etc."[17] Perhaps, it was that "etc." that gave the Babe his "belly ache that was heard around the world" and cost him the 1925 season.

Among professional sports players, Babe Ruth arguably was the first to achieve national celebrity status that went well beyond the game he played. That status is reflected in an advertisement in the *Afro-American* in the December of his record setting 60 home run year encouraging readers to come to Baltimore's Regent Theater to hear the city's "Finest Orchestra" and to watch Babe Ruth in "A Human Heart Drama" titled *Babe Comes Home* with Anna Q. Nilsson and Louise Fazenda. Perhaps, those readers being tempted to pay the "10-15-20c" admission price to the Regent movie house would have been encouraged to do so if they had seen the International Newsreel photo of the Babe that had recently appeared in the *Chicago Defender*. Only a few weeks earlier than *Babe Comes Home*, a nattily attired Ruth in jacket and tie looked out at the black weekly's readers with a winsome smile while holding gingerly in his arms a black baby. In the background, a serious looking black youth looks on. "Two Babes Here" reads the photo caption, with an explanatory note that "Babe Ruth, the mighty king of swat, world's batting champion, visited Wheatly Provident Hospital recently while he was in Kansas City. He is shown here with one of the little residents."[18]

The Ruthian visit to Kansas City that led to the hospital visit could well have been the natural product of a developing relationship with that city's black leadership that would have resulted from several postseason appearances he made in profitable exhibition games against the Monarchs of Negro League fame. The beginning of a baseball relationship with that team and its supporters was announced in bold advertising in the *Kansas City Call* of October 20, 1922.

—BASEBALL!!—

BABE RUTH & BOB MEUSEL vs MONARCHS screams the announcement on the sports page, with details of the game's time and place.[19]

In a spectacular parallel to the EAST (Yankees) v WEST (Monarchs) baseball match reported on the *Call* sports page, another "EAST MEETS WEST" story catches our attention below the report on the Monarchs v Ruth All—Stars game, and above the box announcing next week's Yankees v Monarchs clash. What an "odd" sports page many would say that would report the following welcome accorded a "team" from the East that wasn't the Yankees.

Folk music of the East and West met today on comparable terms when the well trained unique Ukrainian National Chorus dressed in native costumes, and the Hampton Institute chorus and choir composed of Negro voices sang in Odgen Hall at Hampton Institute the famous folk songs of Little Russia and the plantation melodies of Negro hymns of the old South.[20]

The story ends with Alexander Koshetz, the conductor of the Ukrainian National Chorus, promising that on his return to his homeland he will put Professor Dett's (R. Nathaniel of Hampton) composition, "colossal in its significance of the cultural possibilities of Negroes, on my program and have my students interpret Negro folk music." As the Southern journalist Harry Golden was wont to say, "Only in America."

Other kinds of Ruth/Negro League relationships would obviously have been present as well. William Jenkinson, who has written a fine book on Babe Ruth's off-season barnstorming career, reports on the fondness that Negro League great Judy Johnson had for the Babe against whom he played on several occasions. And stories abound, as Jenkinson confirms, of a strong relationship between Babe Ruth and the great Bill Bojangles Robinson, with the later a frequent presence in the Yankee clubhouse where he would sometimes use his "charms" to try to bring his baseball friend good luck at the plate.

Undoubtedly, the most tantalizing of Ruthian connections to the black game is the one alluded to by respected sports scribe Alvin Moses. Writing a major feature piece for *Chicago Defender,* publisher/editor Robert Abbott's short-lived newspaper magazine supplement *Abbott's Monthly,* Moses reports that the great John Henry "Pop" Lloyd, a good friend of Babe Ruth's, could be seen regularly in the Yankee home team dugout on Negro League off days as a guest of the Bambino. In the record as we have it, no one else except Moses reports on the Lloyd presence. At the time of the Moses's report, John Lloyd was a fixture in New York baseball circles having played for and managed the Eastern Negro League and sometimes independent New York Lincoln Giants for several seasons. We have him in April 1931 as "one of the best known figures in baseball, (not just Negro baseball) arriving in Jamaica, N.Y. for a conference with Marty Forkins of the Forkins-Powers publicity agency formulating plans to round up a team that will represent New York and play in Yankee Stadium on the days when the Yankees are away."[21] And we know for a fact that John Lloyd was managing the Lincolns when that team opened up Yankee Stadium to Negro professional play on July 5, 1930, in a benefit game for the struggling to organize Brotherhood of Sleeping Car Porters union. "Instrumental in Opening Yankee Stadium to Negro League Play" reads one credit on John Lloyd's plaque that hangs in the Hall of Fame shrine gallery. One can't help but wonder that whoever wrote that inscription about "the greatest shortstop in Negro League play" for the 1977 Hall of Fame induction may have known more than we do about the extent of the John Henry "Pop" Lloyd/New York Yankee/George Herman "Babe" Ruth connection alluded to by Alvin Moses.

Babe Ruth may never have donned a Negro League team uniform. But the Ruth who played often against Negro Leaguers, found himself as a measurement against which to judge the level of achievement among black players, saw the "House That Ruth Built" occupied by Negro League teams, visited black children in hospitals used by blacks, and lived vividly in the memory of veteran Negro Leaguers like Judy Johnson was clearly a significant presence in the history about which we write.

Maybe in some sense the Babe was a Negro Leaguer after all?

AMERICA'S ONE CONSTANT

We know from numerous accounts that Babe Ruth was the bearer of baseball joy to young children whose troubles invariably touched the heart of their baseball idol. His visits to sick children in hospitals are the stuff of legend. Apparently, his love for children brushed aside the black/white divide that his times drew in such striking terms. We have that photo in the *Chicago Defender* of a smiling Babe holding two little black orphan youngsters in his arms at Kansas City's black Provident Hospital on one of his visits to that city. But from the dark side of that racial divide, at a time when Ruth was enjoying his greatest baseball triumphs, comes a black voice with a heart wrenching message about the price racial discrimination could impose on love of children for those who lived the reality of American prejudice. This was a message decidedly different from what we take from Ruth's oft pointed to love of children. One can't help but wonder how the Bambino would have felt in the face of this jarring note from poet Georgia Douglass Johnson in a review in the black press, "Prejudice against Negroes, the barrier of the color-line, make the modern Negro mother hesitate to bring children into the world says Georgia Douglass Johnson in *Bronze,* a new book of poems just published." In a foreword to the volume, Dr. W.E.B Du Bois declares the poems to be "a revelation of the soul struggle of the women of the race," adding that "those who know what it means to be a colored woman in 1922 must read this book."[22]

Black Woman

> Don't knock at my door little child
> I cannot let you in.
> You know not what a world this is
> Of cruelty and sin.
> Wait in the still eternity
> Until I come to you.
> The world is cruel, cruel, child
> I cannot let you in.
> Don't knock at my heart little one
> I cannot bear the pain
> Of turning deaf ear to your call
> Time and time again.
> You do not know the monster men
> Inhabiting the earth
> Be still, be still my precious child
> I must not give you birth.[23]

Georgia Douglass Johnson was the author of two other books of poetry, *The Heart of a Woman* and *An Autumn Love Cycle.* In an author's note, she declares, "I sit on the earth and sing—sing out of my sorrow. . . . I know that

God's sun shall one day shine upon a perfected and unhampered people."[24] So here again is what we find so often in the age of the New Negro—a potent mixture of hope for the future tempered by the hard reality of a prejudiced present.

And sometimes that prejudiced present would be challenged in the most surprising of baseball places. In an age when the greatest black player of his time, Oscar Charleston, and the greatest white player, Babe Ruth, played in separate leagues, one has to search far afield for the way things should have been. One such place was a baseball game held in Raleigh, North Carolina, in the middle of the summer of 1925. While one team was black and the other white, the writer of this report in the black press took special care to alert his readers that the "race games" that took place every Saturday afternoon were "entirely pleasing to players and fans alike, and have caused no friction." The game ended with a score of 11–7 in favor of the black team before "a great crowd of ordinary spectators and special admirers made more luminous by the rooting of the feminine population." We are told that when "pep was demanded the Negro girls supplied it in quantities utterly strange to the white girls." The star of the game for the white team was home run hitter Ed Gumpton, life termer, who escaped the electric chair by executive grace. His black counterpart, Ezzy Steele Forsythe, life termer, also homered, but unlike his white opponent made it home without a spectacular slide. This game was contested on the penitentiary grounds in Raleigh. It was an event that certainly in later years would have been in violation of laws on the books of some Southern states that forbade public sporting contests between members of the "white and negro races."[25]

A NEW KIND OF LEAGUE

Another far afield place where an effort in the 1920s was underway to make things as they should have been, and not as they were, was in a little remembered undertaking by one of baseball's real characters to set things right. As reported in several black weekly newspapers during the winter months preceding the start of the second season of Negro National League play, there was a second "Negro League" story brewing. It appeared at first glance perhaps just as a curiosity which calls out from the pages of these papers' reportage on the state of black and white affairs in the curious world that was the 1920s American racial scene. The black side of this story can only be pieced together from scattered newspaper accounts. It has in those accounts the tone of *Alice in Wonderland* about it as we enter a seeming twilight zone where what we know to be reality is no longer to be reality. We find in the proposed Continental League of Alfred Lawson, the unexpected racially speaking. Here is something that was considerably ahead of its time—a league made up of black teams playing white teams, with an integrated executive suite.

The Continental story's reported protagonist is sometimes referred to as a father of American aviation. Arguably, Alfred (Al) Lawson is the father of night baseball as well, staging games as early as 1902 under a set of electric lights that he carried right along with his team. The author of a noted novel, *Born Again,* he was more remembered by New York Giants great manager John McGraw as a baseball promoter who left the young player stranded high and dry in New Orleans in 1891 after a failed promotion of a trip to Cuba for winter ball.[26]

Whatever past Alfred Lawson brought to his 1921 doings, black papers were buzzing that spring over a new league that would challenge organized baseball in a fundamental way. The *Baltimore Afro-American* of May 6 got to what was for most the real point of the upcoming Lawson-engineered revolution: "The much talked of Continental League will get underway May 20th. Sporting scribes are wondering at the success of such a venture, for the League will be represented by five colored and five white teams. Teams will be located in the following cities: Chicago, Cleveland Pittsburgh, Philadelphia, New York, Providence, Buffalo, Montreal, and Toronto. Teams will battle for a $10,000 pennant."[27]

There is no record of a Continental League team playing a game against another Continental League team in 1921—or any time thereafter. But "Alfred" Lawson and his league became more than a curiosity to be dismissed, more than something to puzzle over, when we turn to the pages of the *Chicago Whip,* the *Defender*'s chief rival for black Chicago's reading public. The *Whip*'s Dave Wyatt's comments on Lawson's doings, that in turn prompted a Wyatt exchange with the *Sporting News*'s G. Taylor Spink, move us into the mind of a black scribe who, on a seldom plumbed level, opens us up to the thinking of his "New Negro" reading public. We are given what we seldom hear in the telling of black baseball history as just a baseball tale. Wyatt provides a striking black perspective on what this Negro baseball business is all about, beyond the playing field, in the minds and hearts of those who played, those who watched, those who wrote about, and those who administered the black game. Former ballplayer now turned sports editor Wyatt rejected Lawson's league proposal as the impractical wanderings of someone whose head was in the clouds: "Baseball people who are familiar with the mental workings of Al Lawson are not taking his alleged organization of the Continental League seriously."[28]

But it is something more than impracticality that bothers this African American journalist. In an extraordinary broadside aimed at this white man who one might expect would be championed as a visionary by a black scribe, Wyatt alerts us to both the depth of pride among blacks in their league and the distrust by those inside the group of those outside the group who "want to cure on the backs of Blacks all that ails the nation." For Dave Wyatt, too often the message from society has been the black man being viewed as "useful ballast in floating many a dream balloon for a solution to the ills confronting the populace of the USA." Outsiders, some well intentioned, some not, are everywhere. They specialize in telling blacks what is best for them. "They have had us traveling in the wake of Bolshevism, the IWW and many other isms that exude from diseased minds. Now comes this grizzled baseballer with a plan to unite a hundred or more of our honorable dark diamond athletes with a band of outlaw promoters, contract jumping players, gamblers, bribe takers, indicted players and other scum of the baseball earth and palm the nauseating admixture off on the unsuspecting public as representatives of the greatest national game on the face of the globe."[29]

This baseball matter is no small matter. The status of blacks in the national pastime is fundamentally important to the status of blacks in American society. In language that will anticipate by 25 years the impact on American society as a whole of the ebony presence of Jackie Robinson on America's ball fields, Wyatt notes, "Baseball is as old as the freedom of the black man, yet among his marvelous achievements since his liberation, none occupy a lower classification than the dark man's progress in the nation's sport in which more than a 100 million souls are interested and is viewed by more than 12 million of all colors and nationalities annually."[30]

Ominously, for supporters of Negro League baseball, the Continental League seemed to be challenging the year-old Negro National League. "Agents acting for the proposed Continental League," wrote Wyatt, "many of whom are dark people, have placed many an obstacle in the pathway of those who have blazed the trail to success and better things and conditions, not only for those now in the spotlight of publicity, but for generations yet to come."[31]

Dave Wyatt had no need to mention explicitly to his readers who and what were being threatened by what he termed "a campaign of destruction and devastation." The answer to the question he posed in the title to a column he penned on the Continental League—"Which Shall It Be?—could only be to choose the infant Negro National League over this white-led "nauseating admixture" Continental business.[32] In Wyatt's view, everyone who was black knew it was Rube Foster and his new league that were in the sights of Alfred Lawson. The real and ominous challenge from the Continental League was not to the segregated order of organized white baseball, but to the just born and prospering black institutional world of Negro League baseball.

Perhaps, our black scribe might have been as outspoken five years earlier if the same scheme had been put forward then. But in his closing salvo, it becomes clear that he is armed now with new ammunition. The black baseball climate is different than it has ever been. For blacks of the "New Negro" era, let there be no mistake that Lawson's is a mistaken path, for now we have our own. "The National Association of Colored Baseball Clubs is satisfied with their lot, are resting on a solid financial foundation, and are operating in perfect harmony with other organized leagues. About the only interest that Lawson's league has aroused is that many predict an early failure."[33]

In other words, thank you Mr. Lawson, but no thanks!

AMERICA'S ONE CONSTANT

With Lawson's Continental League gone from the baseball landscape, with two leagues now in place, with a clamor for a world series rising, the winter of 1923 appears as a clear highpoint in the history of Negro baseball. From 1920 to 1923, change of an extraordinary sort had been the order of the day for black baseball. It is important again to remember that behind that change—behind the celebration of league baseball by Charles Starks and Rube Currie—behind the stellar play on diamonds across the nation and abroad by the Oscar Charlestons of black ball—behind the impractical visionary maneuverings of Mr. Lawson and his Continental League—behind the great Rube Foster himself—loomed the seemingly constant factor of race prejudice that framed the reality of baseball, and all other realities for black Americans of that age. The separate but equal standard, in place in the highest law of the land since *Plessy v. Ferguson* in 1896, was only just beginning on legal grounds to feel the first blows from a still young NAACP starting out on the long road to *Brown v. Board of Education* in 1954. But even at this early date, it would be clear to some, both black and white, that in baseball, separate would not always be the case. Such a someone appeared at this juncture in a powerful editorial in the bible of baseball, the weekly *Sporting News*.

The occasion of this editorializing was the rise of the KKK, which, the *News* intoned, "has now infected baseball as well as America as a whole."[34] It seems that in the 1923 season, dissention between those eligible to take the

KKK oath and those ineligible to do so had racked the Philadelphia Athletics team. The introducer of the dispute was one Robert Kelly Hasty, a member of the Philadelphia pitching staff, a Georgia native, and, most ominously, someone implicated in a flogging case in his home state.

This situation captured the attention of the *Sporting News* that seized on it to wax eloquent about some time honored across history principles that the American game had lost sight of. "It is a pity," bemoaned the editor of baseball's bible, "that in a democratic, catholic, real American game like baseball-we call it our 'national' game-there ever should arise that hideous monster of racial or religious prejudice that has made martyrs of millions, brought out all the brute that is in humanity, and caused woe though the centuries. Yet, sad to say, there are evidences of it."[35]

Evidences indeed. The writer would go on to note with one glaring exception, the absence of distinctions in organized white baseball:

> In organized baseball there has been no distinction raised except tacit understanding that a player of Ethiopian descent is ineligible-the wisdom of which we will not discuss except to say that by such a rule, some of the greatest ballplayers the game has ever known have been denied their opportunity. No player of any other 'race' has been barred. We have had Indians, Chinese and Japanese playing ball and if a Malay should appear who could field and hit he probably would be welcomed. Shades from lightest blond to darkest brunette have been admitted, with the one exception of the wooly-haired race.[36]

Bemoaning what baseball had become and anticipating, perhaps too faintly for our tastes, that it would not always be thus, the editorialist noted the scope and extent the game had taken on in recent years. After all, baseball, our "national" game, had by now

> taken hold in Canada, Cuba, Japan, and other points east, west, north, and south, and as such couldn't be damaged by any ivory-headed obsession that one man made in God's image is any better than any other man made in the same image, within the limitations that seems to fit the conditions of the day, yet may be in the discard tomorrow.[37]

In the context of those times, this is extraordinary commentary, made all the more so for the caution and hesitation its author exhibits as to how and when things will change, but also for his belief in the inevitability of the change that will come. Throughout this decade, prior to it, and right up through the Rickey/Robinson great integration experiment, blacks themselves shared this sense of the inevitable albeit slow coming of an integrated society. They were however far less hesitant and cautious than the likes of the *Sporting News* in their calls for it to happen.

A BLACK WORLD SERIES

What came in 1924 on the major league level of blackball could hardly have been unexpected. From the perspective of playing the game, that "coming next" was arguably the biggest black baseball event in the history of blackball up to then. With two successful leagues in place after 1923, the next logical step would be the staging of a Negro World Series. Across the many years of independent black baseball preceding the formation of the Negro National and Eastern Colored Leagues, there had been many end-of-season series billed by their promoters as contests for the "World Championship of Negro Baseball." These "World Championship Series" were all, of course, self-proclaimed "championships" promoted by their participants to that status. There could be no true World Series until there was a league structure—and once that league frame was in place, it would seem there could be no avoiding staging such a series.

But there could be calculated obstruction and postponement of the inevitable. As the 1923 season progressed with a real league operating in the East for the first time, and in the West the Negro National League enjoying its fourth season of play, increasing numbers of the partisans of black professional baseball—fans, sportswriters, and executives alike—expressed a growing desire for a Negro League World Series. But the one man whose opinion counted the most wasn't ready—and until he was, there would be no World Series.

Rube Foster had seen several of his league teams lose contracted players to raiding by Eastern clubs across the preceding two baseball seasons. Ed Bolden, the key figure from the East in negotiations for a World Series, had loudly accused Foster of pocketing for the league coffers a $1,000 Negro National League entry fee paid by the Hilldale owner when he joined the Western circuit and not returned on Bolden's withdrawal of his club from the league. So, the grand poobah of black baseball was in no mood for a peace with Ed Bolden and his Eastern blackball cohorts that would be consummated in a Negro World Series that the world of black professional baseball clearly wanted. There would be no black World Series, at least not until Rube's conditions would be met. "It must come in time," a *Pittsburgh Courier* scribe intoned at the height of the clamor in 1923 for a World Series, "But according to Foster that time is not now."[38]

With Foster labeling Bolden as "a deliberate teller of lies" and claiming to show "how little" the Philadelphian "meant to help advance the Negro in his profession," with Bolden firing back in uncompromising terms, and with even the usually reserved John Lloyd quoted uncharacteristically as getting into the fray with a public condemnation of Foster as employing "the common method of time immemorial of men of his class who have preyed on the race by posing as a 'race man,'" one had to wonder if the time would ever be "now."[39] But the idea of a World Series proved stronger than the personal enmity that put at odds the men who had to give it life if life it was to have. The grand World Series idea had to wait until 1924 for fulfillment. And when it came, it came on Rube's terms.

The clamor for a postseason classic reached new heights as the 1924 season unfolded, culminating in a "let us have peace and a world series" meeting between Eastern and Western baseball magnates at the 135th Street Young Men's Christian Association in New York City on September 10, 1924. Rube Foster insisted that before there could be a series, there must be a clear agreement to prevent players from jumping their contracts and signing with the highest bidder. An agreement was reached at the New York City meeting to stage a Negro Leagues World Series to open in Philadelphia on October 3, 1924. The contest would be between the winner of the Eastern League, Hilldale of Darby Pennsylvania, and the Kansas City Monarchs who had won the Negro National League flag after a season-long struggle with the Chicago American Giants.

The competitive baseball playing side of Andrew "Rube" Foster must have left that meeting disappointed that it was the Monarchs and not his American Giants that would set colored baseball history. But his league management side could only have been pleased that it had been agreed that a commission be appointed to arbitrate in reference to players. "No club will have the right to interfere with players under contract with any other club in either league unless by legitimate lawful trade by club owners or by sale,"[40] the agreement declared. It further stipulated that each club in both leagues would be given a list of players on every club in each league. Players seeking other berths whose names were on what we would call today a reserve list would not be allowed to change teams. On paper, at least, the matter of players jumping contracts, which Foster and others claimed had severely hurt Western franchises in Indianapolis, Detroit, and elsewhere, had now come to an end.

While Rube Foster had to swallow any disappointment he might have felt in not having his team in the first Negro League World Series—and publicly he appears to have done that with graciousness and ease of manner—his presence would be strongly felt at that event. The *Courier* may have exaggerated a bit when it headlined a Rollo Wilson opinion piece "Rube Foster Dominating Figure in World Series." But the Wilson portrait seems not far off the Fosterian mark.

> When the big games shall have become history there will stalk across the pages of the record a massive figure and its name will be Andrew Foster. A loud voiced man with a smelly pipe who kids his opponents and makes them like it. The dominant power of the commission and of the leagues. The Master of the show who moves the figures on his checkerboard at will. The smooth toned counselor of infinite wisdom and sober thought. The King who to suit his purpose, assumes the robes of his Jester. Always the center of any crowd, the magnate attracting the brains and froth of humanity. Cold in refusals, warm in assents. Apprising his man the while he dissembles. Known to everybody, knows everybody. That's Rube.[41]

Preseries attention was extensive in the black press. The Monarchs were the clear favorite. But off-the-field results were talked about almost as much as the anticipated on-the-field outcome. The larger picture here was what this World Series means for the future of black professional baseball. One scribe put it thusly: "The first Negro World Series marks the ending of one of the most bitterly fought baseball wars of all time."[42] It was claimed that the successful negotiation that culminated with the scheduling of the series was of vast importance to the future of the black game. A World Series, it was said, will acquaint the fans of both circuits with the teams, be the cause of much newspaper publicity, as indeed it was, and perhaps most importantly show baseball officials the weaknesses of continued strife. This last point, a theme that would be picked up considerably in postseason analysis, was alas not ever to be adequately realized.

A colorful cast of baseball characters gathered in Philadelphia for the series opener. If nicknames were the telling factor, the East had to be favored. On the Monarchs were Bullet and Pep and Yellow Horse and Heavy. But they faced off against a Hilldale team that featured Top and Buckeye, Yank and Uncle Jake, Judy, Mirrow, Bizz, Weasel, Rube, Zoop, Sleppy, Dlbo, Nimp, Fish, T.A., Red, and Script.

By all accounts, those watching the on-the-field series witnessed fine exciting baseball moments. As an old fan put it, "there will never be better baseball than that Hilldale half of the eighth Saturday."[43] With the bases full and no one out, the score 2–1 in favor of the Monarchs, and the big guns of the

Rube Foster and Ed Bolden shake hands prior to first game of the first Negro League World Series in 1924. (National Baseball Hall of Fame Library, Cooperstown, NY)

Hilldale battery at bat, not a runner got home. Saturday's game seven was lost by Hilldale in a ninth inning that saw two key errors lead to three runs, a Monarch victory, and an upset Rube Currie who had brought his club to within a hair's breadth of victory over his former Monarch mates. "The wrath of Mr. Currie was being expressed in the clubhouse in language which beggars description," wrote the *Kansas City Call* reporter. "It was cold outside, but it was plenty hot in the Hilldale quarters."[44]

With four victories apiece, the outcome came down to a final ninth deciding game on Monday, October 20th, played in Chicago. Right up to game time it was a question mark as to who would pitch for the Monarchs. Perhaps, the least likely candidate was the great Mendez himself, aged veteran of many a baseball war, manager now of the Kansas City club, and under orders from his doctor after a recent operation that "he pitch no more ball this season as it might injure him permanently." But his response to his doctor was, "I don't care. I want to win today."[45] So pitch he did, giving what has to be one of the most remarkable clutch performances in the history of America's national game. For seven innings, the game was nip and tuck with both pitchers dominating. The Monarchs broke through in the eighth when

Hilldale's Script Lee inexplicably departed from his up-to-then very successful script, and went from an underhand submarine delivery to overhand
tosses. Five eighth-inning runs produced a final score of Monarchs 5 and
Hilldales 0. Carl Beckwith in the *Call* captures this great baseball moment
for us.

> The temperature had dropped oodles of degrees between Sunday eve-
> ning and Monday noon and fur coats predominated in the stands. . . .
> Murmurs of discontent and surprise created a hum when Mendez was
> announced as pitcher for the Westerners. It was not hot enough for
> Joe so they thought. But they changed their minds. For inning after
> inning Joe kept the Easterners popping up or grounding out. Not a
> man reached second, and only four reached first. It is improbable that
> Mendez will ever pitch another such game. He wasn't there for a strike
> out record; just "cut" any kind of way was what he wanted. He kept
> the Easterners popping up, hitting long flies, or grounding out all after-
> noon. And therein lies the answer to the win. He kept the ball, as cold
> as it was, under his control always.[46]

A fine pitching performance—but considerably more than that as well.
Rollo Wilson got it right: "Old Fox Mendez deserves more than mere credit
for a game won in that final battle. The Cuban manager has a fine sense of
the dramatic. It fitted his Latin humor to do the Frank Merriwell stuff and he
came through to perfection."[47]

When the accounting was done, paid attendance for the nine game series
totaled just under 46,000. Kansas City players received $4,927.32 to split
among themselves. The losing Hilldale players had $3,284.88 for the same
purpose. There was grumbling among some players about the size of their
World Series paycheck. But above and beyond the money, the players were
setting a precedent—the first World Series between East and West. In colorful language, Rollo Wilson scolded the disgruntled ones who were upset with
their meager take: "While praise will butter no bread, it may prepare the way
to secure a whole tub of the oleaginous delight."[48]

Let scribe Wilson have the last word on this game:

> Of the scenes behind the scenes we will not write at this time. Wires
> were pulled and puppets danced to the pulling. These things we know,
> but not to tell—just yet, if ever. Of more interest to the fans is the
> knowledge that the games were "up and up" and that each team tried
> to end the series as quickly as possible. And so—Hail to the Monarchs,
> kings of the baseball world for 1924![49]

JOSE MENDEZ: AN IMMORTAL SUPERMAN

Among the best positioned to assess the Cuban pitching ace among black baseball's pantheon of stars, black baseball's first historian, Sol White, ranked Jose Mendez at the head of the class in an stating that the Cuban pitcher "is far in the lead as the greatest colored pitcher of all times. We hear more about the Cuban flinger than any other pitcher."*

Perhaps, the most telling celebration of Mendez's pitching prowess, as well as a testimony to his character as player and competitor, came in an extraordinary encomium from umpire Bert Gholston on the occasion of the great pitcher's too early death from pneumonia on October 31, 1928 in Cuba at the age of 41:

> It was with much regret that the writer read of Jose Mendez's death. During the time he was manager and pitcher of the Kansas City Monarchs, he was a perfect gentleman at all times on and off the playing field. He was highly respected by the players and fans alike. He was skillful, wily, lion-hearted, courageous and showed a wonderful change of pace and control.
>
> Baseball is a game of heroes. Each summer has brought its new star to flash across the firmament in the panoply of the great; each season has found its meteor riding to glory on the crest of popular acclaim.
>
> Jose Mendez was a World Series superman. It was his wonderful pitching in the last game of the World Series when his pitching staff was apparently shot to pieces that stopped the enemy and turned them back. He was more than a hero. Heroes come in common mold; but supermen are cast from strange clay. He was superman.
>
> History has known but one Colonel Rounge; the stage has but one Bert Williams; the ring has seen but one Joe Gans; and Baseball has but one Jose Mendez. There will never be another.
>
> Senor Jose Mendez was a superman of that long remembered series, attaining the unattainable, accomplishing the impossible, doing the undoable and making it look easy. Yet you can't class supermen as heroes. Heroes are human, and in the attainments of supermen is something of the immortal.
>
> The superman of that World Series was Senor Jose Mendez. May his soul rest in peace.**

---

* *Pittsburgh Courier,* November 8, 1924.
** *Kansas City Call,* December 4, 1928.

The great Jose Mendez. (National Baseball Hall of Fame
Library, Cooperstown, NY)

Ah, if such as that could be the last word on the first black fall classic. But
a reading of the series coverage on the front pages of the "World's Greatest
Weekly," as its masthead proclaims the *Chicago Defender* as being, will not
allow us to leave the baseball story with Rollo Wilson's hail to the kings. As is
always the case in this world that was so different from the world in which we
live, the baseball reader following his game in his newspaper found that paper
screaming at him about a place and time that involved much more than the
joy and escape baseball may have afforded. The World Series was big enough
news to command bold front-page headlines in the October 18th *Defender*.
"Kansas City Wins in 12th," the paper shouts. "Sweatt's Triple and Rogan's
Single Ties up World Series, 3 All." Above the baseball news we are told, in
a head that stretched across the entire page, "Chicago Mob Leader Held for
Murder"—and below that but still just above the competing baseball head,

"Race Riot Brews in Jacksonville." There is simply no way to escape into the comfort of baseball.[50]

But when we turn to the editorial page and have our attention immediately captured by an editorial cartoon depicting a baseball bat, we think for a moment that we have indeed returned to where we want to be—in the midst again of a celebration of the historic baseball stuff that is underway in Kansas City and Philadelphia. However, such is not to be. The caption over the bat brings us back to where unfortunately we always seem to be. This is, after all, a Negro American newspaper reporting on a world where in the next year or so the front page will tell us that the Ku Klux Klan's request for a permit to march down Pennsylvania Avenue in Washington, D.C. has been approved with the proviso that those "noble" fellows march maskless. Above the baseball bat in the midst of the first Negro League World Series, we read[51]

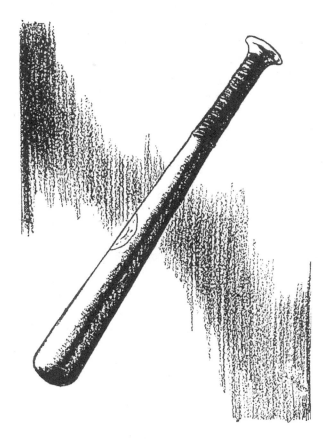

The latest in lynching implements. (Personal collection of Lawrence Hogan)

We are now compelled to return to the front page to peruse the Chicago Mob story that we previously ignored that accompanies the "World Series" headline. It seems that while historic black baseball moments were occurring in the East and in the West, in the city that was arguably the capital of black professional ball, a mob was employing a baseball bat to beat to death one William Bell, Negro.

Lest the use of baseball bats for something other than hitting a baseball be thought an anomaly, see the *Kansas City Call*, April 3, 1925, "White Man Beats Boy with Baseball Bat," recounting an incident where 12-year-old J.W. Baity was struck across the face with a baseball bat and had his arm wrenched upon returning to a ball field to retrieve his bat. He had been chased from the ball field by "a white man named Morris who had come to the field with his two children and ran the colored boys away."[52]

And then there is a letter to the editor of the *Chicago Defender* at the beginning of the 1926 baseball season offering a cautionary word about the nonbaseball use in the 1920s of baseball bats:

In addition to your editorials in the issues of March 3 and 20 entitled "Bug House Fables," I mention this occurrence. Just a few years ago in Palestine, Texas during the city elections Race men and women were clubbed with bats, irons, and guns and were beaten from the polls. One man died as a result of being beaten with a bat. The mob was led by the chief of police and the pastor of the M.E. church and backed up by the K.K.K. These facts can be verified by the ex-mayor of the city, who was defeated by A.L. Bowers. Considerations in the past and present will not justify us in signing our names, as you well know. Success to the *Defender*. I had rather miss my meals than be without the *Defender*.[53]

To come back to the Chicago Mob/baseball bat story in the *Defender* at World Series time. William Bell's only "crime" appears to be that he was in the wrong place at the wrong time—and that he was black. He happened to be outside Shapiro's wine store at 14th and Miller Streets shortly after Otto Epstein (white) and Irving Rockowitz (also white) learned from Miss Betty Greenblatt and Miss Bertha Deutch that two men had tried to kidnap them. The *Defender* reporter tells us that the verdict rendered by a hastily convened coroner's jury "came as a distinct surprise to the large mixed crowd that packed the inquest room. They had expected acquittal." The verdict was that "William Bell came to his death from a blow with a baseball bat held in the hands of Otto Epstein and we recommend that Epstein be held to a grand jury on the charge of murder, and further recommend that Irving Rockowitz be held as accessory until released by due process of law."[54]

Some last World Series baseball word!

DOC SYKES—SCOTTSBORO MAN

A black World Series largely played for the attention of black Americans was one thing; an event marred by American race prejudice that garnered the attention of the nation as a whole, and indeed played to a worldwide audience, was clearly another. The person who takes us from one to the other, star Negro League hurler Franklin "Doc" Sykes, never experienced the thrill of pitching in the Negro League fall classic, but he certainly knew the thrill, if that is the right word, of "pitching" in his nation's race arena to a national, indeed international, audience.

In Sterling Brown's wonderful poem, "Strong Men," we find the kind of man "Doc" Sykes was:

> They dragged you from the homeland,
> They chained you in coffles,
> They huddled you spoon-fashion in filthy hatches,
> They sold you to give a few gentlemen ease.
>
> You sang
> Walk togedder, chillen,
> Dontcha git weary.
> The strong men keep a-comin' on
> The strong men git stronger.[55]

Long after he had taken to dentist office and drill on a full-time basis, Doc Sykes would be recollected with considerable fondness by those who remembered him with glove and ball. When he went North in 1926 from Decatur, Alabama, to Philadelphia accompanied by his sisters, and took home a charming bride in the former Alice M. West, *Pittsburgh Courier* columnist Rollo Wilson recalled with much pleasure just how good a pitcher he had been:

> Ask any of the old bugs who infest the home of Clan Darby who "Doc" Sykes was and they will tell you he was one of the best hurlers who ever toed the slab for the House of Bolden. I but voice the thoughts of baseball folk everywhere when I wish the talented dentist and his bride all the luck and happiness which are theirs by heritage.[56]

Seven years later, Wilson's counterpart on the *Baltimore Afro-American*, Bill Gibson, saw before him in the *Afro* offices "a tall wiry man, the picture of health," who had returned for a visit to the scene of his baseball triumphs. "In bold firm handwriting he inscribed his name on the office guest book—Dr. Frank Sykes, Decatur, Alabama." Gibson summed up his man in precise terms:

> Doc appeared in much better condition to take the mound than some of the hurlers I've seen this season. Quiet and modest, almost to the point of reticence, Doc Sykes, then as now nevertheless believed in getting things done. Action, not words, counted most with him and he wasted neither.[57]

Frank Sykes came to the game of baseball as a child in Decatur, Alabama, playing, as did so many youth of his time, on local sandlots. He attended Morehouse College for two years and was good enough to earn a spot on that school's team. The years 1910 and 1911 found him in Chicago at the beginning of a decade marked by the Great Migration of America's black population in record numbers from the rural South to the urban North. He played in the Windy City's Sunday School League that was already a recreation haven for native and migrant black youth. The fall of 1911 saw him entering the preparatory school at Howard University where he was a member of the varsity team during the years from 1912 to 1915.

"When did you first break into the big game," Bill Gibson asked his visitor in the 1933 visit. "It was back in 1913," Doc Sykes replied, "with the old Lincoln Giants. I had done a little playing around Decatur and in Chicago. I also played on the Howard University nine for four years pitching and sometimes playing in the outfield."[58] From the Lincoln Giants, Frank Sykes took his already formidable spitball to the Brooklyn Royals, and in 1916 and 1917, toed the mound for the emerging top-notch Hilldale club. He came to Baltimore and made his debut in a Black Sox uniform in the summer of 1919, remaining with the Sox through the 1924 season when he left baseball to pursue dentistry on a full-time basis.

Sykes pitched for some fine Black Sox teams in the early 1920s with players like Blaney Hall, Charlie Thomas, Joe Lewis, and Jud Wilson, providing strong support in the field and at bat for their teammate on the mound. The year 1922 had to be Sykes best season, indeed one of the best recorded in the history of Negro professional baseball. In that year's campaign, he took the mound for the Sox 37 times, winning 30, losing 6 with 1 tie. One of those games was memorable enough to recount in detail.

"A No Nothing Game" reads the headline over the *Kansas City Call* piece reporting "Baltimore Pitcher into Hall Of Fame."

> Baltimore, Md, Sept 21—It is the ambition of every baseball pitcher to some time during his career on the mound pitch a no-hit no-run game.

Only a few twirlers are ever able to achieve this feat. And when it is done with the least number of batters that are required to play a regular game, 27, that hurler at once strides majestically into the baseball Hall of Fame.

Last Sunday at Maryland Park, "Doc" Sykes, the ace of the Black Sox staff, felt the urge of achievement stirring within him and decided that this was as good a day as any to cross the portals of the Hall, and forthwith he went to the box against the Original Bacharach Giants of Atlantic City (who by the way are playing a far better brand of ball than the New York team of the same name), in the first game of a twin set-to, and hurled a no-hit no-run game, doing it with the additional feat of having only 27 men face him, three in each inning and without a single pass. Only two men were retired on strikes, and the game was played in exactly one hour and twenty minutes.[59]

Sykes crowned his 30-win no-hitter season with a victory in October, the account of which again captures our baseball imagination. "Dentist Hurler with Fine Support by Team Mates Hold Big Leaguers to 4-0 Victory" reads the headline over this *Afro* report:

Showing more than the fine brand of baseball that they are capable of when they so mind to play, the Black Sox administered a brilliant coat of kalsomine to the All-Star baseball aggregation composed of a number of big league players and some stars from the minors at Maryland Park before 4000 enthusiastic fans last Sunday.[60]

Once again Sterling Brown is apropos:

> They cooped you in their kitchens,
> They pened you in their factories,
> They gave you the jobs that they were too good for,
> They tried to guarantee happiness to themselves
> By shunting dirt and misery to you.
> You sang:
> Me an' muh baby gonna shine, shine
> Me an' muh baby gonna shine.
> The strong men keep a-comin' on
> The strong men git stronger.[61]

Sykes's dentist's degree, and the status it gave him, lent themselves to colorful prose when it came to recounting his pitching prowess. Such was the case on a warm baseball Sunday in October 1921 when his Sox traveled "out Westport way" to square off against a select team of all professionals. The account in the *Afro-American* was particularly florid in its description of a game that pitted against Doc Sykes a lefthander

> whose pitching for the past season had led his teammates and several hundred rooters who had accompanied the later to expect him to thrall the Sox's colors in the dust in short order. But they, as the saying goes, had reckoned without their "host," which is to say exactly they had reckoned without the aforesaid Doctor of the drill and forceps. And be it said here and now that the elongated tooth puller administered the visitors a brand of "gas" that had them gasping for breath during the entire first session. Joe Lewis (catcher) was selected to hold their "feet" while Doc applied the gas, and between these two the patient didn't have a kick left.[62]

In his baseball career, Sykes would win more than just great games. While apparently he wouldn't admit it, it was generally known that Frank Sykes brought about an improved economic status for Baltimore ballplayers. "The Alabama born pitcher opposed co-plan or percentage ball, insisting at all times that baseball of the salaried variety was the only real kind. At one time Doc was drawing down a cool $300 per month for his efforts."[63] In at least one instance, his willingness to insist on receiving what he felt was rightly his due, as well as what was due his teammates, cost him a bit of money.

> He recalled an occasion during the annual post season series between the Black Sox and the major league All Stars when he found that the white players were getting $20 to $30 each more than the home players were. Incensed because he did not receive a share as large as his opponents, Sykes remained at his office the following Sunday. "Imagine my surprise," he said, "when I found out my teammates received $15 more than they did the previous Sunday."[64]

For all his great and memorable baseball moments, none would quite compare to the moment recorded in the photo of the well-dressed, legs-folded, calm-demeanored Frank Sykes that appears in the *Afro-American* photo section for April 8, 1933. The caption below the picture calls attention to "the dead aim one spectator (in the background) has on the spittoon. They spat over the rail until the court stopped them." And in that same background at the right a fellow with his feet upon the rail is giving Dr. Sykes a "funny look."

For his testimony in a Decatur court that day, Frank Sykes would receive more than just a threatening look. The Ku Klux Klan in his home area of

Decatur, incensed over what had become an expose of and international uproar over the Southern system of justice as revealed for all to see in the infamous Scottsboro trials of nine black youths ranging in age from 14 to 21 who were charged with the gang rape of two white women traveling in a railroad boxcar from Chattanooga to Memphis, burned a cross on the dentist's front lawn hoping to intimidate him into silence. In this Scottsboro instance, the man of action was also the man of words, and he wasted neither. For all his calm outward appearance, there must have been a fire burning inside hotter than that set by the Klan on his front lawn. The defendants' Northern lawyers, needing local assistance to support the point they were arguing that jury selection process was inherently biased in its systematic exclusion of clearly qualified blacks from the pool of jurors, found that support in our old spitball no-hit perfect-game conqueror of that better Original Bacharachs team from Atlantic City. "Says There Are Eligible Colored Jurors in Morgan County, ALA," reads the bold print below the photo. "Dr. Frank J. Sykes, Decatur dentist and former Baltimore baseball hurler, holds a list of names which he testified were O.K. for jury service should they be needed."[65]

"You can bet," Bill Gibson tells us, "that took more nerve than it required for him to set down the Bacharach Giants in 1922. Yowsah!"[66]

> Today they shout prohibition at you
> "Thou shalt not this"
> "Thou shalt not that"
> "Reserved for whites only"
> You laugh.
>
> One thing they cannot prohibit—
> The Strong Men . . . coming on
> The strong men gittin' stronger
> Strong men . . .
> Stronger . . .[67]

AMERICA'S ONE CONSTANT

If the Doc Sykeses of professional 1920s baseball knew what it was like to play their baseball on uneven playing fields, so too, the *Chicago Defender* would tell us in 1927, did the Eddie Graboskis of that era—except the latter, while doing that, really didn't know they were doing it:

Eddie Graboski, captain of Lane High School championship baseball team of Chicago, has signed a contract with the St. Louis National League club as a shortstop.

Lane won the title Saturday—Tuesday Graboski appeared in a Cardinal uniform in St. Louis and went through batting practice with the big fellows.

What a difference color makes. Had Phillips won the title and had Jones or Walker or Roberts stood out even as well as Graboski, where would they go?

The big leagues draw the color line-have done so since Grant played with the New York Giants at second base as an Indian. John McGraw tried hard to break the ice, but Old Pop Anson whose body has "done rotted in de grave" knew the Chicago team couldn't win against New York with Grant hitting the old apple, so he got the color bar placed on the brown skins.

Frankie Frisch came out of Fordham to make the New York Giants club as shortstop and stayed there until this same John McGraw and he came to a parting of the ways and Frankie went to the Cardinals in a trade that involved Hornsby.

Frankie is like Eddie, both white.

No such luck for our boys. No future. Nothing. Perhaps they could make one of the hundreds of teams of Giants but the best he could ever work up to would be $200 per month while Frisch and other boys can see $15,000 on up to Babe Ruth's $70,000 per year.

And yet there is a certain crowd that dump their money into the coffers of the big league magnates each day the teams play, even in the South where they are content to be "Jim Crowed" into the far off bleachers and they wonder why our boys don't get a chance.

We don't demand it—that's why.[68]

THE DISTAFF SIDE OF BLACK BASEBALL

Like Eddie Graboski and Frankie Frisch, you had to be among the "ins" in professional white baseball to have an opportunity to be called out. Throughout the history of black and white baseball, that "in status" was overwhelmingly reserved for the male of the species, and only rarely attained by those on the distaff side of the baseball scene.

If the quantity—and in certain interesting ways the quality as well—of coverage in the black press of women in sports is our measuring stick, for the 1920s clearly, the sport of basketball was a black women's world much more than that of baseball. Paucity of baseball coverage should come as no surprise, for such was simply a reflection of the infrequency of the female athletic presence on ball fields across the nation throughout the 19th and through much of the 20th centuries. What is interesting and instructive is to see how the limited coverage that was present reported on its subject.

An interesting contrast emerges. The female athlete stories that are written about sports other than baseball tend toward straight reporting of athletic performance. Less so seems to be the case with baseball where the tone of the writing tends to be one of stunned surprise at the presence of the female of the species in what apparently was often seen as an exclusively male domain. There was, for instance, no place on a baseball diamond for the idealized black woman we find in the *Baltimore Afro-American,* November 11, 1923.

> An "If" For Girls
> If you can dress to make yourself attractive,
> Yet not make puffs and curls your chief delight;
> If you can swim, and row, be strong and active,
> But of the gentler graces lose not sight;
> If you can dance without a craze for dancing,
> Play without giving play too strong a hold,
> Enjoy the love of friends without romancing,
> Care for the weak, the friendless, and the old,
> If you can master English, Spanish, Latin,
> And not acquire as well a priggish mien;
> If you can feel the touch of silk and satin,
> Without despising calico and jean;
> If you can ply a saw and wield a hammer,
> Can do a man's work when the need occurs,
> Can sing when asked, without excuse of stammer,
> Can rise above unfriendly snubs and slurs;
> Can sew with skill and have an eye for dust;
> If you can be a friend and hold no grudges,
> A girl whom all will love because they must;
> If sometimes you should meet and love another,
> And make a home with faith and peace enshrined,
> And you, its soul—a loyal wife and mother,
> You'll work out pretty nearly to my mind
> The plan that's been developed through the ages,
> And win the best that life can have in store;
> You'll be, my girl, a model for the sages,
> A woman whom the world will bow before.[69]

While picturing the ideal black woman as someone with physical qualities to be put to good use, that use does not seem to include competition of the keen sort found on a baseball diamond. She might not play, but she could attend. And when our ideal black "If" woman attended ball games, it was important for the men who were present to act like gentle-men, as the sportswriter would note, who "observed on several occasions at Olympic Field, Dexter Park, and other grounds where Sunday baseball is played, the attitude of some of the fans who use indecent and profane language in the presence of women. To be brief and to the point, it is not fair, and to say the least ungentlemanly. Any male individual who considers himself living up to the requirements of a man will not degrade himself to this extent."[70]

If the ideal woman's place was not on the field, but in the stands, we learn that in those stands she did not have to be just a fan. In the spring of 1922 in a full column of "Pop Ups from Mr. Wiselogy" that present close to three dozen news worthy items about the upcoming Kansas City Monarchs season, we learn in the bold headline for this piece—"Girl Ushers for the Monarchs"—that "young lady ushers will be used at all of the Monarch games this season. Those desiring places should communicate with Secretary Gilmore at once."[71] Might one wonder why among all the other stories that item commanded the headline?

In the middle of the decade, one detects something of a tone of surprise in the *Pittsburgh Courier* story headlined "Female 'Pitching Ace' Is Main-stay of Southern Ball Club." Here we have an Elizabeth—no last name is given—nicknamed "Lizzie" who obviously can hurl the horsehide. She fans her opponents with regularity and dispatch. In a recent game, she was credited with seven strikeouts as well as a hit batsman. For three innings, no one got on base. When the leadoff man finally did land safely on a scratch hit in the fourth inning, "the girl whiffed the next two up and caught the runner napping." With a colorful superlative that sounds "Satcheless" in its praise, the team's 165-pound catcher tells us "that girl can biff an ant off a caterpillar's back at a hundred feet, and never raise a hair."[72] One might expect a fine baseball future for this young "Lizzie" of an athlete. She is only 15 years of age. We know her here only as Elizabeth. Her last name is not given.

For that we will have to wait two years for a short piece that appears in the *Chicago Defender* late in March 1927. Short too was the baseball career of Elizabeth "Lizzie" Hawkins who, the paper tells us, will not grace the dia-monds in Kingston, North Carolina this summer. Her absence was obviously not due to a poor performance in her second season. "Lizzie," the reporter notes, "had a better record here than any other mound artist, professional or amateur."[73] Talented though she was, there would be no organized baseball in her future. Local acquaintances report that the young lady had gone to one of the South Carolina or Georgia resorts as a maid, a vocation presumably seen as more fitting for a black woman. Spring training for Elizabeth will be a trip accompanying her employer to the North.

Baseball playing of "a sort" would be left to the "Lizzies" of Baltimore. "Bloomer Girls Play Saturday" is the announcement over the small story in the August 18, 1922, *Baltimore Afro-American*. The expectation is that the "fur" is bound to fly in what promises to be "one of the most interesting games of the seasons at Maryland Park."[74] The source of the interest appears to be threefold: The game is between two girls' teams; the New York Bloomer Girls, white, are playing the Black Sox Bloomers, the later team name indicating a likely affiliation with or sponsorship by the Eastern Negro professional team of the same name; and while the New York club is a known entity who performed well in a previous Baltimore contest, the hometown girls have yet to show their wares on a local diamond.

Indeed, the fur did fly—mostly off the backs of the locals as the "N.Y. Bloomer Girls Swamp B.S.B. Birl."[75] Yes that is a B where G should be. A case of a journalist inadvertently adding insult to injury? The final score? Ye gads, is this "real" baseball? 48 runs on 40 hits for NY—two runs on three hits for Baltimore.

As to what comes next, we wonder again whether this is "real" baseball? To have your game reported in 1922 in an almost full-page length column written by an important black sports editor in a major black paper might be thought to be a highpoint for woman's baseball reportage in the early 1920s. To top it off, your team is coupled in the opening paragraph with Rube Foster's Chicago American Giants. But one has to listen directly to where the reporter takes us with this one:

> Djever see a girl base ball team? No. We have. And I just want to tell you old boy you've missed half of your life pleasures. We saw our first game Sunday on our way back from the American Giants ballpark where we saw the Giants wallop a bunch of whiskered fathers, The House of Davids. How we stood all this misery in one day I can't say, but never the less we did.
>
> The game was played at 36th and Wabash Avenue. The teams were the Broads vs. Narrows. The latter team is a bunch of young boys who play a snappy game of anything other than baseball. While the former is a collection of Flappers who are evidently trying to prove that women should be allowed to vote, or perhaps they were trying to play baseball.
>
> The game was full of features. The outstanding ones were: a sister pitching and a brother playing short; another was a catch by the center fielder who borrowed a chair and crawled up on the elevated railway and got a fly ball for the third out with the baseball.

The final score was eleven eleventy eleven to nine ninety nine in favor of the Broads.

They might have scored more, but had no place to mark them.[76]

This eyewitness account next gives us an umpire who has no knowledge of the most rudimentary rules, players who wear glasses to be able to count the score, and a game that was great "because you could leave whenever you wanted to without disturbing anyone."[77]

One has to assume that it is mere coincidence that this story appears over an advertisement from The Pelvo Medicine Co. of Memphis Tennessee that announces to the paper's female readership that they "May Be Made Well and Strong Again" if they suffer with "Female Troubles," and have that tired, worn out, nervous, and run down feeling so common to women.[78]

The next woman's baseball story raises as many questions as it answers. It is one of those tantalizing tales about which we wish we could know more. An easy one for a reporter to write, as its protagonists are doing the unexpected. It is clearly a read between and behind the lines story—and what we get when we do so read, while revealing of the male/female role divide in the sports life of the America of the 1920s, is far less than we would like to know.

"Girls Game Is Attracting Much Attention" shouts the article in the middle of the sports page of the August 14, 1926, *Pittsburgh Courier,* announcing that the Youngstown Nine, best known in the sport as the South Side Bloomer Girls, will battle McKees Rocks Lockhart Bloomer Girls Lassies the following Saturday at Grayber Field at 3:15 P.M. The story's headline does exactly what it claims its subject is doing—and in so doing confirms for us what we know about the limited space and place that women claimed in baseball in the mid-1920s. Indeed, because of its novelty, such a story about such a game would attract considerable attention, and be given prominent space in a black newspaper. For after all how often did women play "real" baseball?

Pardon us. These women baseball players are "Maidens Fair" who are representing Youngstown, Ohio. These are "Bloomer Girls who are crossing bats." This event is "something entirely new in the way of a baseball game." In fact, some will undoubtedly think that this "announcement may appear as a joke." And then playing against what he knew had to be the expectations of his readers, the reporter assures us that "fans who turn out for this inter-city combat are in for the surprise of a lifetime."[79] The surprise of course is that women will be playing serious baseball in a serious way.

We are assured that such is the case by those men who are managing these maidens. What is interesting is the black professional baseball connection that is present in this promotion. Claudie Johnson, former member of the

Homestead Grays and now Keystone guardian of the Brown Stars, a top re-
gional professional team operating out of Youngstown, is coach and manager
of the Youngstown "lassies." Johnson reassuringly sends advance word that
he is bringing a "baseball team" to Pittsburgh. His counterpart, W. P. Young,
who is also a former Gray, is handling affairs in the Lockhart camp. His advance message is also one of reassurance. He means to have his girls ready to
"entertain the visitors with baseball first." Both managers can be confidant
that their players will be treated fairly and professionally on the field of play.
For underscoring the seriousness of the contest, Tom Brown, owner and
manager of the Youngstown Brown Stars who "lately have been cutting such
a figure in semi professional ranks," has agreed to "handle the indication as
umpire-in-chief."[80]

The *Courier* report tells us nothing about how this game came to be
scheduled—nothing really about the players on the two teams other than
their novelty status and apparent serious baseball demeanor. How had they
come to play their nation's game at a time when it was decidedly not their
gender's game to play we are not told. How much baseball had they actually
played remains a mystery. Nor do we know what prompted the ex–Negro
League professionals and their baseball boss to assume the roles they play
here. Most frustrating of all, we do not learn in future issues of the *Courier*
the outcome of this "intercity combat." But then why should we? Novelty
by its very definition is something that only fleetingly occupies our attention.
The 1920s was not, after all, the age of the female baseball player.[81]

THE BLACK FAN

It was however a decade of significant black male versus white male on America's professional baseball diamonds. The golden decade of American sports
proved to be a time when on a frequent basis black teams faced off against
white teams in profitable exhibition contests that flew in the face of our nation's then-prevalent racial norms. Fans in large numbers feasted on interracial game of this sort that were the pure gold that made the decade for the
black sporting populace so golden a time. Who were those black fans who
turned out to see their own, more than hold their own, against those others
own? Not surprisingly, they were a varied lot indeed.

For white sportswriter Henry "Whitey" Gruhler, sports editor of the *Atlantic City Daily Press,* black fans were different from white fans in the way
they communicated with their players:

> There was a communication between the fans and the players in black
> baseball that didn't exist in white baseball. The fans were kidding the

players, and the players were kidding the fans. There was a communication between them that I always admired.[82]

For *New Jersey Afro-American* reporter Bob Queen, black fans were "just public" like white baseball fans—interested in the same things about their ball heroes as their white counterparts:

We had the ratings, the batting averages, the home runs. Every game had the box score. The same as you see in the daily papers. And that wonderful corps of sports writers you saw all over the country. They would write human interest stories about the ball players. They would tell you about something that happened in their hometown. They would even print it in the paper if one of them got caught speeding in his car. That never reached the daily press. And that's what the public likes to hear about. We were just public. Just because we happened to be a black public we had the same interests and felt the same way about our sports heroes.[83]

And for Newark Eagles baseball fan Leonard Wilkerson, Negro professional baseball was something you went to see to admire the quality of the play as much as to root for a favorite team:

I just went to enjoy the ball game regardless of who won. And a lot of times at these games there would be two teams from two different locales. Not necessarily a home team. Say it would be the Homestead Grays and the Crawfords, two teams from out of town. So you just picked one that particular day and say, well I am rooting for this one or that one. But the main thing was to go to see these guys perform.[84]

When we turn to our 1920s sources for our impressionistic picture, not surprisingly, we find all of what Gruhler, Queen, and Wilkerson tell us was present—and considerably more as well.

Black fans, like white fans, would at times be the objects of criticism from management for their weak support. Sometime that criticism might be especially pointed, as was the case in a particularly sharp August 5, 1921, *Baltimore Afro-American* barb aimed at Black Sox fans by Sox owner Charles Spedden who was disappointed in lack of turnout for the quality of baseball he was providing. But perhaps, only the pointedness of Spedden's criticism distinguishes it from what one might have heard from a white owner of a

UNSER JOE GETS A FACE LIFT

On occasion, the black press would report on white heroes in that other "Big League" for its readers. Here we have in 1926 from that "other World Series" the interesting tale of one Joe Harris. Known as "Unser" Joe, he was a World War I veteran. One of Joe's favorite pastimes in his war days, Rollo Wilson tells us, was to "make faces at every Boche machine gun he espied. One morning one of those German war tools spat a leaden stream at our hero, rearranging his face to give Joe's visage the appearance of an ex prize fighter from the knock-down drag-out era. But this story has a happy ending. Beauty trumps disfigurement. A skin graft operation after Hilldale's 25 series triumph by a skillful surgeon was a success. Big League fans and writers are to be forewarned. When you see a familiar squat figure slouching toward the plate, but with a strange map above those shoulders, content yourself in peace. It's the same Joe Harris."

Source: Pittsburgh Courier, January 20, 1925.

major league team that wasn't enjoying the fan support he thought his club deserved.

We do find however a kind of criticism aimed at black baseball fandom that is considerably different from what can be found at fans of white baseball teams. In reading through the black press of these years, one comes across a sense among the scribes, which they hoped their black reading public shared, of what was involved in the ownership and management of "our own" leagues—and what needed to be protected. What distinguishes black baseball from its white counterpart in this regard is seen in two stories from 1922. Both came from the then center of the blackball world—Rube Foster and his Chicago American Giants as reported in the pages of the *Defender*. It seems there was a hot pie man appearing regularly at the American Giants home field, Schloring Park, who had enticed a considerable following for his delicious sweet potato, fried and raisin pies. In the opinion of the *Defender* writer, the pie man's pies were just fine—but not so the black and yellow skull cap he wore that had made him a laughing stock for some of the white patrons. The black reporter feared that the "ignorant folks" who come to baseball games would make a remark some day about the pie man, and a fight would result. So the pie man's cap had to go. "Let us have a different kind of hat or cap—not one of those monkey affairs. Our game is too important to be put in danger of being besmirched by the foolish and the ignorant."[85]

Earlier in that same year, black baseball made the front page of the great Chicago black weekly with a headline "Near Riot Stops Baseball Game!" An overflow crowd of some 17,000–18,000 fans had spilled out on to the field along the foul lines, surging into fair territory time and time again during this game. Playing conditions became so intolerable that into the eighth inning opposing managers Foster and Crawford mutually decided to call the contest. An uproar resulted with disgruntled fans throwing cushions and pop bottles onto the field, and female fans being placed in danger of bodily harm.

The article reporting this melee outlines steps that were agreed to in the aftermath of this near riot to prevent something like that happening again. But it is the closing "editorial" statement of the *Defender* reporter that brings home his principal concern. He notes "that in all the years of semi pro and professional baseball in this city never have the fans disregarded the rights of others at this park." And then our reporter, turned editorialist and scold, issues a serious warning to the baser element among fans and brings home the special regard that he and presumably his readers held for what they had built in their Negro National League: "The game shall continue for the good of the game, and for the pleasure of the thousands that have patronized this institution which has taken time and money to build, and the hoodlums and the lawless element shall not break it down."[86] As more than a passing aside, one should note the closeness of these concerns to the Chicago race riot of the bloody "Red Summer of 1919." In that event, foolish actions by the "hoodlums and the lawless elements" had brought disastrousness in their wake in terms of extensive property damage and loss of life.

This special black concern about fan behavior is echoed in sharp terms in the *Kansas City Call*'s headline "Rowdyism May Cause Monarchs to Lose Park." In early June 1922, upset at a small element of fans who had been criticized by some of the whites who regularly attended Sunday games by the hundreds, the editorialist, as well as Secretary Gilmore of the Monarchs, laid down the law to those responsible for the bad behavior: "Betting and drunkenness will be eliminated. Foul language in the presence of our women will not be tolerated. The offense of the few is all the more great when the fact is taken into consideration that there are always several hundred white fans in the crowd at the Sunday games, who see a good game no matter who is playing, and who have hitherto shown no signs of being

affected by the lack of discrimination in seating, but who only use such in-
cidents such as those which occurred Sunday to prove their arguments that
they're all bad."[87] When journalists Sam Lacy and Wendell Smith in 1947
famously cautioned black fans about the need to be on their best behavior
when they went to see Jackie Robinson play, they were only highlighting
and echoing a white-fed reality that had always been a part of the world of
the black fan.

If black fans had to be smart and on their best behavior in the ballpark,
they would also demonstrate keen baseball judgment as seen in an account
from an unexpected quarter. Rollo Wilson notes in a 1926 column that the
veteran baseball scribe and critic Calvin Cain has shown that "although it
is not generally known, the Colored baseball fan is one of the most astute
judges of big-league timber in the country."[88] It seems that when Eddie
Rommel, the ace of Connie Mack's Philadelphia Athletics pitching staff, was
a rookie, Cain was given the inside dope on Rommel by "the first critics who
pronounced him great":[89]

> There were a dozen promising rookies with Connie that spring, and
> I was anxious to send word back North as to who would make the
> big-league grade. One evening while having my shoes shined in front
> of the Colored barber shop in the Negro section, I bethought me
> that there was always a score or more of these Colored boys who were
> deeply interested spectators at every practice game. So I asked the boy
> below me with the brush who was the best of the young players on
> the squad.
>
> "Eddie Rommel," he answered quickly and with a finality of accent
> that closed all debate and caused all doubt to vanish away. Two or three
> other Colored boys added their "Yes indeed" to the declaration.
>
> From the unexpected to the UNEXPECTED!
>
> At the Detroit camp in Augusta, Georgia, the next year, Ty Cobb
> came to me just before a practice game and said to me in all seriousness:
> "I wish you would go over there and sit in that bleacher with all those
> Colored boys and listen to them a while. I want to find out who is the
> best rookie in my squad." Remembering the Rommel selection, I went
> without comment.
>
> Driving away from the park that evening Cobb asked me, "Well who
> is my best boy?"
>
> "Lew Blue" I answered, without hesitation and with all the confi-
> dence in the world.
>
> "Those Colored boys are uncanny in their judgment on a young
> player," declared Cobb. "If I had their gift I could win the pennant
> every year."[90]

ALVIN WHITE—WITNESS AND TESTIFIER: "DYED-IN-THE-WOOL FANS WHO KNEW THE GAME"

Ty Cobb's thoughts about knowledgeable fans are echoed by an old John Lloyd talking with Alvin White about how the game of Lloyd's day was different from what they were viewing in the early 1950s. Lloyd, speaking through his amanuensis, reporter Alvin White, tells us how much the game had changed, not just playing wise but fanwise as well from when he had played it: "Today you have no iron men pitching double headers. And you have no pitchers playing infield or outfield when they aren't pitching. We did. Today's players are pampered. The game has gone fancy. Even the fans are different. Many of them hardly know what's happening unless the ball is knocked out of the park. Our followers were dye-in-the-wool fans who knew the game."

Source: Al White, *Our World,* July 1953

One would think it would be a difficult, if not impossible, task to get into the deepest recesses of the heads and hearts of blackball fans and see what they were thinking where their thinking counted most. Perhaps, it is not possible to go there. But then perhaps if we ask the right questions, we may gain interesting insight into the thoughts found in those deepest recesses.

The *Amsterdam News* for the July 11, 1923, prints in its POET'S CORNER on its editorial page the ever-moving words of James Weldon Johnson's *Lift Every Voice and Sing,* titling it here as it is so often titled, "The Negro National Anthem." Is there another American people, who, from their experience with their country, have felt the need to have their own national anthem? Might we wonder a bit about what that need is about?

Two weeks later, in the middle of the 1923 baseball season, the same newspaper carries a story whose bold announcement immediately captures our attention. Hardly a sports story—but there it is on the sports page. It is placed next to a piece headlined "Lincoln Giants Defeat Famous Bacharachs in Double Bill." The scene for this tale is the conclusion of a concert in Paris. The background is a France that as it appears regularly in the pages of the black press is, from a black American point of view, a place remarkably free of color discrimination. So free in fact that Southern tourists from the United States, "capitalists and petty bourgeoisie" as this writer labels them, have caused numerous furors by trying to impose their "savage" racial customs on "French gentlemen of color." The white Americans resent the presence of French Colonial Negroes as guests and customers in cafes, restaurants, hotels, trains, and sightseeing buses, and are apparently not at all timid in making their resentment known. Frequent rows are created, the writer tells us, by "the crackers in Montmartre cafes because the management permits dancing between white girls and Negro men."[91]

Present at the concert were a large number of black and white Americans. At the conclusion of the musical program, the whites, with considerable enthusiasm, burst forth into a rendition of the Star-Spangled Banner, while the coloreds stood by in sullen silence. "Join in your National Anthem!" hollered one of the whites toward his "fellow colored citizens."[92] And to add effect to the "invitation," he waved his arms conductor-fashion and had his companions hold their voices to give the blacks present an opportunity to lead off with the anthem.

Join in they did in sonorous rich-throated song. But what they sang was not America's national anthem, but the international song of all oppressed people, the *Marsellaise*. In a scene eerily presaging the famous moment in the movie *Casablanca* when Paul Henreid, playing the resistance fighter Victor Laszlo, leads the patrons of Ric's Café in a resounding Marsellaise rebuff to the Nazis occupiers of French Algeria, the concert orchestra members who had ignored the singing of the Star-Spangled Banner, now whipped out their instruments and accompanied the dark Americans. The Parisian crowd, which had been speeding toward the exits to escape the infliction of the American anthem, stopped in their place to join the colored men in their rendition of the *Marsellaise,* and thunderously cheered them at its conclusion.

What we sing easily, what is difficult for us to sing, and what we refuse to sing can be very revealing about who we are. It is the taken-for-granted custom today to begin each major and minor league ball game with a rendition of America's National Anthem, the Star-Spangled Banner. Such was not the case either in white or in black baseball in the 1920s heyday of the first Negro Leagues. The singing of the anthem at the outset of athletic contests began in the dark days of World War II—and persisted thereafter. At a much later time on America's racial front, a great American, a former major league baseball player, who had also been a Negro Leaguer, and was a patriot in the full sense of the word—i.e., both as he should be perceived by those who looked at him then and look at him now, and as he perceived himself—would say that he could not salute his country's flag nor sing its anthem.

One wonders how far the black American baseball fan of our 1920s days was ever really removed from the deeply negative judgment about his country's flag and anthem that a momentarily disillusioned or simply deeply angered Jackie Robinson was as he surveyed the turbulent racial scene of the America of 1972. When those 1920s fans turned their attention from the sports pages of their weekly paper to the front pages, they saw in glaring headlines and attention-riveting pictures the injustices that their country was meeting out to their kind. Indeed, sometimes they encountered those injustices right on their newspaper's sports pages. All through the early 1920s, great numbers of them listened with rapt attention to a Black Moses try to sing and speechify them away from their "adopted" country to the lands of their ancestors. "Rise Up You Mighty Race!" Marcus Garvey would intone, as he did to 20,000 followers gathered in Madison Square Garden at the end of August 1920.

> We are striking homeward toward Africa to make her the big black republic. . . . We say to the white man who dominates Africa that it is to his interest to clear out now, because we are coming, not as in the time of Father Abraham, 200,000 strong, but we are coming 400,000,000 strong, and we mean to retake every square inch of the 12,000,000 square miles of African territory belonging to us by right Divine.[93]

And even the most Americanized of those who were listeners, not followers of the black demagogue, such as the national Republican committeeman and one-time assistant attorney general in William Howard Taft's cabinet, Henry Lincoln Johnson, would testify how deeply the Garvey message penetrated into the black masses. Those were the same masses after all who were attending baseball games played by those of their kind who clearly had the ability, if not the opportunity, to play on the white side of their nation's baseball divide.

Yes, those black fans did love their country, and, echoing their great leader Frederick Douglass, would say in word and deed on many an occasion that it was their nation as much, indeed more than it was their white fellow citizens' country. Every time they sang their own Negro National Anthem, they pledged to forever stand "True to Our God, True to Our Native Land," which was decidedly America and not Africa.

But one can't help but think that the editor of the *Amsterdam News*, in placing his "Black Americans Respond with the 'Marseillaise'" story on his paper's sports page, is perhaps inadvertently signaling us about feelings that at least a few of the black citizens attending Negro National and Eastern Colored League games, or, when they were allowed, attending games held at white parks where they sat in segregated accommodations, must have harbored for at least a moment or two in their heart of hearts. If at some of those games they had been "asked to sing the Star Spangled Banner by crackers who were discriminating against them," one wonders if they might have been tempted to give the "sharp and thrilling rebuke" that their comrades in France had given to those concert goers.

A letter to the editor of the *Chicago Defender* from John Gray, 116 Atlantic Avenue, Brooklyn, New York, December 3, 1927, titled "America," speaks volumes to this point about feeling rebuke:

> Editor, the Defender: Will you find time for these few remarks?
> I am a Negro, and want to know how a Negro, supposed to be intelligent with just common sense can sing "My country tis of these, sweet land of liberty" or put out a gorgeous display of flags, or wear a Red Cross button with the same enthusiasm as the white man?

After detailing a litany of abuses and injustices endured by the Negro at the hands of his countrymen, Mr. Gray concludes:

> I can't see where we are obligated in any way, shape or form to anyone. The Red Cross actions during the Mississippi flood have cooked me.

Fans of the Negro Leagues. (National Baseball Hall of Fame Library, Cooperstown, NY)

When money was given to them to give to the Negroes and whites alike, it was "charged up" to Negroes or they had to work for food: hence no Red Cross buttons for me. While we don't have to destroy flags, I can't see any cause for waving them every time we turn around. It looks ignorant when you compare America's attitude toward you with it.[94]

So indeed the 1920s was a Golden Age of Sport for black Americans. But theirs was a "gold" that was unfortunately more than just a bit worn and tarnished by an American racial prejudice that continued to shape and dominate so many areas of their lives as black and white baseball fans unknowingly waited for Jackie.

AMERICA'S ONE CONSTANT

But there were seeming "I have a dream" baseball times when the tarnish, on the oddest of grounds, would be replaced by hope. Here we have J. A. Jackson of the *Baltimore Afro-American* reporting at mid-decade in an article titled "Rival Organizations Select Colored Umpire for Big Sports Event."

The writer has an all-abiding confidence in the God we acknowledge. Sometimes we are cast into a rather deep despair, but when this occasionally happens along comes some sort of a tonic that restores our hope for the world and its people. Recently race troubles, intolerance, and the lack of harmony between the peoples who make up the population of this great U.S.A. has been disturbing the writer quite a bit. As we read a copy of another trade paper with a sort of blue spirit, we came across this boxed story with a Dayton, Ohio date line.

The local Ku Klux Klan has challenged the Knights of Columbus to a baseball game, the proceeds to go to charity. Max Brunswick, a Hebrew lawyer, is in charge of the affair and Claude Johnson, a Negro athlete, has been named as umpire.

The story may or may not be true, but the fact remains that if enough of the spirit of friendliness and of the clean sporting instinct remains in any community, to even suggest such a project, there is undoubtedly a big foundation upon which one may base some hopes for an end to intolerance some day.[95]

BLACK HANDS ON WHITE BODIES

A wonderful and surprising thing this Negro press. Langston Hughes captured the reality of the black newspaper of the Golden Age of Sport when he claimed that "there is nothing printed in the world like the American Negro Press. It is unique, intriguing, exciting, exalting, low-down and terrific. It is also tragic and terrible, brave, pathetic, funny and full of tears."[96] And for today's reader, it is also full of surprises. How for instance is a black trainer like Ed LaForce serving with the white Pittsburgh Pirates on the major league level? Surprising as that may appear to 21st-century readers, it is doubtful that such would have surprised the 1920s black baseball observer and reader of his people's papers. It was whistling in the dark in the 1920s to think that *Chicago Defender* reporter Juli Jones's notion that the pick of the best whites could square off with the pick of the best blacks in a real "blood and sand American sporting contest" for a real World's Championship.[97] There was a place however in organized white baseball where black hands "up against" white bodies was an accepted fact no matter how strikingly out of place and inconsistent with the racial tenor of those times this might seem. Here in the spring of 1926, one finds this place in the happy visage of Rogers Hornsby, seen by many as prejudiced, smiling broadly as the New York Giants black trainer "Doc" Jamieson holds a mirror so Hornsby can admire the cap of the team that he will now manage. Seemingly more in tune with the 1920s racial climate, in a few months' time, it will be charged in the press that Hornsby's "southern prejudice" is behind the veteran trainer's firing.

ALVIN WHITE—WITNESS AND TESTIFIER: "HORNSBY WAS THE NADIR"

I talked with Leo Durocher, Al Dark, Rogers Hornsby, Dizzy Dean. The strangest thing. There was always some kind of chemistry developed immediately between most of the boys from the South and me. That made talking with them easy. Always they answered questions spontaneously and friendly. That is the biggies. There were some pretty lousy guys from the South too. But the absolute nadir was Rogers Hornsby. I don't think the man actually had a friend. When the New York Giants got him from St. Louis in a big trade, the first thing Hornsby did was to have the Giants fire their trainer, a black fellow names Jamieson whose uncle had the job before him. All Harlem knew this and the Giants lost those rooters until Hornsby left. He told McGraw no nigger was to check what time he went to bed.

Source: Alvin White to Lawrence Hogan, January 14, 1977.

But here is what appears to us as that surprising inconsistency again—this time in heartfelt and deeply moving tributes paid by Damon Runyon and numerous other white New York reporters to Jamieson's uncle, Ed Mackall, on the news of his sudden and unexpected death. These white scribes testify in the most fulsome terms to Mackall's skill, character, dedication to his work, and to the fondness in which they held him during his long tenure as chief trainer for John McGraw's New York Giants.

Might one not reasonably wonder that if Pop and Top and Cannonball and Smokey Joe and Rube can't play in the majors, how can Ed Mackall train in the majors—and Bill Buckner "keep the arms of the White Sox pitchers as limber and smoothly working as oil"—and Ed LaForce do the same for 22 consecutive years with the Pittsburgh Pirates—and "Doc" Jamieson, Compton White, Walter Irvin, and Emmett Parker have training stints with the Giants—and "Doc" Lambert work with the Detroit Tigers of the "fair minded and unprejudiced" Tyrus Raymond Cobb? Black trainers in the majors, for long stints of prized and lauded service? How can that be? Apparently, if you are black, you can rub them down, but you can't play with them. Perhaps, the only answer is that one should never look for consistency when it comes to drawing something as ridiculous as the American color line, and deciding who is to stay on one side and who on the other.

Likely, the oddest black training moment of the 1920s is found in a letter written on June 10, 1928, by Philip K. Brown to Ray Schalk, wherein two black trainers anticipate crossing through what they hope is not an impenetrable color line. At the time, Schalk was the manager of Chicago White Sox. Mr. Brown's "musings" are well worth our attention for their indication of how distant the racial landscape of the 1920s is from our own times.

My Dear Sir:

Pardon me for interrupting you at this crucial moment. I am writing to ask you whether or not you can employ two Africans who can train your players, and get your club out of the cellar. We have our own remedy to rub the men with. I am sure if you give us a chance to show you what we can do, you will surely find out what it is all about. We may prove a luck to your club to beat the Yankees out of the pennant.

We are demanding no set price for our service, but sooner or later we will let you know we are worth something. We need no pay, but our train fares back to New York City, if we fail to make good. I have been a Sox fan since 1917 when the Sox and the Indians of Cleveland were engaged in an eighteen innings game. I am still a Sox fan even with its disgraceful showing.

Mr. Schalk we are Negroes from Africa, but I should not think that being Negro would have any bearing on the proposition. It should not have any bearing, since I am not, or we are not to participate in the game, and the main basic being commercial. That is as long as Sox can run for you. No doubt you would wonder why I make mention of what we are; well there are some clubs which will not allow Negro trainers.

By the way we have not applied to others for work as yet. I figure that the Sox needed men of our type to help it through. Now, please let me hear from you before the Yankees come to Chicago.

I am yours truly,

Philip K. Brown

38-30 W. 128th St.
New York City, N.Y.
P.S. Please no Publicity[98]

We have no indication of a reply from Ray Schalk. The Yankees finished the 1928 season in first place for the third year in a row. The Philip K. Brown–less White Sox ended up a distant fifth with a 72–82 record.

BLACK HANDS ON BLACK BODIES

These black newspaper sports sections reported as well the "darker" side of the porous trainers' color line. We find there for instance, James "Jew Baby" Floyd, who it is reported in 1926, "has had the physical welfare of the Kansas City Monarchs in his capable hands since the organization of the league."[99] In a remark definitional of Negro League pitching conditions, the *Kansas City Call* noted that Jew Baby's "long, strong fingers have rubbed the inflammation out of more sore arms that had to be used the same day than can be numbered. If the trouble was muscular, his funny little bottles of home made liniment were all that was necessary to chase it."[100]

The most renowned black trainer in black baseball was the aforementioned William "Doc" Lambert. He worked both sides of the baseball color line as a trainer for the Detroit Tigers, along with numerous stints with Negro professional teams in the Florida off-season, in spring training, and in the Northern regular season. Lambert served as a personal trainer for several Negro League veteran stars, and for many years, had his own gymnasium and conditioning quarters in Philadelphia. Rollo Wilson gives us a wonderful description of that popular retreat as it appeared in the mid-1920s:

> Here, from early morning till late at night there is a constant stream of athletes who want Lambert to iron out a kink or treat a charley-horse. Here, also, gather the fans who like to talk trade with the men who have made or are making history in Negro baseball. Pictures of the great teams of the past adorn the walls of his loafing room, and you can always get an argument out of somebody by asserting that present day stars eclipse such oldsters as Nate Harris, Pete Booker, Buckner, Bowman, the original Home Run Johnson, Pete Hill, Johnny Hill, Monroe, Foster, Sol White and the likes of them.[101]

But all of these star players, as a matter of course with no consideration of their ability, were not welcomed in major league clubhouses. That kind of welcome for men of their color was limited to those who had the ability to rub down whites, while those who were capable of playing with and indeed outplaying their white counterparts had to be content with testing their skills against the supposed best in baseball in barnstorming and exhibition contests. Go figure![102]

THE NESTOR OF BLACK BASEBALL

So where finally does this business of a black Golden Decade of the New Negro as occupier of new ground find its baseball center? How does one get to the writing and thinking and analyzing of the Charles Starks and Rube Currie sort found on the sports pages of a major black weekly newspaper? Where does the pride of possession—the joy and celebration—the defensive combativeness in the face of perceived and real put-downs come from? The most direct answer is the existence from the decade's outset of a Negro National League, and the pride and possessiveness that sprang up from a people who for too long, and in too many ways, had been told that they were second rate and deserved and would receive a second-rate place in any and all parts of the American order.

It was fine and good that the poet laureate of black America, Langston Hughes, might say just about this time in his "The Negro Speaks of Rivers" that he and his kind had "bathed in the Euphrates when dawns were young." Indeed, in what has to be one of the most precious and audacious lines in all of American poetry, that he and his people had known "rivers ancient as the world and older than the flow of human blood in human veins." But for the fortunate few who were alerted to Hughes's wonderful poetry, his claim that they and he were "present" at significant points in the history of mankind was likely a vague assertion about someplace "back there" in history. What increasing numbers of black Americans clearly wanted was something right here right now that said to them in unambiguous ways, "you count for something." Thousands, indeed perhaps millions, found their "you count now" in the Marcus Garvey inspirationally led Universal Negro Improvement Association's "build-your-own-world" separate from white America episode of dreams and chimeras. And thousands would come to find it in a "built-by-our-own" Negro National League baseball world that by its founder's claim had garnered by 1925 more than $2 million in fan revenue—and paid players more than $1 million.

But before there could be that world of "big money," record setting crowds, and prodigious baseball feats that would be heralded across the nation; before there could be a National Association of Colored Baseball Clubs; there had to be, as one sportswriter put it, a Nestor of colored baseball: It is said of Homer's Nestor

> Sweeter than honey from his tongue the voice flowed on and on.
> Two generations of mortal men he had seen go down by now,
> Those who were born and bred with him in the old days,
> In Pylos's holy realm, and now he ruled the third.[103]

Those lines of Homer are, by 1920, an apt description of the man dubbed the "Father of Black Baseball." Andrew "Rube' Foster is, without argument, the central black baseball figure for the 1920s—and certainly in many ways for well before, and well after.

Prior to his founding of the Negro National League that more than anything else he did earned him his "Father of Black Baseball" title, Andrew Foster was a player extraordinaire. In September 1912, a white paper, the Albany *Times Union,* characterized him as the "Black Mathewson of the National Game, a Great Ballplayer Despite His Resemblance to a Barrl."[104] In 1912, no greater praise could be paid to a pitcher than to be compared to the great Matty. The stories abound of the playing days of this black baseball giant. There was the time he led his Philadelphia Giants to a 5–3 victory over the other Rube, the great Waddell of the Philadelphia Athletics. He reportedly struck out Mike Dolan three times in one afternoon's work for the Leland Giants. The fine major league batsman Jack Stahl "couldn't get within speaking distance of Uncle Rube's curves."[105] Foster claimed that in a long career in baseball he lost only six games to opposition blacks teams.

Similar testimony lauds his managerial and executive abilities. When his great team came to Kansas City for an important series in the 1920s, it was his name rather than his American Giants team name that was featured in game advertisements. "It is claimed," *Pittsburgh Courier* sports reporter Ira Lewis wrote, "that the Germans learned some of their spy system from the propaganda Rube Foster used to steal away Bingo (player Bingo DeMoss) from C. I. (fellow league owner C. I. Taylor)"[106]—an unreal throwaway line that could be said of no one else in black baseball. In saying it, Lewis captures the respect in which his contemporaries held their black baseball father.

The great Rube's contemporaries would listen as well to the stuff of poets who would sing in their newspapers Foster's praises as a baseball man they could count on when the money was on the line.

> FAITH'S REWARD
> It was on Decoration day,
> The sun was shining hot
> When thousands sat to see the fray
> On Schorling's baseball lot.
>
> There was a faithful "Fosterite,"
> His name I won't repeat
> Who made some think he was not "bright"
> By saying Rube would beat
> Now all the fellows round about
> Began to jeer at him.
> Some said: "He's bugs, beyond all doubt."
> Some said: "His mind is dim."
>
> But just to show his loyalty,
> His confidence in self,
> He drew a roll of bills, and he
> Just staked it right and left.
>
> So when the game was over and
> The crowd began to go
> That fellow was in clover, for
> His hat was full of dough.[107]

As is so often the case with legends, there are numerous accounts of his beginnings in his chosen craft. What there can be no dispute about was Rube Foster's prowess as a baseball player. Early black baseball impresario Ed Lamar remembered the Foster he first saw play when the young Rube joined

Lamar's Cuban Giants in Zanesville, Ohio, in 1900 or 1901 as the team came East from a Western trip. Lamar compared Foster favorably in speed to major league star Amos Rusie, and took particular note of his fine curve ball. It appears that at the time of his initial contact with Lamar, the young pitcher was relying too much on his physical prowess that got him in trouble in his first game with the Hoboken Club, arguably "the best white independent club in that area."[108] He lost in a rout 13–0. "From then on," Lamar notes, "he made a study of the game and every chance he had he would go out to the big league parks and watch the big clubs in action."[109] He must have been a fast learner. Later in that Cuban X Giants season, he beat the Hoboken Club twice, and would never lose to them again. But then he seldom lost to anyone in his prime as the anchor for staffs on the Philadelphia Giants, Chicago's Leland Giants, and finally his own American Giants club.

If Rube Foster had done nothing else but play his game the way he did, he would be remembered in baseball annals. But he did much more than play his game so wonderfully well. He was the creator of the Chicago American Giants, America's first national sports team. His success with that effort would propel him into becoming the key figure in bringing together on February 13 and 14, 1920, at the Negro YMCA in Kansas City the group of men who established the first national major black baseball league. It was a gathering Ira Lewis characterized as "perhaps the most singular and noteworthy meeting ever held in the interest of our sport life."[110] Rube Foster was aptly characterized as the league's "active, militant, fighting head."[111] He and his cohorts were acting out of a history that had seen several efforts at organizing a black league die a quick death. Suggestive of the boldness of the move, it was said at the time that only three of the eight founding teams were paying their players a regular salary. A contemporary claimed that Rube Foster acted as he did at this time "sensing the death of semi-pro baseball."[112] While such a motivation may well have been present, given all that he and like-minded cohorts like C. I. Taylor, J. L. Wilkinson and Edward Bolden had done baseball wise with their teams from 1910 to 1920, a league of national scope was a natural next step.

Such a league was heralded at its outset as a great advancement for the race as a whole. According to journalist Lewis, considerably more than his people's sports life was involved at the Kansas City doings: "It is indeed a source of much satisfaction to know that after years of work on the right track but in the wrong direction, the big men in colored baseball are at last brought face to face with the same alternative which in time will eventually face every big Negro enterprise of the country-*Organization*. . . . The workings of this league will be watched with more than passing interest by everyone. If it is successful, as we all hope, look for a further merging of colored business interests on a national scale."[113]

Rollo Wilson, whose reportage and commentary in leading black papers of the 1920s illuminates in exciting and insightful prose the doings of the black sports fraternity, once said that it was as hard to get Rube Foster to talk about baseball as it was to look at Mr. Ziegfeld's beauty choruses. That comment came from an evening session in January 1926 after a league meeting when Wilson caught the "Honorable Foster seated contemplating a filet mignon—no make it two. Except for a crowd of about five deep around his svelte person, he was alone. Now and then his silent chuckle, comparable only to the disappointed roar of a bull elephant as his lady escapes the amorous embrace of his trunk, rattled the Dresden set up of the dinning dancers."[114]

One can't be surprised that someone who lived baseball in the way Rube Foster did could be found talking it into the wane hours of the evening over good food and drink. What is remarkable is that when it came to showing off his baseball identity, which was of course a large piece of the identity of black baseball itself, Foster was much more than good talk. In an extraordinary series of long articles found in black papers across the nation in 1921, beautifully written, substantive, appearing at a time when his ascendancy in the black game was confirmed but still on the rise, he laid bare his baseball soul to the sports-reading public.

Foster was, he tells us, first and foremost a baseball man: "Even at my present age I have not lived at any place continuously as long as I have been associated with ball players."[115] It seems appropriate then to let the baseball man define himself as the baseball man he was. That he was more than willing to do that in the most public of ways undoubtedly says something significant about the largeness of the man we deal with here—large both in physical size and in force of personality, and certainly large in his commitment to baseball.

Foster announced his intent at the outset of his series. It was an easy matter he said for someone who had followed baseball for 24 years "to go over the ups and downs of a career, and to tell the things necessary for permanent success."[116] To do that would take four detailed articles filling up considerable space on the sports pages of the many black weeklies in which they appeared, while undoubtedly adding much to that winter's hot stove leagues discussions.

The title of the first piece, "Rube Foster Tells What Baseball Needs to Succeed," was enough by itself to attract the undivided attention of readers and of hot stove leaguers. While anticipating disagreement over his outspoken views, he quickly established a pedigree that no one could dispute: "Much weight must be given to what I say as I have dealt practically with the subject longer, made a greater success and have been the only man of Color to remain continuously in the game for such a length of time."[117]

The first article is nothing if not pointed in its criticism of his fellow league owners. He does not name names—but for any owner reading this one, it had to be easy to recognize if his own feet were being gored. If it were nothing else, it is clearly a self-serving piece. Organizing the league was, according to Foster, the result of "a duty I owed my own Race to advance along the same lines as other baseball clubs." He made baseball a profession and a business from what it was when he came to it. That was a time when the national game "was put in disfavor by the narrow ignorance of leading people all over the country who believed baseball was a game to be patronized only by the sporting element and not fit for their girls and boys to see."[118] But he is now to the point where he can't even see his team practice because he is so busy with league affairs.

After laying out in specific detail the difficult tasks he is involved with—how hard it is to work with the men he has to work with—but how profitable in financial terms baseball can be—he comes back to being the race man with the large vision—and concludes with an advertisement/invitation to "first class men to communicate with me" so that he can serve them as a consultant. In that role, he will give them the plans to formulate and effect an organization that if managed from a straightforward business proposition point of view will show a profit on an investment of $10,000, and "at the same time raise the Race (man) from the thought of being a thing of sympathy crying that the world is against him when he has made no effort to improve conditions." If Foster's invitation is accepted, "many sites will be able to boast of a real baseball club."[119]

This first piece in the series in particular, but the others that follow as well, give us an Andrew Foster who has a large vision for himself, and for his people. That vision has led him into a situation where he says baseball is paying him considerably less money than in his independent days, and claiming considerably more of his time in tasks that are considerably less rewarding. He gave a detailed analysis of costs to him to run his team in the league rather than as an independent, and of the losses he has suffered in doing so. He is tempted to go back to those independent times when all that concerned him were the fortunes of his own team. He is strongly critical of the small-minded men he has to work with. He is defensive about their criticism of him. There is nothing lighthearted about Rube Foster. He can't easily dismiss his partners' behavior. He is combative. Overly sensitive. Wound tight. Pontificating.

Moralizing. And ready, indeed seemingly eager, at times to let someone else do this unrewarding and unappreciated league business, while he goes back to being an on-the-field baseball man.

Rube Foster had a tiger by the tail. Or did the tiger have him? While he complains, it seems he enjoys immensely what he is doing, and that those baseball doings feed the ego that drives this extraordinary man to do what he has done. But what is also apparent—and to be tragically confirmed in just a few short years—what he is doing is extracting from him a personal price of considerable scope.

In three subsequent articles that range across a wide swath of subjects, and draw effectively on his unique experience in the game, Foster explained "Why Colored Baseball Managers Have Been a Failure"—"they have failed to learn the fundamental principles that would assure success in any undertaking"—and Rube Foster clearly knows what those principles are. He goes on to describe "Colored Baseball Players as I Have Known Them"—three of whom from his generation, Sol White, Grant Johnson, and William T. Smith, he berates for squandering the legacy they should have given to the present generation "by passing out of baseball without leaving anything for today's players to take up except their ability to think and hit." In his last piece, "Colored Umpires," he responds with an incredible argument to the thousands who have urged him to employ race umpires in his league. In asserting that blacks were not yet ready to be umpires, the great Foster compares the situation facing potential race arbiters to the cruelty and injustice involved in "turning loose four million uneducated and ignorant slaves without safeguarding the necessary things in life for them, and preparing and fitting them for the duties necessary as citizens and a free people."[120] This is an argument he will shortly abandon.

"Easy" it may have been for him to write these articles. But who else in the history of the game, black or white, leaves us such a public testament. Did Anson write like this? Did Spalding? Did the revered Judge Landis? If we could bring anyone back from the Valhalla of black baseball for one night of good ball talk into the wane hours over "two filet mignons" and a good bottle of wine, who would it be other than Rube?

Despite all his complaining in the pages of the black press, Foster and his cohorts could look back in the winter of 1921 with considerable satisfaction on their league's performance. The *Chicago Whip* claimed "one million persons supported their initial effort in 1920."[121] For 1921, only one team, the Dayton Marcos, was missing from the original eight—but it would be eight again for the second league season with the addition of the Columbus Buckeyes. With the twists and turns, and ups and downs natural to an undertaking of this sort, success both for his team and his league would be the Founding Father's story through mid-decade.

But as the old saying goes, all good things come to an end. When word came North to Chicago in 1902 that there was a fine pitching prospect playing for the Waco Texas Yellow Jackets who was worth going after, Jerry Williams, a stockholder of the Chicago Unions, wrote to Andrew Foster inviting him to join that club. Williams told him that they played all white teams, mostly league clubs, and that he would be put to a severe test. Foster answered as follows: "If you play the best clubs in the land, white clubs as you say, it will be a case of Greek meeting Greek. I fear nobody."[122] By the middle of the 1920s, "fearing nobody" was no longer an option for Rube the Great. After 1926, when a "nervous breakdown" took him permanently away from his life's love, Rube Foster, along with the reality of league play that he was so instrumental in bringing into being, were rapidly becoming its past. The future, if there was to be one, of black professional baseball now lay with Cum Posey and his Homestead Grays.

Black baseball began the decade of the 1920s—America's fabled Golden Age of Sport—with what was seen at the time, and afterward as well, as a golden moment, the organization of the Negro National League with the then seemingly indomitable Andrew Foster at its center. We end it with Rube no longer at the center, with his league in decline and soon to disappear altogether, and with a dawning realization that at least for now there is no longer a center, with the game and its participants about to go through times that were arguably tougher on the domestic scene than any their nation had ever faced. But for now, it is enough—indeed it is fitting and proper—that we wonder over what we have lost.

That wondering takes us back to where we began our journey with Rube the Great. What did that ancient Greek poet say about that Nestor fellow?

> Sweeter than honey from his tongue the voice flowed on and on.
> Two generations of mortal men he had seen go down by now,
> Those who were born and bred with him in the old days,
> . . . and now he ruled the third.[123]

But now our Nestor is down too. His ruling days are gone. The recorded date of death of Andrew "Rube" Foster is December 9, 1930. As Christmas loomed near, there were of course many fine words of parting praise. The question for us is what epitaph do we write to his memory, and to the memory of the black baseball over which he loomed so large?

At Andrew Foster's funeral, 3,000 people packed the main part of St. Mark's church and annex in Chicago, and outside in the snow stood 3,000 more who were unable to gain admission but patiently awaited their turn to view the remains after the conclusion of the service. News of the death of the baseball giant filled the front pages of all the major black papers, and warranted fine comment on their editorial pages. While the praise was great, and the sorrow fulsome and sincere, the death that counted the most for our story, his baseball death, had occurred four summers earlier when illness took him from the presidency of the Negro National League, and removed from his control the managerial reins of his beloved Chicago American Giants. The epitaphs that count the most—the ones that speak most directly to who he had been, and what he had done with the game that was his life's work—had really been written back in August 1926 when it became clear that his baseball career was ended. Let us listen to what his peers said then. How appropriate was Carl Beckwith's choice of words to open his "The End of a Great Career" piece in the *Kansas City Call* of September 10, 1926:

> The passing of Rube Foster from the baseball stage means the termination of the career of the best-known Negro baseball player in the entire world. Baseball was his work and his pleasure. On the field, on the corner, anywhere he happened to stop long enough to talk, the subject of his conversation was almost always the same—baseball. He took it to bed with him, and he got up with it in the morning. It was both his life and his living, and his heart was in it.[124]

Without Rube Foster, the Kansas City scribe tells us, there would never have been a Negro National League.

The respected Ira Lewis, noting Foster's varied baseball career as a star player and then as club owner, manager, and league executive, took note of the debt baseball owed Rube Foster, and expressed a hope that was not to be that "both his physical ailments can be cured and the genial character again restored to normalcy."[125] The *New York Age* struck a hopeful note for the future of black baseball if not for Rube himself: "The Negro National League has suffered a tremendous loss in the all but fatal illness of its leader. His passing is a hard blow for colored baseball, but somehow the teams under his supervision will survive."[126] Other papers sounded a chord of criticism for his autocratic ways, while giving fulsome acknowledgment to his great accomplishments as player, and then as astute owner and manager of the Chicago American Giants, and as the key figure in the establishment of the first Negro major league.

Even though he wasn't dead, these reports of his baseball death were not exaggerated at all; for from 1926 on, he was at best a yearned for memory in the ranks of black baseball. At Foster's funeral in 1930, Mrs. Mabel

Malarcher, the wife of "Gentleman" Dave Malarcher, the Chicago American's Giants much-admired third baseman and manager, sang a solo of "the Rosary." If the occasion had not been so solemn and sensitive as a funeral, she might well have sung about Andrew Foster's story of ups and downs that were both his and the game he loved what youngsters on the streets of Harlem had sung about another great New Negro hope who had fallen from the heights, had served a term in the mid-1920s in the federal penitentiary in Atlanta, and was now in exile in his native Jamaica:

> Marcus Garvey black as tar
> Tried to go to heaven on a Hershey Bar
> The Hershey Bar broke and down he fell
> Instead of going to heaven he went to hell.[127]

But hell is not a place to leave the Foster story, and the larger Negro baseball story to which our Nestor was so integral. While the "Father of Black Baseball" died in the midst of hard times for his game and his nation, there would be glory days again for the dreams that Rube Foster and Ed Bolden and their cohorts had given powerful reality to in the 1920s. Leaving alone what the future might bring or not bring, perhaps the epitaph spoken by Henry Lincoln Johnson about Marcus Garvey's attempts to translate his grand dreams into grand realities, and ride that Hershey bar all the way to heaven, applies as well to this 1920s story of the rise and fall of our Nestor, and of the black professional league baseball to which he was so integral. "If every Negro could have put every dime, every penny into the sea, and if he might get in exchange the knowledge that he was somebody, that he meant something in the world, he would gladly do it. . . . The Black Star Line (Garvey's major enterprise) may have been in the end a loss in money, but it was also 'a gain in soul.'"[128]

In the baseball story we tell, substitute Negro National League and Eastern Colored League for Black Star Line, while recognizing that whatever might have been the monetary gains or losses, the baseball part of the golden decade of New Negro sports was a gain in soul for those who by their athletic prowess and achievements made it happen, for those who were there to witness and give witness to it, and for those who visit its playing fields through the lens of history.

AMERICA'S ONE CONSTANT

If by the decade's end, with Rube Foster's absence, baseball things were as different as they could be from when the decade began, America's racial constant it seemed hadn't changed. In July 1929, the *Associated Negro Press* would headline a story "This Is a White Man's Country Bellows Georgia Congressman":

> Sylvania, Ga., July—(By The Associated Negro Press) With no war apparently in the offing, Congressman Charles G. Edwards told his constituents here Tuesday that "This country must not only be protected against the hordes of undesirable immigrants who would not make good citizens, but it must go on its course as a white man's country."
>
> Continuing his remarks which were prompted by the disturbance caused in the white ranks by the White House Tea Party, the Georgia solon bellowed to his vast audience, which was fringed on one side by a group of Negroes, many of whom were mulattoes and "almost white," "The great dominant white race, proud of its unblemished blood for thousands of years, will not tolerate social equality, even in high places without giving rebuke. Negroes should have justice, fair play, and equality before the law, but there should never be anything like social equality of the whites and blacks."[129]

The reference to the "White House Tea Party" was to a controversial reception given by President and Mrs. Hoover to the new Congressman from Chicago, Oscar DePriest and Mrs. DePriest upon his taking up his duties in the House of Representatives. DePriest, a Republican, was the first black elected to the national Congress since the departure of George White in 1901.

The reference to there never should be anything like social equality between whites and blacks would begin to be rejected in organized white baseball on April 18, 1946, in Roosevelt Stadium in Jersey City, New Jersey, and the next year at Ebbets Field, Brooklyn, New York, United States of America!

CHAPTER 6

Hard Times for America and for Blackball, 1930–1940

SETTING THE SCENE—THE BEST OF TIMES BECOMES THE WORST OF TIMES

If it was the "best" of times for baseball and otherwise in the 1920s, that decade was followed in the 1930s by the worst of times. During America's greatest internal economic challenge for blacks, the good times "last hired became in bad times the first fired," and extracted its economic Great Depression downward toll on African Americans. Americans caught up in the hope that Franklin Roosevelt's New Deal brought to the nation's troubled multitudes would, in their letters to the president, address the architect of that "deal" with salutations like "My Pal!" "Dear Buddy," and "Dear Humanitarian Friend of the People." Black professional baseball, like so much else of the America of Great Depression time, was sorely in need of being rescued by its own "Humanitarian Friend of the People."[1]

With Rube Foster, C. I. Taylor, and J. L. Wilkinson in the lead in a baseball West that saw the establishment in 1920 of the first Negro major league circuit and in the East with the Eastern Colored League after 1923 anchored by strong franchises in Philadelphia, New York, and Baltimore, the decade ahead held out the promise of being the best of times. To follow Mr. Dickens's lead, at its end the 1920s had descended to the worst of times. It seemed at its outset to be an age of wisdom. Its ending, with only the Western league barely holding on to a precarious existence, made it look like an age of foolishness. What had started as an epoch of belief with Rube Foster waxing eloquent about the future of the black game turned into an epoch of incredulity with Foster, felled by illness, removed from the game after 1926 and his successors not able to capture the magic of the Foster era. The season of light it seemed to be ushering in at its opening gave way to a season of darkness. It began in a spring time of hope. With the beginning of the disintegration of its league structure after the 1927 season, it would end in a winter of despair, a reflection in many ways of the widespread despair felt by the one-third of the nation Franklin Roosevelt would memorably characterize as "ill housed, ill clad, and ill fed," as America sunk deep into the worst economic depression the nation had ever experienced.[2]

Harlem as America's black metropolis is a good place to take the measure of the ill times that black baseball and the nation as a whole were experiencing. "Superficially," David Levering Lewis tells us, "Harlem itself appeared to be in fair health well into 1931." Certainly, from a literary point of view, she had been in considerably more than just fair health for nigh on a decade. And she still seemed to be such. With the publication in late 1930 of *Black Manhattan*, America's best-known "black metropolis" was celebrated in print as she had never been before. "Harlem is still in the process of making," its author James Weldon Johnson declared.[3]

ALVIN WHITE—WITNESS AND TESTIFIER: THE WORLD COMES TO HARLEM

Harlem was an exciting place to be for a reporter like Alvin White who lived there from the early 1920s through the late 1930s before taking up duties in 1939 as the first black news bureau correspondent in the nation's capital for the *Associated Negro Press*. White describes Harlem colorfully as "much more than an entertainment oasis where whites could enjoy a quality of music found no where else. It was also the northeast corner of 135th Street and 7th where Southern collegians, with time off from summer jobs as bellhops and waiters on overnight steamships to Boston or Albany, or from hustling bags at Grand Central and Pennsylvania stations, would gather to shoot the breeze and plan for their return to school. And Harlem was 116th Street and Park Avenue at the international market of an international community with foreign born blacks—British, French, Dutch, Danish, Spanish, and even a few Swedes—proud of the separate heritages they brought with them from the islands, and celebrating, of all things, Queen Wilhelmina's or Juliana's birthday, or singing the Marseillaise on Bastille Day."

Source: Alvin White to Lawrence Hogan, April 14, 1981.

But few folks, black or white, there or anywhere in the Depression America of 1931 felt like waving flags. Johnson and his talented 10th friends like NAACP chief Walter White and Howard philosopher and literary critic Alain Locke might still celebrate the Harlem of a Renaissance—and the great Harlem still to come—but it was hard to be optimistic in the face of the harsh economic reality of those Great Depression years.[4] While they and their like continued to laude, and rightly so, the artistic, literary, cultural, and economic achievement of black Americans since the ending in 1918 of what was then called the Great War—and tried to remain optimistic that prosperous times would soon return to their nation—there were Harlems all across the nation, one for instance on the south side of Chicago, another on the Hill in Pittsburgh, that were facing the bleakest of times. By the third year of the Depression, Lewis tells us, "for the great majority of the population, Harlem, New York was in the process of unmaking."[5]

Lewis, the author of the landmark study of the Harlem Renaissance, *When Harlem Was in Vogue,* points us at the 1931 *Report on Negro Housing* presented to a president, Herbert Hoover, who would soon be swept out of office with the assistance of a considerable percentage of Negro voters who knew too well the conditions this report documented.

> Nearly 50 percent of Harlem's families would be unemployed by the end of 1932. The syphilis rate was nine times higher than white Manhattan's; the tuberculosis rate was five times greater; pneumonia and typhoid were twice that of whites. Two African American mothers and two babies died for every white mother and child. Harlem General Hospital, the single public facility, served 200,000 African Americans with 273 beds. A Harlem family paid twice as much of their income for their rent as a white family. Meanwhile, median income in Harlem dropped 43.6 percent by 1932.[6]

By the late 1920s, coming into a depression that turned out to be the greatest economic downturn ever experienced in their nation, "last hired first fired" was the old line that must have sounded in the minds and touched the hearts of many in the Negro working class. The job gains blacks had made during World War I, while not expanding relative to their population growth in the postwar years, had to a considerable degree been retained through the first part of the decade. But that hard-won job position would be swept away in the wave that was the Depression. African Americans began to feel the coming downturn well before the crash of 1929, and subsequent soaring unemployment figures impacted on them in especially severe ways. They would continue to feel the economic hard times more acutely than their white fellow citizens all through the 1930s.

On the political front, even before the onset of the Depression, change seemed to be the order of the day. In national politics as black Americans entered the last years of the 1920s, there were clear signs that the Grand Old Party Republican ship they had been sailing on since Reconstruction was ripe for abandoning. In mid-decade, Roscoe Dungee captured the growing mood of black leadership and many among the masses when he called into question the political mantra uttered by the great Frederick Douglass in the 1870s—the one about the Republican Party being the ship, and all else the sea. The radical Dungee would tell his *Oklahoma Black Dispatch* readers that the Negro had laid down and gone to sleep in the backyard of the Republican Party for 60 years, and it was past time for a wake up call.

That sentiment was something that blacks in increasing numbers were beginning to share as the decade moved toward its conclusion. The national political wake-up call began to come in muted tones in 1928—and then resoundingly in 1932 and 1936. And when it came, they answered the ring. In the 1928 national election, two black national weeklies, the *Baltimore Afro-American* and the *Chicago Defender,* did the previously unthinkable—something that only a radical like W.E.B. Du Bois and his NAACP crowd would have advocated up to then. They urged their readers to jump off the Republican ship to support the Democratic candidate Al Smith.

If 1928 was a muted call limited to a few major black voices, in 1932 the call was clear, loud, and effectively spoken and heard. The *Pittsburgh Courier* had reached by then the position of leading black newspaper that had been the purview of the *Chicago Defender* since that paper's move to national status in the 1910s. *Courier* owner and editor, Robert Vann, was a black Republican stalwart who had been in charge of the Colored Division of the National Republican Party organization in the previous two presidential contests. In 1932, he jumped ship. In his famous *The Patriot and the Partisan* speech delivered throughout black communities, he drew the line clearly for all his listeners to see and hear: "Go home and turn Lincoln's picture to the wall. The debt has been paid in full."[7] And so they did on Election Day when a record percentage of the black vote went into the Democratic column.

FDR's New Deal was ushered in with a flourish of legislation unprecedented in the nation's legislative history. And while the discrimination that was prevalent through all of American society meant that blacks would fare less well from this legislation than their white counterpart "Forgotten Americans," they would fare better than ever before from a government that since the few years of post–Civil War Radical Republican control had been largely deaf and blind to their plight.

Four years later, the long ride on the Republican elephant was clearly over. It was now time to saddle up and mount the Democratic donkey. Historian Leslie Fischel captures this story well.

> By midway through his first term, FDR had captured the admiration and affection of the Negro people and, with that, their votes. During the campaign of 1936, Negroes were outspoken in support of the Democratic national ticket. Sixteen thousand Harlem residents traveled to Madison Square Garden in September of that year to attend a political rally, and sixty other cities held similar and simultaneous rallies. The New Yorkers mixed a rich fare of music and entertainment with leading New Dealers talking politics, but it was an African Methodist Episcopal Bishop, Reverend Reverdy C. Ransome, who symbolized the affair and its meaning by reading a "New Emancipation Proclamation." The vote in November was anticlimactic; the second Roosevelt had weaned the Negro away from the Republican Party.[8]

From the outside looking in the problems that black baseball would encounter during the Depression years of 1929–1932, as the league structure of the glory days of the 1920s disintegrated, might seem pale in comparison to the larger picture of a society whose political, economic, and social institutions, many were arguing, were in need of radical transformation. But for those within the game, the problems were very real and very significant, made all the worse by the problems that beset the nation as a whole. The always pinched and precarious financial underpinnings on which the black baseball establishment rested were to be all the more pinched and precarious through a good part of the coming decade. In such a climate, the prospects for prosperity for black baseball were not good. During the era of the Depression, black baseball, like the nation as whole, and most especially the nation's black citizens, would follow a path of precipitous decline—but also undertake a search for new direction, with renewed hope for the future. If for an America that went down into and then began to emerge out of the Depression, there would be an FDR to start the engine again—so for a baseball that went down into and then began to emerge out of decline there would be, at least for the immediate task of restarting and regeneration, a Gus Greenlee who in his Pittsburgh Crawfords of the early to mid-1930s arguably had the best professional team in the entire history of professional baseball—and over the longer haul a Cumberland Posey whose Homestead Grays could well have been the greatest baseball dynasty in the history of our national game.

HARD TIMES REQUIRE A SENSE OF HUMOR

All would not be doom and gloom during the Depression times. A good sense of humor could go a long way toward getting one through those hard times. Listen to Rollo Wilson in his "Sports Shots" column of January 24, 1931, who gives us Negro League legend Chappie Gardner as a grower of beards.

A rose by any other name would smell as sweet, so one imagines that the Cuban House of David will play the same brand of baseball as did the Havana Red Sox. For the C.H. of D. is but Romiro Ramirez and company with hirsute adornments.

According to my boyfriend Syd Pollock of the dear Tarrytown NY, owner of the club, the boys are at Santiago Cuba industriously tending their individual crops of facial alfalfa. Syd has offered a prize to the lad who grows the longest and heaviest beard err the ids of March. Unlike the mustaches affected by sundown college athletes, these beards are being shaped for commercial and not social purposes.

I should suggest to Syd, en passant, that he see the great Chappie Gardner resident in New York who has written a brochure on the various methods for growing beards for various purposes-evangelistic, theatrical, publicity and detective. The great Chappie has also perfected a preparation for growing hair on blockheads and ivory domes. It well may be that the great Chappie's nostrum will cause hair to sprout from a catcher's mask, and this would be a wonderful convenience to the backstop. Think of how many fouls will be lost forever when the catcher is trying to untangle his hair from the mask.

Then too it might be possible to prevail on the great Chappie to go South for the spring rearing of the beards. None knows better than he how to teach a young and tender beard the way it should grow and blow. Among the great Chappie's most prized possessions are testimonial letters from George B. Shaw, Chief Justice Hughes, Moses, William Cullen Bryant and Chester L. Arthur. It was he who made it possible to "swear by the beard of the prophet."

Source: Pittsburgh Courier, January 24, 1931.

Negro Leaguer Gabe Paterson, in what sounds like a resurrection analogy, called Gus Greenlee "the Jesus of Negro sport."[9] For several of those Depression era years, Greenlee's Pittsburgh Crawfords fielded as fine a combination of baseball talent as has ever occupied a baseball diamond.

The 1936 squad, perhaps his best, could boast of the likes of future Hall of Famers Josh Gibson, Satchel Paige, Cool Papa Bell, Judy Johnson, and Oscar Charleston.

At the end of the 1932 season, *Pittsburgh Courier* sportswriter Rollo Wilson wrote that Cumberland Posey, the Homestead Grays owner he called "my boy friend from the Monon[gahela] Valley," who was Gus Greenlee's baseball competitor, had just "finished the most disastrous year of his baseball career. He made enemies of men who had once been his best friends; he saw himself become the mighty somnambulist of a vanished dream when his personal league [the East–West League] crashed about his head. He lost his grip on a profitable territory. He saw his club raided by the same ruthless methods which he had employed against other owners in the history years." But, Wilson told his readers, "Posey will rebound."[10] Rebound Posey did with a Homestead Grays club that by the end of the decade would be on its way to as remarkable a string of first place finishes as any team in the history of sports.

By the decade's end, a revived two-league structure with the renewal of a Negro World Series, a new crop of outstanding players who would come to rank among the all-time legends of the sport, and a midsummer Negro League All-Star game that had become the sporting event of the year for black fandom announced that black professional baseball had rebounded.[11]

BLACKBALL IN BIG LEAGUE PARKS

A good part of the economic rebound black professional baseball would experience in the 1930s came from the game's penetration into major league baseball space as big league owners began to realize that there was a good buck to be made while on road trips by renting their empty stadiums to top flight Negro baseball teams. On rare occasions, for what they deemed to be good causes, they even donated their facilities. Such an occasion occurred in the decade's opening summer at what we will now call "The House That Ruth Built, and Pop Opened!"

For over 80 years, the now consigned to the dustbin of history old Yankee Stadium served as the site of great moments in the history of our national pastime. As special a moment as any occurred on July 5, 1930. In late June of that year, advertisements in leading black newspapers put out the cry to "Fill the Yankee Stadium!" for a July 5 doubleheader between the NY Lincoln Giants and the Baltimore Black Sox. These games would be a benefit for the Brotherhood of Sleeping Car Porters (BSCP) and the first appearance of Negro professional baseball at the stadium.

"BABE RUTH" YANCY

Bill Yancy had the distinction of being the first black player to set foot on the turf at Yankee Stadium. Yancy's excitement was such that he ran out on the field early, pretended to catch fly balls in right field like Babe Ruth, and stood alone at home plate pretending to hit home runs into the right-field stands like the Babe. Bill Yancy counted playing in Yankee Stadium as one of his biggest thrills.

Source: Robert Peterson interview with Bill Yancy, National Baseball Hall of Fame.

To have been the inaugural black baseball moment at the house that Ruth built would be significant in itself. But a benefit for the BSCP makes the occasion especially noteworthy. The union that A. Philip Randolph was struggling to establish is an epic story in American history. And the name Randolph keeps company with that of Martin Luther King, Frederick Douglass, and Booker T. Washington at the apex of African Americans who have impacted our nation's history.

The day was a grand success. As manager/first baseman for the Lincolns, Pop Lloyd stole a base, went 4–8, and handled 24 putouts without an error. Between games Bojangles Robinson running backward outraced YMCA track stars. A band from Harlem's famous 369th infantry entertained the large crowd. When receipts were tallied, Randolph's brotherhood treasury was $3,500 to the good. After the July 5th opening, there would be a substantial Negro baseball presence at Yankee Stadium through the 1930s, up to the integration of the majors in 1947, and all the way into the early 1960s. When the Yankees were on the road, teams from the Negro Leagues played there with a regularity that is surprising only to those who do not know their baseball history.

"Instrumental in Opening Yankee Stadium to Negro Baseball" reads John Lloyd's Hall of Fame plaque. And yet there is no recognition of this at today's Yankee Stadium. Pop Lloyd's baseball world was a place hidden by a color line that had whites seeing stereotypes, while blacks celebrated the talent of men with colorful names like Cannonball, Smokey Joe, Dandy, and Lloyd himself, El Cuchara. The "color line" today at Yankee Stadium seems to be one of historical amnesia. Every year at an Atlantic City ballyard named after Pop Lloyd, we celebrate the memory and legacy of those who played their ball in "leagues where only the ball was white." Wouldn't it be wonderful, and historically appropriate, if that other Pop baseball site—the one he opened on July 5, 1930—would see fit to honor the man who could have been the greatest shortstop . . . wait a second, maybe the "greatest player of all time"?

Isn't it time for the Yankee Stadium history that was Phil Randolph and his BSCP, the Negro League World Champion Cubans of 1947, and most of all America's baseball great, Pop Lloyd, to be recognized? In their own Yankee Stadium baseball moments, Negro Leaguers, playing behind the veil of race, were every bit as good as the Ruths and Gehrigs of Yankee lore. And as deserving of permanent recognition at the "House That Ruth Built, and Pop Opened!" as the poet Andy Razaff put the case in a poem penned to baseball commissioner Kenesaw Mountain Landis after taking in a Negro League contest at Yankee Stadium in the mid-1930s:

To Judge Landis

(About Colored Ball Players)

Dear Mr. Landis, just a line
About last Sunday's baseball game
At Yankee Stadium. Were you there?
Now if your weren't, it's a shame!
You should have seen those colored boys,
Crack players from the East and West
Who showed that crowd a brand of ball
As good as any of your best.
For hitting, fielding, nerve and speed,
For pitching of the finest sort,
For class and perfect showmanship,
Those boys did credit to the sport.
And more than thirty thousand fans
Were there on hand, which goes to show
That keeping big league baseball white
Means losing lots of punch and dough!
The first club owner smart enough
And BIG enough to find a place
For colored players on his team
Will seldom lose a pennant race.
It's time you and your crowd woke up
In this new and enlightened age—
Oh, by the way your Schoolboy Rowe
Should see those pitchers, Jones and Paige![12]

DADDY BLACK IN RHODE ISLAND

Yankee Stadium was not the only new venue for black baseball in the early 1930s. In the midst of the Depression, with the collapse of the Negro major leagues, players of the caliber of future Hall of Fame candidate Oliver "Ghost" Marcell and veteran Negro Leaguers Jesse Hubbard, Luther Farrell, and Robert "Highpockets" Hudspeth became available to those who could afford to bid for their services to play in places like Providence, Rhode Island, where they never would have thought of playing previously. The pay they received was considerably less than what they received during the 1920s heyday of league competition. But especially in hard times, players went where the money was, however meager that money might seem to what they had received previously.

For one year, Arthur "Daddy" Black was the go-to man for a handful of scrambling for employment now ex–Negro leaguers, and his Providence Giants were the go-to team. The "Daddy" Black Depression payday would prove to be, like its provider, short lived. The *Boston Chronicle* of October 1, 1932, tells us this story in a front-page piece headlined "20,000 File by Bier of 'Daddy' Black."

> Providence, R. I.—It is safe to say that fully **20,000** persons reviewed the remains of Arthur J. (Daddy) Black, slain Number's King, war veteran and benefactor, during the time that the body lay in state from Monday noon until funeral time on Wednesday. Thousands called at the Montgomery Funeral Homes during the hours the body was there. Many, many more persons, school children, men and women, black and white, from all walks of life, viewed the body as it lay in state at the Elks Home, 881 Westminster Street from Tuesday noon until Wednesday. Faces were pale and sad. Women cried and in some cases strong men broke down and wept—and some of these men were white—as they looked on Daddy's face for the last time.
>
> The dead man reposed in a plain but beautiful quartered oak casket draped with the American flag, and flanked on all sides by beautiful floral tributes, sent by admirers, relatives, friends and business and fraternal associates. He was laid to rest in the uniform of a chief machinists mate of the U.S. Navy, on his arms stripes denoting years of service, and on his breast service bars denoting participation in foreign service while in the Navy—the Boxer Rebellion, and the World War. Wednesday morning the American flag was removed from the casket, and a blanket of flowers was substituted bearing the words "Husband" and "Daddy."

At the time of his slaying by five armed men who broke into his house in an attempt to rob that day's lottery receipts, the *Providence Journal* noted that two years ago he organized the Providence Colored Giants. Measured by the talent on its roster, that club was the best Negro professional team in the history of New England. The journal went on to note that Daddy Black "was one of the chief figures in the Boston Twilight League, a fast circuit. In baseball circles Black was always known as a free spender. He bought a large bus for his team and always was prompt in payments to his players."[13]

BLACK BASEBALL AND BLACK MUSIC

If it was a "Daddy" in Providence in the midst of Depression times with the bucks to bankroll a fine team of now ex–Negro League baseball players, it was a "Pops" with a golden horn and many of his musical cohorts who we turn to next as we journey into Depression era baseball. Gerald Early tells us that "there are only three things that America will be known for 2,000 years from now when they study this civilization: the Constitution, jazz music and baseball. They're the three most beautifully designed things this civilization has ever produced."[14] Robert Cvornyek sounds a similar chord: "Baseball functioned as the athletic counterpart to the innovation and cultural expression found in jazz."[15]

If blackball after Pop Lloyd and 1930 would be a game played beautifully and wonderfully at Yankee Stadium, it was also then, and well before and after then, a black–owned and orchestrated event that offers a special path into the heart and mind of America's citizens of color. "The Negro Leagues," the poet Amiri Baraka tells us, "are like a light somewhere. Back over your shoulder. As you go away. A warmth still, connected to laughter and self-love. The collective Black aura that can only be duplicated with Black conversation or music."[16] The great blues and jazz historian, Albert Murray, takes us magnificently down that baseball and music road both visually, and in prose that moves and jumps, and surprises like a good knuckleball when he tells us and shows us in *Stomping the Blues* that black baseball was Satchmo's game too.

> The enthusiasm for baseball that has long been so widespread among blues musicians is remarkably in character with their involvement in rituals of elegant endeavor and perseverance in unfavorable circumstances. The overall attitude toward the nature of things that is implicit in a baseball game is not at all unlike the pragmatism that underlies the blues statement. Not only are there bad times as well as good times, but even during the best of seasons when your team wins more games than its opponents, most of its efforts end in failure. The very best batters are not only hard put to hit safely on an average of three out of ten times but miss the ball more often than they hit it when they swing

the bat. Most base runners do not score. They very best pitchers not only give us bases on balls and have their best pitches end up as hits and even home runs, but also get knocked out of the box from time to time. And yet the competing players and partisan spectators alike accept such adversity as part of the game, which otherwise would not last the customary nine innings. In fact, the whole point of sportsmanship is to condition people to win without arrogance and with grace. As deeply disappointed as a team and its rooters are when its most dependable hitter strikes out in the ninth inning with the tying and winnings runs on third and second base, everybody would be scandalized if he then became so embarrassed that he ran off and spent the rest of the day crying and cursing himself. What is expected is that he realize that for all his great skill, past record, and heroic effort, you cannot win them all.[17]

Across the entire history of the black game, ballplayers and musicians played off of each other in what became for many a lifetime mutual admiration and inspiration society. They were constantly meeting on their travels, these fellow troubadours of the road, crossing paths as they crossed back and forth across their country and abroad as well. They enjoyed, indeed loved what each other did—and they enjoyed each other's company.

We find this music and baseball identity connection in the lit up eyes of Monte Irvin and Buck O'Neil, when they wax eloquent about the music and musicians that meant so much to them at so many points in their baseball careers. It is there in the Nat Cole who, his wife tells us, loved his family and his music most of all, but there were moments when she wondered if baseball might have been first. What wouldn't we give today to listen to that identity connection as the "Black, White Sox" band led by the White Sox best-known fan, the "Big Boy" the *Chicago Whip* crowned as the champion Sox rooter of the city, filled the stands of old Comiskey in the early 1920s with jazz sounds that were "fresh and new. His loud and humorous voice could be heard above the din of doubles and triples, and his Sox band in their last World Series was termed an innovation in jazz music"? Or to be present as the Newark Eagles' Effa Manley, the only woman ever elected to the Hall of Fame, put together special music moments to benefit the New Jersey NAACP that she served as entertainment chairman? Or to listen to Satchmo urge on his secret nine, and likely after the game, win or lose, serenade them with his precious trumpet sounds? Or to have been there in Harlem looking out our apartment window when the 369th struck up the Army Blues as they headed off to the "House That Babe Ruth Built, and Pop Lloyd Opened" to entertain the fans at another Negro league doubleheader?

The story of the intersection of black baseball and black music is a story of special places at special times. It is Chicago in the late 1910s when Rube Foster's American Giants ruled the baseball day as the likes of Freddie Keppard, King Oliver, and the young Louis Armstrong began to rule the music scene. It is Kansas City in 1924 when the Monarchs won the first Negro League World Series and such legends of the music world as George E. Lee, Jay McShann, and Benny Moten were establishing their own "World Series" reputations. It is Pittsburgh in 1935 when the legendary Crawfords of Gus Greenlee announced the return of top-level professional black baseball after the down years of the Depression, and in the Hill section of the Steel City such jazz and blues greats as Earl Hines, Billy Eckstine, and Art Blakey were playing a special brand of music that made listeners forget all about any depression. It is Newark in 1946 when Effa Manley's Eagles won what is arguably the last of the great fall Negro League World Series classics, while in music venues in Newark and close by in New York City the likes of the great Ellington and Basie, and voices like Ella and Sarah dazzled new generations of lovers of this quintessential American music.

Ask players like Monte Irvin to talk about those special black music and black baseball times and places, and you are liable to have several hours of wonderful conversation ranging across something that began to get into him as a youngster in the 1930s growing up in East Orange, New Jersey. Get him to tell his story about a taxi ride in Japan in 1953 with Hank Thompson, baseball player, and Ben Webster, magnificent saxophonist, where Ben broke a communications barrier with some language that was universal in its understandability! Or to describe the scene when that same Webster, wont to emphatically poke at someone when he was making an important point—and apparently with Ben many points were to be made with emphasis—found the dinner he had just consumed on the floor after over "emphasizing" Joe Louis, and you will find yourself in a world where music and baseball went together like love and marriage and that proverbial horse and carriage.[18]

STANLEY REMEMBERS THE MUSIC TIMES

Stanley "Doc" Glenn was a fine catcher with the Philadelphia Stars of the Negro National League during the 1940s. He became in the recovery of Negro League history one of the best sources to draw on.

At night, the players frequented Philadelphia's lively clubs and cheap restaurants. In the '40s, the city had many small jazz and other music venues, which attracted black and white audiences alike. We always used to go hear jazz at the Blue Notes on Ridge Avenue, or big band music at a particular hotel at Broad and Lombard Streets.

And come evening, we were welcomed at all the culture hubs. We hung out with the patrons at jazz clubs, and you could always find a theater where the big bands and top vocalists were playing to enthusiastic crowds. We'd mingle with the other athletes there, and after we saw the shows we'd go up and introduce ourselves to the musicians and celebrities who were touring those cities at the same time. For example, bandleader and vibraphone player Lionel Hampton was a huge baseball lover. Singer and movie star Lena Horne was starting to have great success, and often performed in the nightspots of Pittsburgh. Oh, she was gorgeous! Both were loyal fans of Negro League baseball, and as far as they were concerned, we ballplayers were stars in our own right. We'd always hang around and talk with them wherever they were having a show.

Source: Stanley Glenn, *Don't Let Anyone Take Your Joy Away: An Inside Look at Negro League Baseball and Its Legacy* (Bloomington, IN: iUniverse Inc., 2006).

THE INCOMPARABLE ONE

And then there was Satchel. In fact, everywhere you look after 1926 in this story, there seems to be Satchel. When the author of this work first came to the topic of Negro professional baseball in the early 1980s, he was told by someone who was already there that you could always learn a lot by simply asking any of the veteran players to tell you their "Satchel story"—because, he said, everyone had one, and they were all good.

The factual baseball story of Robert Leroy Satchel Paige is better known than that of any other Negro professional ballplayer. It began on the professional level in 1926 with Chattanooga in the Negro Southern League. And then it stretched across a seemingly endless swath of the American landscape and time from Birmingham to Baltimore to Cleveland, Pittsburgh, Kansas City, down into the Dominican, over at least in name to Newark, New Jersey; on a colorful plane barnstorming with his own all stars; into Cleveland again at the age of God only knows to help the big show Indians win a championship; to a major league rocking chair in St. Louis, and one day and night stands here and there and just about everywhere; to three innings with the Kansas City Athletics at the questionable age of 59 to become the oldest man to pitch in the majors; to pitching both for and against the Indianapolis Clowns during the late 1960s; and finally to a little village in upstate New York where in 1971 where he experienced the proudest moment of his life with his election to the National Baseball Hall of Fame as that shrine's first Negro League inductee. And in the face of all the ball playing, all the traveling, all the glory, all the hardship, and all the fun, one can only say, My Goodness!

The Satchel of wins and losses, strikeouts and earned run averages, exists as well as he can be found in the wonderful statistical compilation Negro baseball historians Larry Lester and Dick Clark did for the Hall of Fame project "Out of the Shadows." Here we try through probing questions and challenging statements to have readers capture the larger Satchel of lore and legend; for it was as lore and legend that he was best known to the thousands of fans throughout the country who saw this marvel pitch, read about him in black and white newspapers, and heard countless stories told about this Methuselah of the Mound. Turning to those stories is the best place to find Robert Leroy. How much of what follows is true in a strictly factual sense hardly matters at all. For Satchel, like all great legends, was his own truth.

How Old Would You Be If You Didn't Know How Old You Are?

One reporter got his mother to estimate he was five years older than he said. "She must have got me mixed up with my older brother," he shrugged.

The St. Louis Browns official roster for 1953 lists Paige's birthday as "September 11, 1892,* 1896,* 1900,* 1904.* (*Take Your Pick)."[19]

How Can He Be Immortalized?

If the purpose of the Hall of Fame is to preserve the memory of the game's immortals as advertised, then it is clear that Paige belongs there. For he is truly an immortal in every sense of the word.

The only trouble with the idea at all is the fact that the sculptor commissioned to carve the colorful mound wizard's features would have an impossible task. Trying to pack 6ft 3in of rail thin bones into a stoop-shouldered, serious-faced piece of marble and have it look anything but comical would certainly drive anyone to distraction.

He is the possessor of a record that is entirely without equal in the game's history. Had he been a white man, Paige would have made the Hall of Fame long ago.[20]

At Heart He Was a Humble Fellow

Dizzy Dean says: "If Satchel and me pitched on the same team we would win 60."

Satchel says: "Aw, that Dizzy is too modest."

Dean once said that Paige was the best pitcher he ever saw, "and I been looking in the mirror a long time."[21]

Control Was the Essence of His Game

At his first professional tryout, he knocked 14 out of 15 cans off a fence from 60 feet.

While touring, a favorite trick was to set a ball on a box at home plate and bet he could hit it at least once in three tries. He usually won.

With two batters facing each other 6 inches apart, he would pitch between them, even knocking cigars out of their mouths.

From a St. Louis fan: "One day I saw a pigeon land on Paige's raised foot just as Satchel was about to deliver. He went through with the delivery, struck out the batter, and held that pose while the catcher fired the ball back and killed the pigeon."[22]

He Talked as Good a Game as He Pitched

"When he was with the St. Louis Browns in 1951 he inquired politely of his manager Rogers Hornsby, 'Mistah Hornsby. There's something puzzlin' me. Are you training Old Satch for pitchin' baseball, or are you trying to train him for the army?' "[23]

His pitching mate on the St. Louis Browns, Ned Garver, remembers that

[P]eople often asked Satchel Paige about his age, and he enjoyed telling them a different story each time. Because he had pitched in more games than anybody else, I asked him if there was one that he considered his finest effort.

Without hesitation, he said it was when he was called in from the bull-pen with the bases loaded—nobody out—three balls and two strikes on the hitter—and his team leading 1–0.

He said he arrived at the mound with the ball he had used to warm up in the bullpen in his back pocket, then threw a few warm-up pitches with the game ball. When the ump said "play ball," he got the ball from his back pocket, so he had a ball in each hand . . . gave them his "wind-mill" wind-up-threw one ball to third-one ball to first-picked a man off at each base-and his motion so confused the hitter that he swung and missed and the side was out! You hesitate to ask questions after that.[24]

He Pitched, and Pitched, and Pitched

In 1934, he was in top form. In the fall, he fanned 16 out of 18 barnstorming big leaguers in Cleveland. The next day at Columbia, he struck out Mickey Heath, Danny Taylor, and Nick Cullop of the same team after deliberately loading the bases. He later won a 13-inning 1–0 battle against Dizzy Dean.

In 1941, he reportedly took the mound for 30 straight days.

In 1942, he recorded four straight wins over the Grays. Nabbed by a policeman for speeding on the way to the last game, he took the mound with no warm-ups in the third inning with the Monarchs behind 4–3. To give himself time to get ready, he settled on the solution of trying to pick a runner off first. He would throw one to the plate, and three or four to first base. He blanked the Grays without a hit the rest of the way to a 9–4 victory.

He Was a Mystery to His Fellow Players

His oftentimes opponent and fellow Negro Leaguer Max Manning tells us that

> Satchel Paige as everyone knows is the epitome of pitching. There was something strange about Satchel's ball. Satchel's ball always looked small no matter where you looked at it. No matter what angle you looked at it, it was always small. It never looked like the size of a normal ball. It had to do with how he threw it, the speed and velocity with which he threw it, and where he threw it. You would look at it and you would say, what happened to the ball and why is it so small. And it became very hard to hit.[25]

James Riley, in his fine *The Biographical Encyclopedia of the Negro Leagues*, informs us that "Biz Mackey had the best story about how small Satchel's fastball looked. He said that once Satchel threw the ball so hard that the ball disappeared before it reached the catcher's mitt."[26]

And then we have an eyewitness account from an unimpeachable source. Malvin Goode, *Pittsburgh Courier* reporter and ABC TV network newsman, knew Satchel well.

> You hear a lot about Satchel Paige. I'm not talking about what someone told me. I'm talking about what I saw myself at the West Field ball park in Homestead right next to the hospital. I saw him deliberately walk three men and then turn to third and say, "You stay there." It was a show. "You stay there." "You stay there." And then strike out the side.[27]

He knew he was part of a history much bigger than baseball. Come with Buck O'Neil as he takes us to a special history place:

> Everybody knows Satchel Paige. Or, rather everybody knows *who* he was. But few of us actually knew him, and I count myself one of the lucky ones.
>
> Mention Satchel nowadays, and people will remember that he pitched in the majors when he was fifty-nine, or that he was a colorful showman, or that he had those six rules of living. While all those things are true, they make him out to be more of a clown than a man, and I just want to set the record straight.
>
> Let me start out with a story that shows a part of Satchel that no one ever hears about. One time we were on the road with the Monarchs in Charleston, South Carolina. When we got to Charleston, the hotel rooms weren't ready yet. So he said, "Nancy, c'mon with me. We're gonna take a little trip." Well, we went over to an area near the harbor called Drum Island. That was where they had auctioned off the slaves, and there was a big tree with a plaque on it, marking the site of the old slave market. Satchel and I stood there, silent as could be, for about ten minutes, not saying anything, but thinking a whole bunch of things. Finally, Satchel broke the silence.
>
> "You know what Nancy?" he said.
>
> "What's that Satchel?"
>
> "Seems like I been here before."
>
> "Me too, Satchel."

That was Robert Leroy Satchel Paige. A little bit deeper than most people thought.[28]

SATCHEL PAIGE'S RULES FOR RIGHT LIVING

Avoid fried foods which angry up the blood.

If your stomach disputes you, lie down and pacify it with cooling thoughts.

Keep the juice flowing by jangling around gently as you move.

Go very lightly on the vices, such as carrying on in society. The social ramble ain't restful.

Avoid running at all times.

Don't look back, something may be gaining on you.

Source: Larry Tye, *Satchel Paige: The Life and Times of an American Legend* (New York: Random House, 2010).

HOW FAST WAS COOL PAPA

If Satchel was the epitome of pitching speed in his prime, so was the Cool man for speed on the bases.

James Thomas "Cool Papa" Bell, 1922–1946, St. Louis Stars; Detroit Wolves; Kansas City Monarchs; Homestead Grays; Pittsburgh Crawfords; Memphis Red Sox; Santo Domingo; Mexican League; Chicago American Giants; Detroit Senators; and Kansas City Stars.

How fast was "Cool Papa"? Some of it is obviously just good story telling. He was so fast that when he hit a ball through the pitcher's legs, it would hit him in the back as he slid into second for a double.

And some of it seems like just good story telling, but on closer inspection turns out to have some fact in it. "He was so fast that he could hit the light switch in a hotel room and be in bed before the lights went out." Seems Cool was rooming one night with Satchel, and when he discovered a slight delay in the light switch, won a ten spot from his roommate when he bet he could reach the sack before the light went out.

And then there are the recollections of those who played with and against him:

"If he bunts and it bounces twice, put it in your pocket," says "Double Duty" Radcliffe.

"If he hits one back to the pitcher everyone yelled, 'Hurry!'" claimed Jimmie Crutchfield.

Bill "Ready" Cash remembers what it was like to play the Homestead Grays when James "Cool Papa" Bell was cavorting around the bases:

Lots of time I tell people when we played the Homestead Grays and Cool Papa gets on second base and Jerry Benjamin comes up and lays a bunt down the 3rd base line that's all you need cause Cool gonna dust off at home plate. That ain't no lie.[29]

Perhaps, the historian John Holway captures best just who this James Bell was. Holway recollects a story from October 1948 when

Satchel Paige got together one more club of youngsters to barnstorm against his world champion Cleveland Indian mates, Bob Lemon and Gene Beardon, plus Murray Dickson, Al Zarilla, Roy Partee, and others. To bolster the youngster's morale, he added forty-five year old Cool Papa Bell to the squad to play a few innings and lend his experience. In the final game, with Lemon on the mound, Bell walked and Paige laid down a neat sacrifice that pulled the third baseman off the bag, a classic example of the hit-and-run bunt that Rube Foster had perfected almost half a century earlier. Bell was almost to second when ball hit bat and almost on third when the third baseman picked the ball up. When the startled catcher, Partee, ran down the line to cover third, Bell brushed right past him and raced across the wide-open plate. He had scored from first on a bunt! Rube Foster must have looked down and smiled.[30]

AMERICA'S ONE CONSTANT

While Satchel pitched, and pitched, and pitched his wonderful assortment of curves and change ups and fast balls and hesitation balls, and while Cool ran the bases with an abandon that was a sight not to be believed, others were throwing pitches of a different sort. Four years into Satchel's professional career, seven into Cool's, a bill was introduced into the Congress of the United States that proposed "to repay slave owners for slaves freed." Justice was to come at last for those whose property had been taken from them by a hooligan president and his bands of armed hooligans—better known to history as Abraham Lincoln and the U.S. Army.

> 6/25/30 Washington D.C., (By The Associated Negro Press) As an opposition measure to the one offered by Senator Hatfield of West Virginia which would provide a pension for ex-slaves, Representative Larson of Georgia has been urged to present a bill to authorize the government to reimburse Southern slave owners for the slaves freed under the Lincoln emancipation proclamation.
>
> While those urging the presentation of the bill evidently feel that such a measure would never be passed, it shows just how much the Southerners actually thought of the slaves who proved loyal to them during the war despite the fact that the defeat of the confederate states meant their freedom.[31]

THE JOSH MAN

If Satchel was the black baseball attraction on the mound, and Cool on the bases, clearly Josh was such at the plate. More than 40 years after he played against him, Charlie Biot remembered him well.

> Josh was in a class all by himself. He was an uncanny hitter. He never had to do a lot of digging in or moving around at the plate. He just took his back foot and dug it in. And you remember him always rolling up his sleeve. He always rolled up his right sleeve. And then he was set. He took one or two little swings for exercise and held his bat back. He

was a perfect hitter. I think he was born with that. Some people say you can develop it, but I think Gibson was more just a natural born hitter. And he swung with such great ease. I never saw him swing, get off balance, fall. I never saw him do the things that I see every day among the major league ball players.[32]

Biot recalls a game between Gibson's Homestead Grays in Richmond, Virginia, that entered the ninth inning with the Pittsburgh club and Biot's Black Yankees tied at two apiece.

I'll never forget it. The lights were very expensive to run at that time. It looked like we were going past nine innings. The Grays were coming to bat for their last half. Gibson was the lead-off hitter. So the manager ran out, and they got together like they were going to change pitchers, and he said, "Please, for God's sake, get the game over with. This game is going on too long. We won't have any money left. The electricity bill will beat us. Give Josh a pitch right down the middle and let him end it cause the people would love to see that." And that's what we did. McDuffie was pitching and the first ball he pitched was right down the center and went right over my head about 50 feet in the air into the trees 420 feet away. We laughed and kidded about it later that night when we got in the restaurant. We said to Josh, "We let you hit that one." And he laughed too. But you did not have to let him hit it.[33]

What about the ones they didn't want to let him hit? John Holway tells us that Josh Gibson "hit what he called his longest home run in 1932. It was a measured 512 feet against Sug Cornelius in Monessen, PA. 'Why didn't you call for a curve?' the players asked catcher Larry Brown after the inning. 'Goddamn!' Larry replied, 'If I'da known he was gonna hit the fastball, I wouda' called for the curve.'"[34]

Mal Goode would take issue that the Monessen shot was Josh's longest, for he saw one with his own eyes that was special.

One day Ralph Kiner hit one just barely over the center field wall in Forbes Field. I sat beside a fellow who said, "I bet no one's ever hit one that far." I said, "Oh yea. I saw a fellow on a team a few years ago, a fellow named Josh Gibson. In August, 1938 I saw him hit a ball 20 feet above that wall which was marked 440 feet which meant it had to be 700 feet into the tress in what they called Schenley Park."[35]

But was there one of Josh's that was even longer? Read John Craig's wonderful *Chappie and Me* for a colorful description of a reported

Gibsonian dinger that was even longer than the prodigious blast Mal Good remembers.[36]

"Let me tell you 'bout somethin' I seen with my own eyes," Chappie said. He went on to recount a tale about playing a game in Pittsburgh some years back when he and Josh Gibson were with the Homestead Grays Playing the Crawfords.

"Come down to the ninth inning' that day and we was losin' 4–3. Our first two guys got themselves out, but then Layton Hope got a single, and Josh came up to the plate."

He paused for a moment to sip his beer.

"The first pitch was a curve, which the ump called a strike. The next was a fast ball, and I don't know why their pitcher threw it. I guess he don't either. Anyway it was a mistake. Come in around the letters, and Josh sure took a likin' to it."

"Now I seen some long tatters in my time, don't think I ain't, but nothin' that was took hold of like that."

"Lawd, God, it just climbin' and takin' off out of there 'till it went into the clouds. Well, we all stood around, lookin' up, waitin' for that ball to come back down, only it never did."

"Ump got tired of waitin' after about fifteen minutes and ruled it a home run. Nothin else he could do."

"You won it 5–4," I said.

"Yes and no," Chappie said.

"How is that?"

"We come right back at it the next day in Philadelphia, Same teams, same umpire. We just moved over there."

He took an extra long pull at his beer.

"We was in the second inning, when a ball come down out of the sky.

"Oh, oh!"

"Their center fielder got under it. Everybody was screamin' and yelling.' Don't know why it didn't drive him right into the groud, but he hung onto it somehow. Musta come from a mile up, that ball."

We were all laughing.

"And then," Jim Stewart managed to ask.

"Umpire looks over at Josh, who is sittin' on our bench," Chappie said, "and he hollers: 'You're out yesterday in Pittsburgh.' "[37]

THE BLACK LOU

And after Satch, Josh, and Cool came the Black Lou, who confessed in his retirement to having played the game for "the fun of it. We got little pay. They said it wasn't too much fun, but we thought it was fun, because we were doing what we wanted to do."[38]

Part of Walter Fenner Leonard's memory of the baseball of his youth were minstrel shows that regularly came through his Rocky Mountain, North Carolina, hometown in his growing-up years. A. G. Allen, the Florida Minstrels, the Georgia Minstrels, Silas Green—they all had baseball teams. "They would parade in the morning," Leonard would tell historian John Holway, "play a game against a local team in the afternoon, put on the minstrel at night, and take all our money away. Well, that's what we used to say. They used to get all the money from the sporting people in the afternoon, get all the money from the show people at night—and then they had doctors with them selling medicine to take that part of our money too!"[39]

As a youngster, he first got interested in baseball watching it illegally through a crack in the fence of his hometown stadium. When the police made him and his buddies move five feet back from the fence, they got boxes to stand on to look over the fence. The police came back and told them that was against the law too. There was nothing left to do but to play the game themselves.

Walter Fenner "Buck" Leonard came to play it probably as well as anyone has ever played it. He started out as a right fielder. The experienced Negro League first sacker, Ben Taylor, was "the owner, manager, everything" of his team. Still a great hitter, but getting too old to play in the field, Taylor groomed his young pupil to play his own first base position. He must have taken some pride in the fact that the boy he mentored came as a man to be compared most often to Lou Gehrig. From all accounts of the way Buck Leonard came to play that position, Gehrig would have been proud too.

Historian Jim Riley captures well the best liked player in the game with his description of Buck Leonard.

Possessing a smooth swing at the plate, he was equally smooth in the field. In 1941 one media source described four or five sensational stops that were "way beyond the reach of 99 percent of major league first basemen." Sure handed, with a strong and accurate arm and acknowledged as a smart player who always made the right play, Buck was a team man all the way. Respected by his teammates, he was even-tempered and professional, and his consistency and dependability were a steadying influence on the Grays. A class guy, he was the best-liked player in the game.[40]

As adept as he was in the field, he was even more adept at the plate. While teammate Josh Gibson was slugging tape measure home runs, "Leonard was hitting screaming line drives both off the walls and over the walls. Trying to sneak a fastball past him was like trying to sneak a sunrise past a rooster." And when he hit them, he hit them! Black Yankee pitcher Bob Scott thinks that one or two typical Buck Leonard line drive home runs he gave up to the "Black Lou" might still be going.[41]

If he could play the game well, he could also talk it well and recollect it well. He became an important and delightful source for historians like John Holway to go to as they began in the late 1960s to recover and construct a history that had been "lost, stolen or strayed."

I talked to Buck Leonard in 1969 and 1970 in his comfortable brick home in Rocky Mountain NC. He was such a rich fountain of stories about the black ball days. He talked easily in a slightly high pitched voice, punctuating his tales with a broad and gleaming smile. He was such a good storyteller that I went back to talk to him again and again.[42]

One of those many agains gave Holway as good an account as we have of what it was like to play over 200 games a year and travel those highways and byways on those old rickety buses. Buck's remembering captures what has been called the romance of the road—but what was also the hard times the road gave to those who had to travel it:

Sometimes we'd stay in hotels that had so many bedbugs you had to put a newspaper down between the mattress and the sheets. Other times we'd rent rooms in a YMCA, or we'd go to a hotel and rent three rooms. That way you got to use the bath by renting three rooms. All the ball players would change clothes in those three rooms, go to the ball park and play a double header—nine innings the first game, seven innings the second.

The second game would be over about 6:15. We'd come back to the hotel and take a bath, then go down the street and eat and get back in the bus to go to Pittsburgh. The bus seats would recline—you'd be sitting there, and the drone of the motor would put you to sleep. We'd get back to Pittsburgh 7:30 in the morning, go to bed, get up around three o'clock, go up the river somewhere about twenty-five or thirty miles, play a night game, come back. Next evening the same thing. We logged 30,000 miles one summer. Of course you'd get tired around July or August. The people didn't know what we went through. They'd see us dragging around, and they didn't know we ridden all night to get there.

We used to play at Bushwick in New York on a Sunday evening. And go out to Freeport or out to somewhere on Long Island, and play Sunday night. Man, you're spent when you play a doubleheader at Bushwick or Yankee Stadium or the Polo Grounds. Then you go out there at night to play, you're still tired and you're just forcing yourself.[43]

As hard as his baseball could be, it had its special rewards. One of those came late in life for Buck Leonard—but when it came, it was indeed something to treasure:

I was in Cooperstown the day Satchel Paige was inducted, and I stayed awake almost all that night thinking about it. You know, a day like that stays with you a long time. It's something you never had any dream you'd ever see. Like men walking on the moon. I always wanted to go up there to Cooperstown. You felt you had a reason, because it's the home of baseball, but you didn't have a *special* reason. We never thought we'd get in the Hall of Fame. It was so far from us, we didn't even consider it. We didn't even think it would some day come to reality. We thought the way we were playing was the way it was going to continue. I never had any dream it would come. But that night I felt like I was part of it at last.[44]

Walter Fenner "Buck" Leonard and baseball commissioner Bowie Kuhn at Leonard's induction into the National Baseball Hall of Fame. (National Baseball Hall of Fame Library, Cooperstown, NY)

LEON

If the big four of Satchel, Cool, Josh, and Buck are the ones you always hear about, there were other big ones like "The Putting Something on Your Mind Man" who deserve our attention as well.

What kind of pitcher appears in a record seven East–West All-Star games and sets an All-Star record by striking out a total of 14 batters?

What kind of pitcher carves out a 12–1 record in Venezuela in 1940 while pitching his team to the championship?

What kind of pitcher logs a perfect 6–0 record with Vera Cruz in the Mexican league with a 3.79 ERA contributing a .298 batting average while annexing his second pennant of the 1940 season?

He was the kind of pitcher who would recollect in his senior years that "when they told me they was gonna pay me to play baseball, I said they must be crazy. I said I'd play for nothing."

What kind of pitcher strikes out five of the seven batters he faced in the 1942 All-Star game without giving up a hit?

What kind of pitcher plays six winters in Puerto Rico establishing the league's single game strike out record in 1941 by fanning 19 batters in an extra inning game?

What kind of ballplayer is it who is the starting pitcher on opening day of 1941, moves to center field when his teammate who stared there was drafted, and after returning to the mound later in the season moves to second base to fill in for an injured teammate and forms a double play combination that historian Jim Riley tells us was unchallenged?

> He was, his teammate Clarence "Pint" Israel remembers, the kind of ball player who believed in what he called putting something on your mind. And that was when you came into that batter's box you were getting paid to hit the ball and he was getting paid to pitch. And the best easiest thing on his mind was to keep you from hitting the ball. If that meant putting some rosin on it, cut it, lick it, whatever he had to do. And then Leon pitched you close and tight. That's the kind of ball player Leon was.[45]

What kind of pitcher is taken on as a gun for hire by the Homestead Grays to secure a five-hit victory over Satchel Paige in the 1942 Negro League World Series?

What kind of pitcher is it who lands on Utah Beach in the Allied invasion of France, and a year or so later pitches his Army team to victory over a white major league laden squad in a packed stadium of cheering fans in Nuremburg where 100,000 Germans had, only a few years earlier, cheered Hitler? He took a 2–1 four hitter into the ninth. When the first batter tripled, he proceeded to strike out the side, all three of that side being major leaguers.

He was the kind of competitor who didn't hesitate to throw a chin whiskers pitch to a one-armed ballplayer. Pint Israel remembers a game one night around Ocean Cliff, New Jersey:

> They had this Pete Gray. He was a one armed ball player. He was the leadoff hitter. We kind of nonchalantly looked at him. He got the first hit off of Leon. He is standing over there at first base. Leon looked over at him. "I'll tell you what. Wait till you come up the next time." I guess it was the third or fourth inning he came up again. And Leon threw it right under his chin. And he didn't hit anymore that night.[46]

What kind of a pitcher in 1946 after returning from service opens the season with a 2–0 no-hitter against his team's arch rival, and leads his club into the World Series with a 13–4 record topping the league in strikeouts, innings pitched, and complete games?

What kind of pitcher is it who holds the strikeout record in the Negro National League, the Puerto Rican League, and the East–West All-Star game?

> He was the kind of ball player who when asked joshingly in the twilight of his career by the Gene Benson who he faced many times when both were in their prime, "Was they paying him to throw at me?" He would say without hesitation, and with emphasis in his voice, and a smile on his face. "Yes!"[47]

Leon Day was one of the funniest and gentlest of Negro League veterans this writer has had the privilege of knowing. When his former teammate and dear friend Max Manning brought him the news to his hospital room in the spring of 1995 that after so long a wait he had finally been given his just due with election to Cooperstown, Leon could accept that news with a wry smile and a gentle thank you. Within a few days, he would pass to a more important hall of fame than the one that immortalizes great baseball players—and that summer, his wife, now widow Geraldine, would bring tears to the eyes of the thousands who gathered for the Cooperstown Hall induction ceremony when she delivered an acceptance speech that could have been more magnificent only if Leon had delivered it himself.[48]

TROUBADOURS OF THE ROAD

Satchel, Cool, Josh, Buck, Leon, and countless other predecessors and successors were all barnstormers—baseball troubadours of the road traveling the highways and the byways of the Americas. The constant play outside league schedules from early spring through late fall in large cities and small hamlets across the length and breadth of the nation, and abroad as well, had the Negro professional player constantly on the move. This type of play occupied a far larger part of their baseball playing than did league games. And it challenged a player's stamina and resolve to continue to play the game. Bill Cash recalls those days with a shake of his head and a wonderment that testifies to the strength and élan of young men who played a game they could only recollect in their old age as something they loved to do:

> This is a different era all together than what it was when we came along. I feel the major league player of today, he couldn't have played in our league. No way for him to play with the traveling and the way we had to play. Get to the ball park an hour or half hour before the ball game and you dress in your bus, not in the ballpark. You go out on the ball field and the umpire says play ball. You don't have a warm up. You finish a ball game like we finish. You play in Chicago and we got a double header to play in Philadelphia. We get to the ballpark at 5:00 o-clock, 5:30. You got to be on the ball field at 6:00. These ball players couldn't do that. They don't want to play a doubleheader on get away day. They don't want to play a day game after a night game. They are tired. We play 3 or 4 games a day and had to travel 1300, 1400 miles. They just couldn't do it. But there was nothing like baseball in those days. We just loved the game.[49]

This "storming of barns" would put the Negro professional player on fields that by today's standards could only be called makeshift at best. Charlie Biot recalls a memorable moment on one of those fields:

> I got hurt in a place called Pittman New Jersey. I crashed into a light support. In those days they had light supports on the playing field. I was playing shallow and the pitcher hit the ball over my head. I went back about 15 yards trailing the ball, which is a bad habit. I wouldn't have done it, but the light system was very poor that night and when I went back my right fielder crossed over and he said you can get it. And I kept running and trailing it and the lights went out. I ran into this light support which is about three, four feet all around, made of concrete. I tipped it. I knocked all my teeth out. I was unconscious two

hours. They thought I was going to die, but I survived. All the fellows that helped me that night, they are all gone. They've passed on.[50]

The constant wear and tear experienced by players on long road trips for Negro teams like the Monarchs and American Giants of the 1920s was matched and sometimes bested in the late 1930s for black clubs like the Newark Eagles. Historian Bob Luke recounts such a trip made by the Newark club across two weeks in August 1939:

They played nineteen games while covering three thousand miles and making sixteen stops. The team rode out of Newark on a Saturday and played an afternoon game in Wilmington, Delaware, and an evening game in Baltimore. On Sunday they played two games in Richmond, Virginia, and headed back to Baltimore for a game that night. The western swing began the next day with a twilight game in Bellefonte, Pennsylvania. Then it was onto Buffalo where they arrived at 5:30 in the morning. They had the day to rest before playing an evening game there. After Buffalo it was on to Pittsburgh for a Wednesday afternoon game, then a Thursday game in Altoona. Then it was onto to Canton, Ohio for a Friday game, and back to Pittsburgh for a game on Saturday. They played a doubleheader in Indianapolis on Sunday. Their scheduled Monday game in Yorkville, Ohio was rained out, giving them a short

The 1939 Newark Eagles. (National Baseball Hall of Fame Library, Cooperstown, NY)

respite before a Tuesday night game in Akron. They then road 450 miles back to Newark before playing the Homestead Grays in Tremont, Pennsylvania on Thursday and Friday. From Tremont the Eagles drove to Philadelphia for two games against the Philadelphia Stars on Saturday, and then back to Ruppert Stadium for two more games against the Stars on Sunday.

Nah, this just couldn't be. But it was. From a distance of 70 years our breath is taken away, and we feel a tiredness that goes deep into our bones.[51]

CHAPTER 7

The Seasons of Change, 1940–1947

SETTING THE SCENE—TIME FOR DOUBLE V

Langston Hughes's wonderful comic character, the Negro leader Dr. Butts, had a penchant for softening the injustices of American segregation by comparing the situation blacks faced in the United States to oppression abroad: "They bomb folks in Florida, but Hitler gassed the Jews—Mississippi is bad, but Russia is worse."[1]

Hughes's Jess B. Semple had a counter for all the "buts." "Dear Dr. Butts: I take my pen in hand to write you this letter to ask you to make yourself clear to me. When you answer me, do not write no 'so-and-so-and -so-and-so-but. . . . I will not take but for an answer. Negroes have been looking at Democracy's but too long. What we want to know is how to get rid of that but."[2]

The position taken by black leadership from the outset of World War II was clear. There would be no buts. It was time to up the ante. If the nation wanted Negroes to fight abroad in defense of freedom, shouldn't the nation see that Negroes experienced freedom at home? It was not to be like World War I. This time there would be no putting demands for racial justice on the shelf of "first win the war." "Double V" was the rallying cry—Victory abroad, but also Victory at home.

Increasing militancy took numerous forms. A. Philip Randolph's March on Washington Movement in the spring of 1941 threatened to put 50,000 Negroes on the streets of Washington, D.C., to protest discrimination in the armed forces and in the home-front burgeoning defense workplace. The trumpeted Double V demand at the war's outset rapidly expanded the NAACP to a point where it spoke for the Negro masses. The black press highlighted discrimination in the armed forces and discrimination at home in papers that reached record circulation numbers. The Congress of Racial Equality pioneered the sit-in tactic.

The historian Richard Dalfiume argues convincingly that World War II was a watershed period. These were years of transition in American race relations that because of the attention given to the dramatic challenges posed by the civil rights movement of the 1950 and 1960s, and the dramatic results attained by that better known period, have become "The Forgotten Years of the Negro Revolution."

James Baldwin said of the period, "The treatment accorded the Negro during the Second World War marks, for me, a turning point in the Negro's relation to America. To put it briefly, and somewhat too simply, a certain hope died, a certain respect for white Americans faded."[3]

Gunnar Myrdal, writing during World War II in his monumental *An American Dilemma* study of the U.S. racial scene, predicted that the war would act as a "stimulant" to Negro protest. The Swedish sociologist felt that there was "bound to be a redefinition of the Negro's status in America as a result of this War."[4]

E. Franklin Frazier, Negro sociologist, regarded the war as the point where "the racial structure of society was cracking," and the equilibrium reached after the Civil War seemed "to be under attack at a time and under conditions when it is particularly difficult to defend it."[5]

The historian Charles Silberman, looking back on World War II from the vantage of the turbulent 1960s, pictured the war years as a "turning point in

---

CORE SIT-INS

Black and white activists from the Christian pacifist movement, including James Farmer and George Houser, created the Chicago Committee of Racial Equality, the first chapter of CORE, in 1942. The interracial group advocated nonviolent direct action to address racial discrimination. Not a mass membership organization, CORE depended on a small group of disciplined activists to conduct their campaigns to desegregate public accommodations, workplaces, and housing. Pioneering the use of sit-ins and other civil disobedience for civil rights causes, the Chicago chapter reached a high point when the organization desegregated White City Roller Rink in 1946.

American race relations during which the seeds of the protest movements of the 1950s and 1960s were sown."[6]

TWO GAME CHANGERS

One of the most significant of those seeds had been planted by professional black baseball's long witness against the segregation of our national game. Another would now be planted by a talented baseball player and a bold white general manager. In the person of Jackie Robinson, and in the instrument of Branch Rickey, a revolution in baseball was coming that was to change the national pastime forever.

But like all true revolutions, it was a long time in coming—fought for on fields as disparate in time and place as the makeshift ball diamonds of plantations of the old slave South; on the pages of newspapers with names like *Defender* and *Afro-American* when Jim Crow ruled the day; in ballparks, both professional and amateur all across the Americas wherever blacks could find the time and resources to play an American game that they loved to play. And certainly seen in photos that capture for us those who played their version of America's national pastime on fields of their own during their nation's long season of segregation, during so many baseball seasons in the sun.

Jackie Robinson signing his first contract with Branch Rickey. (National Baseball Hall of Fame Library, Cooperstown, NY)

The newsman and commentator Charles Osgood, in recollecting his early baseball years in Baltimore, captures well some of the last moments on the Negro baseball side of the Robinson/Rickey revolution that was finally now in sight.

> One Sunday at Memorial Stadium, as the guests of Tommy Thomas, my father and I saw an exhibition game between the Orioles and a black team called the Baltimore Elite Giants, pronounced Eee-lite. For the closet Confederates in Memorial Stadium that day, the visiting team was not seen as a group of baseball professionals but as Pullman porters out of their league. And out of their league they were. They were far better than the Orioles.
>
> "Why aren't those Negroes playing in the major leagues?" I asked my father.
>
> "Well, Charlie, they're flashy all right" he said, "but they're not steady enough to play the whole season."
>
> My father was a decent and intelligent man, but that observation wasn't one to be bronzed. Like the rest of Baltimore, he never dreamed that his own Babe Ruth might not have been as good as the black Josh Gibson, a catcher who in one season hit eighty-four home runs; or that the great Red Ruffing might not have been as good as Satchel Paige, whom a Ruffing teammate named DiMaggio called "the greatest pitcher I ever faced" after trying to hit against him in an army camp game.
>
> My father and I both had a lot to learn. In just four years, one of our lessons would be a Montreal second baseman named Jackie Robinson.[7]

ALVIN WHITE—WITNESS AND TESTIFIER: A REMINDER TO WRITE THE YANKEES

Segregation on the baseball field was, of course, more than matched by segregation off the baseball diamond. Al White wrote to his boss, Claude Barnett, in September 1939 asking for help with a reporting problem he was facing:

> Dear Chief:
>
> Just a line to remind you to write the Yankees, E. G. Barrow, 103 West 42nd St. for our press reservations for the World Se-ries—reminding them that Mr. Dawson denied our application when the Yanks and Giants played, the first time that was done.

Mr. Dawson is not as liberal as Daniel Daniel (World Telegram). Mr. Dawson is from the Times and a sort of warped person.

Al White went to Washington later in 1939 to serve as Associated Negro Press executive correspondent for the first black permanent news bureau in the nation's capital. He describes in striking terms what it was like to be a black reporter covering a national scene where his kind was not welcomed:

> I was denied an application to the Congressional Press galleries although the requirement could be met. The principal requirement was that I represent a daily paper. Mr. Barnett made arrangements with the Scotts of Atlanta to have me represent the Atlanta Daily World. This was unacceptable to the committee. No area I though newsworthy was closed to me—only there were few doors open. Much important material came via messengers employed in various departments—anything marked "special" or "confidential" that they were called on to deliver was discreetly opened and read.

Source: Lawrence Hogan, *A Black National News Service: Claude Barnett and the Associated Negro Press* (Haworth, NJ: St. Johann Press, 2002).

AMERICA'S ONE CONSTANT

The poet Countee Cullen, in his oft-heard "INCIDENT," takes us movingly to the Baltimore where Charles Osgood and his dad had some lessons to learn.

> Once riding in old Baltimore,
> Heart-filled, head-filled with glee,
> I saw a Baltimorean
> Keep looking straight at me.
>
> Now I was eight and very small,
> And he was no whit bigger,
> And so I smiled, but he poked out
> His tongue, and called me, "Nigger."
>
> I saw the whole of Baltimore
> From May until December;

Of all the things that happened there
That's all that I remember.

The Changing Process

For Jackie Robinson to become Charles Osgood's lesson, others had to grow
and learn as well, none more so than the man most instrumental in the making of Jackie. And his growing and learning—the making of Branch Rickey—
into the architect of what arguably is the most important appearance ever
of a baseball player on the fields of major league baseball, came in ways
often not observed by students of the "Mahatma." June Fifield, widow of
Rickey's pastor, Reverend L. Wendell Fifield, shares with us such a growth
moment:

> News of the passing of Branch Rickey, a treasured friend of my late
> husband, Rev. Dr. L. Wendell Fifield, came to the world on the day
> I sat writing an anecdote about a game we saw with him at Ebbets
> Field, for one of the chapters of a book based on my husband's life
> and works.
>
> It was a strange, mystical experience to me to have been so sur-
> rounded by the spirit of Mr. Rickey that I should be writing about him
> at that time. It seemed, somehow, a sign that the time had come to tell
> a story I had long hesitated to write because it seems privileged mate-
> rial. Dr. Fifield had shared the feeling that Jackie Robinson and the rest
> of the world should know the story but that it should not be told in
> Rickey's lifetime without his permission.
>
> I had always felt that Mr. Rickey would be the first to approve,
> for his own life was so bound up with this young man, his affec-
> tion so deep and his expectations so high. His affection, shared by
> his wife and "Auntie," the sister in her eighties who never missed a
> game and keep an impeccable box score, was evidenced to us many
> times. "Auntie" gave us her own witness once when we dinned at the
> Rickey's home. She said, "When we have the team over for refresh-
> ments, Jackie is the one who offers to lend a hand, and he unfailingly
> says a word of appreciation when he leaves. He has the best manners
> of the bunch!"
>
> I write this in the spirit of a tribute and a plea: a tribute to Branch
> Rickey and L. Wendell Fifield—two men, strong of character, pastor
> and a parishioner, whose rapport was a quick mutual outpouring of
> meaningful forces that drew them together inextricably as friends; a
> plea to Jackie Robinson to realize what went into the launching of
> his career—that someone cared enough to grope for wisdom beyond

himself, to call upon God's guidance—and that the man who did this was, in common parlance, "white."

One day as my husband sat working at his desk in the study of the church house, his secretary buzzed to say, "Mr. Rickey is here and asks to come in." No appointment was ever necessary for someone with an urgent problem, and my husband's "Certainly, show him in," carried with it more than casual interest. He was always warmed by the presence of this friend whose busy schedule of travel and activity allowed him little time for communication on a social level. In high hopes of a long chat, Dr. Fifield rose to greet him at the door.

"Sit down, Wendell," said Mr. Rickey. "Don't let me interrupt. I can't talk with you. Keep right on with your work. I just want to BE here. Do you mind?"

Without another word, Branch Rickey began to pace the floor. He paced, and he paused, he paced and he paused. Occasionally he gazed out the window at the sooty gloom of Brooklyn Heights, slightly relieved by the church garden struggling for beauty below. Pace, pause, pace, pause; turn, gaze, turn, gaze, pace, pause.

Once in a while my husband looked up from his work, but he spoke no word. He knew that whatever brought Mr. Rickey to his presence was an extremely important and personal matter, and he gave him the privacy of his struggle. Mr. Rickey stood with eyes closed and seemed to draw his great frame up to new height. Then he'd sag again and pace. As the pauses grew longer, my husband once caught a kind of glow about Mr. Rickey as he stood in silence. Then, back to the pacing and pausing—and silence.

Forty-five minutes of this can be a long, long walk. I believe, on the average, allowing for pauses, about three miles. It proved to be a might significant three-mile hike, in the equally significant atmosphere of a minister's study. At the end of the time, Branch Rickey, his face aglow under those famous outthrust eyebrows, bent over my husband's desk, his eyes piercing, and cried:

"I've got it!" He banged his huge fist on the desk, rattling everything from fountain pen to intercom. "I've got it!" he banged again, elated, transported.

It was too much for Dr. Fifield. He'd waited long enough to know what was going on in his home base. "Got what, Branch? How much longer before I find out what you're up to—pacing around here and banging on my furniture and keeping the whole thing to yourself? Come on, out with it!"

Branch sank, exhausted, into the nearest chair, fortunately big and overstuffed, as he was himself in those days of generous teeming good health and vigor.

"Wendell," he said, "I've decided to sign Jackie Robinson!"

Moisture glistened in Mr. Rickey's eyes. He blew an emphatic blast of his famous big nose, while my husband awaited the end of the story.

I hope Jackie will see his fellow man in a new light, knowing this story. May he ever remember Branch Rickey's soul-searching in the presence of the God of us all, on his own "Days of Decision."[8]

Jackie's baseball beginning proved to be an auspicious one. In his first at bat, he grounded out to short. But with two runners on base in the third inning, with his bat cocked high in what was to be as memorable a batting stance as ever seen in the majors, a powerful swing sent a high fast ball into the left-field stands. The fun had only just begun. A bunt single in the fifth was followed by a steal of second. Then over to third on a groundout, followed by what was to become a signature Robinson move, dashing down and up the line that ended with a run scored via a balk by the rattled pitcher. In the seventh, the now–Negro Leaguer singled, stole second again, and scored on a triple. In the eighth, he bunted his way on, raced all the way to third on an infield hit, and drew another balk to score another run. In his debut in what mainstream sportswriters referred to as "organized baseball," Jack Robinson had four hits, scored four runs, drove in three, and had two steals in Montreal's 14–1 victory. The long wait for a Phoenix to return that had begun in the 1880s with the exclusion of his kind from the ranks of "organized baseball" had finally ended with a day of glorious play on April 18, 1946, in a Roosevelt Stadium that appropriately bore Jackie's own middle name.

Before he was a major leaguer, Jack Roosevelt Robinson was a Negro Leaguer. And so were major league players with names like Doby, Mays, Newcombe, Banks, Aaron, Irvin, Campanella, and Jethroe who would shortly follow the trail blazer into the majors, and whose accomplishments fill up the record books with MVP, Rookie of the Year, and Cy Young awards in the 15-year period from 1947 when the Dodgers started this thing called integration to 1959 when finally, if even only on a token level, the Boston Red Sox in bringing up their first Negro player, Pumpsie Green, began to catch up with where American baseball and America the nation were going. In the euphoria then and now over what Jackie Robinson and Branch Rickey did, it is often forgotten that along with the entire first generation of great black major leaguers, Jackie Robinson learned to play the game of baseball in a segregated world where the only opportunity for professional play had been on those teams that played their baseball behind the veil of race separation.

His fellow Negro Leaguer and Hall of Fame member Monte Irvin re-members well what the world that Jackie and he grew up in was like when he recollects a childhood in East Orange, New Jersey, filled with dreams of playing baseball.

> I just wanted to be a real good ball player. I didn't know if I'd ever play professionally. I didn't know if I'd ever play in the major leagues. I certainly wanted to play in the Negro Leagues. You see at that time we aspired to play in the Negro Leagues. That was as high as our aspirations could go. I would say, now one of these days I would like to play for the Homestead Grays; I would like to play for the Newark Eagles; I would like to play for the Pittsburgh Crawfords, or the Lincoln Giants. If you were a baseball player you did aspire to play for those clubs. We never knew that later on we would get a chance to play in the majors. But those were our inspirations at that time.[9]

That Negro League world must have been a good teacher, for his one year with the Kansas City Monarchs of the American Negro League prepared the first Negro major leaguer since the 1880s well in two important ways. The first was the ability to play the game of baseball on a skill level that made him more than ready to hold his own in the majors. Supposed smart judges of baseball talent on the white side of the "can Robinson make it" debate felt the talent wasn't there. *New York Daily News* columnist and strong proponent of integration, Jimmy Powers, labeled him a 1,000 to 1 shot to make the grade. Bob Feller was widely quoted as thinking that Robinson the baseball player was too thick and broad shouldered and would be tied up by a good fastball put in the right place in his strike zone. Baseball's Bible, the *Sporting News* predicted that "the waters of competition in the International League will flood far over his head."[10]

Jack Roosevelt Robinson baseball player would let his bat and glove and arm and speed a field be his answers to the doubters. In his first season with the Dodgers' top farm team, the Montreal Royals, with the "flood" somewhere other than "far over his head," the ex–Negro Leaguer led the International League in batting (.349), runs scored (113), and fielding percentage (.985). Robinson also stole 40 bases and drove in 66 runs. These would be extraordinary numbers under any circumstance—but especially so with the weight of a "Great Experiment" on your shoulders. His baseball numbers were even more impressive considering that Robinson missed 30 games due to injuries, often the product of a rookie, and a black one at that, being the target of close pitches and hard slides at second base. He led a team that set a league attendance mark, bested their closest rival in the pennant race by 19½ games, and then easily claimed the Little World Series title over the American Association's Louisville Colonels. Some flood!

But he was prepared well by his Negro League experience in ways other than just playing quality baseball. His teammate on a Negro League All-Star 1946 postseason barnstorming club, Gene Benson, remembers telling him one night that "where he was going was easier than where he was coming from."[11] Benson meant that what Robinson had encountered playing baseball in the Negro Leagues was as tough—no, indeed tougher than what he would face with the Dodgers. But the veteran Negro Leaguer probably meant something else as well. Jack Robinson's Negro League experience, as well as all that had led up to that experience, must have nurtured in him an attitude of dealing with adversity and challenges of a sort that had filled his entire life and would now crescendo with what the sportswriter who would become known as Jackie's scribe, Wendell Smith, wrote about on December 29, 1945, in the *Pittsburgh Courier*. Robinson, Smith opined, had "the hopes, aspirations and ambitions of 13 million black Americans heaped upon his broad, sturdy shoulders."[12]

Those hopes were tinged by doubts that to someone outside the community might seem paranoiac. Anyone who followed Negro League baseball knew that Jackie wasn't the best. There were easily several other prospects who were more tested and experienced baseball wise. Was Jackie chosen by the wily and not to be trusted white owner Branch Rickey because he wasn't good enough to make it, and his failure would bring to an end any thoughts of "niggers" as major leaguers? One man's paranoia is another man's reality.

There were many who felt that all this "extra weight" would be too heavy to carry. Veteran Negro League great Dave Malarcher, a product of the Rube Foster school of baseball smarts, encountered such doubts in an incident in a "Negro man's neighbor store in Chicago." His response was firm and definite:

One day, as I went into a Negro man's neighbor store here, he—knowing my baseball background—said to me, "Eddie Collins, former white Sox second baseman says that Jackie Robinson will not make it in the major Leagues. What is your opinion as a baseball man?" I replied, "As a baseball man, and an expert in the game, I have seen Jackie play. I know his ability as a player, and his spirit as an athlete. I have seen him demonstrate his great courage and sportsmanship in tight competition.

The only thing that will cause him to fail will be, if all of the ball players on all of the teams, and all of the managers of all of the teams, and all of the umpires, and all of the owners, and the presidents of the leagues, and the commissioner, and then all of the baseball fans in all of the cities 'turn thumbs down' on him, he might not make it; all of this would be too much against him. But, if he is given just half a chance, he'll make it easily." And he did![13]

What Jack Roosevelt Robinson did was of course of considerable importance beyond the playing field of America's national pastime. The black journalist Mal Goode sitting in a Yankee Stadium press box 40 years after the Robinson debut remembered with a passion that was palpable how special visually and emotionally it was to see this fine, beautiful black specimen of an athlete take his place on major league diamonds at a time when that American place for people of his color was so proscribed and limited by his nation's racial norm. Author Robert Peterson placed that Robinson baseball integration moment in the same historically important context as *Brown v. Board of Education*.

Another kind of context, one that is seldom brought forward when the discussion turns to the Robinson/Rickey moment, is offered by black poet and man of letters, LeRoi Jones/Amiri Baraka, as he recollects his growing up years in Newark, New Jersey, and the wonder filled Negro baseballness that marked that growing up time.

For Baraka, the best times were when his father took him on Sundays to the Ruppert Stadium home of the Negro National League Eagles. Very little in his life was as heightened in anticipation and reward. The recollection of those black men playing baseball carries memories and a politics that to this day make him shudder. He pictures the scene standing in lines with his old man, "lines of all black people! Dressed up like they would for going to the game, in those bright lost summers. Full of noise and identification slapped greetings over and around folks."[14]

Easily understandable was such a recognition level given that folks of Baraka's color in the Newark of the 1940s "worked together, lived in the same neighborhoods, went to church together, and played together." "We knew," he tells us, that the players "*were* us—raised up to another, higher degree." Fans talked to the Eagles before and after the game. "That last fabulous year they were World Champs. They had Dobby, Irvin, Pearson, Harvey and Pat Patterson, a school teacher, on third base. Leon Day was the star pitcher. He showed out opening day! Coming into that stadium carried a sweetness with it. The hot dogs and root beer have never tasted that good again. A little big-eyed boy holding his father's hand."[15]

From how they played and how they looked, the Newark Eagles had this young boy's heart. They were professional players, real black heroes. And he could be intimate with them as an extension of himself in a way that he could never be with the Yankees and the Dodgers.

Such was the old Amiri Baraka's memory of a time and place of his youth that would always haunt his memory, and never be repeated. In this baseball recollection, he felt a sense of completion for he was participating in something at a much higher level than anything else he knew. Here was a part of America where this young boy was not excluded from either identification with or knowledge of what he was watching, what his black players were doing.

> We all communicated with each other and possessed ourselves at a more human level than was usually possible out in cold whitey land. . . . We were wilder and calmer there. Louder and happier, without hysteria. . . . In the laughter and noise and easy hot dogs there was something of us celebrating ourselves. In the flying around the bases and sliding and home runs and arguments and *triumphs* there was more of ourselves in celebration than we were normally permitted. It was *ours*.[16]

And then this poet of black America takes us on a flight to places and spaces in the mind that make one think that this is not the young LeRoi Jones back then experiencing the coming of Jackie and Branch, but the old Amiri Baraka whose thoughts now are those of one who has seen and experienced things post-Jackie that he does not like and cannot accept.

> But you know, they can slip in on you in another way, Bro. Sell you some hand magic. I heard the wheels and metal wires in his voice, the imperfected humanoid, his first words "Moy nayhme is Jeckie Rawbeanson." Some Ray Bradbury shit they had mashed on us. A skin coloreed humanoid to bust up our shit.[17]

And then going to those places and spaces in the mind gets downright political as Baraka paints integration as "a straight-out trick," a "rip off of what you had in the name of what you ain't never gonna get." The poet bemoans the bitter side of the breaking of the color barrier in white baseball that ushered in with Jackie and his fellow black major league pioneers the destruction of the Negro National League, of the destruction of the Eagles, Grays, Black Yankees, Elite Giants, Cuban Stars, Clowns, Monarchs, and Black Barons. That was the price to be paid for going to the big leagues. The poet is on a rhetorical roll. Is that what the cry was, he asks, "on those Afric' shores when the European capitalists and African feudal lords got together and planned our future? ' We're Going to the Big Leagues!' "[18]

But the final word here needs to be not poet Baraka's ideological and spiritual disgruntledness with what he sees as the baleful results of Jackie Robinson's breaking of the color barrier in "organized baseball." Rather let us listen again to the special voice of a special Negro Leaguer as "Gentleman" Dave Malarcher recollects for Bob Peterson, the author of that American sports classic, *Only the Ball Was White*, what Jackie and his doings had come to mean to him in his own and in Jackie's twilight years:

> When I review baleful attempts, and the mental and spiritual punishment which he (Jackie) underwent in quietly "standing the gaff" in order to make good for us and for democracy, I think of him now, in these latter days of his life, as a greater and more powerful hero than ever—a symbol of courage, patience, fortitude, and great mind and ability, and unfaltering stamina, demonstrated under the most trying of circumstances. For he truly performed and excelled!
>
> I am sure that the facts concerning the things which Jackie had to endure and overcome, as revealed for the first time in your book, will raise the image of Jackie Robinson higher and higher still in the estimation of the American People for the destruction of the bars of evil and segregation which he achieved for the image of American democracy.[19]

And finally a gentle reminder from one more voice of the Negro Leagues for the historical context that always needs to be referenced. Jackie may have been the way, but as James Joe Green, first baseman, Kansas City Monarchs, tells us: "Jackie didn't pave the way. We did."[20]

LAWRENCE EUGENE DOBY, AMERICAN LEAGUE GAME CHANGER

There was another trail blazer right along side Jackie. The on-the-field baseball record speaks for itself. In a pitchers' era, Lawrence Eugene Doby led the American League twice in home runs, with 32 in both 1952 and 1954. He hit at least 20 home runs in eight consecutive seasons and drove in more than 100 runs five times, including a league-leading 126 in 1954. Doby played in six consecutive All-Star games from 1949 to 1954, debuting in 1949 as the first African American to play in the mid-summer classic for the American League. During his time, he was also one of the best defensive center fielders in the game, with a 164 game streak of no errors in 1954 and 1955—a record that stood for 17 years. If we could ask Dizzy Dean what was the best catch he ever saw in all his years in baseball, he might well say, as he did from the broadcast booth, that it was Larry Doby climbing up that fence on a warm late July day in 1954 and pulling back onto the field his own body still clutching the baseball that otherwise would have been a home run.

As the first black to play in the American League—debuting with the Cleveland Indians only three months after Jackie Robinson—Doby experienced the negatives of prejudice without the preparation, attention, and support accorded Robinson. Late one evening in the winter of 1971, he would sit with sportswriter Jerry Izenberg and share some of the memory scars he was still carrying from his pioneer days that till then he had kept to himself. Izenberg remembers that

> He told me how on his first day, he stood for five embarrassing minutes because no one would warm up with him, until Joe Gordon tossed him a ball. How he sat alone at the end of the dugout, ignored by all teammates except for Gordon and Jim Hegan, and a coach, Bill McKechnie. How when Lou Boudreau, the manager, asked him to play first base, no one would lend him a first baseman's mitt. How Boudreau sent him up to pinch-hit for a batter who was already behind 0–2 in the count. How a guy from the Philadelphia Athletics spit tobacco juice in his face as he slid into second base. How more than a few pitchers threw at him. How he heard the word "nigger" from the opposing dugouts and the huge white-only sections of the segregated parks. How the fans in Boston, St. Louis and Detroit were especially vile.[21]

And then there was the day, Izenberg learned, when it almost all came apart. As a redneck fan in St. Louis kept zinging him with sexual remarks about his wife Helen, Doby had more than he could handle.

> He started going into the stands after the guy, but McKechnie got to him and pinned him to the ground. "Don't try to move," Doby remembers him saying. "If you get into those stands, we won't have another black player in the league for another ten years."[22]

Doby's baseball record, along with his pioneer status, finally spoke loudly enough to qualify him for induction in 1998 into the National Baseball Hall of Fame. When he was urged by his friend Jerry Izenberg to tell a story at his induction ceremony that he had told Jerry about a black Georgia doctor who had befriended him during spring training and how years later he read that the doctor had been shot at a lunch counter sit-in during the civil rights protests, Larry Doby demurred, choosing instead to remember a glorious baseball moment he cherished all his life.

He would say on the induction stand in Cooperstown that the photo "came at a time when America needed that picture, and even today I remain grateful that I could play a part in giving that to my country."[23]

Similarly to Robinson in another aspect, Doby would be advised by Cleveland Indians owner Bill Veeck about the reality he had to deal with as a baseball player, for their partnership was as much an experiment in race relations as it was about playing fine baseball.

> When Mr. Veeck signed me, he sat me down and told me some of the do's and don'ts. . . . "No arguing with umpires, don't even turn around at a bad call at the plate, and no dissertations with opposing players; either of those might start a race riot. No associating with female Caucasians"—not that I was going to. And he said remember to act in a way that you know people are watching you. And this was something that both Jack Robinson and I took seriously. We knew that if we didn't succeed, it might hinder opportunities for the other Afro-Americans.[24]

Looking back from the late 1990s on what his experiences as a pioneering baseball player meant to him, he would say to students at a Carleton College forum sponsored by former baseball commissioner Fay Vincent that "if we all look back, we can see that baseball helped make this a better country for us all, a more comfortable country for us all, especially for those of us who have grands and great-grands. Kids are our future and we hope baseball has given them some idea of what it is to live together and how we can get along, whether you be black or white."[25]

And to the end he cherished his memory of his time as a young man with the Newark Eagles in the Negro National League, for before he was a major leaguer, he was a Negro Leaguer. He came across the years to have a reputation as a private person, someone who did not seek the limelight, and often kept to himself. His former Negro League teammates would cherish a different memory of the young fun-loving man they knew who had a ready smile and who was so comfortable with himself. And they would wonder if some of what they knew about Lawrence Eugene Doby had been lost in the ordeal of those years of having to deal with much more than just being as good a baseball player as he could be. "Although you were segregated in terms of hotels, restaurants, that sort of thing, you had fun and you had a lot of people come to see you play. And that part it was as good, better than my beginning in the major leagues. Because of freedom. I had more freedom, more comfortability."[26]

THE NEGRO LEAGUES AS MEMORY

As the Negro Leagues faded away after Jackie Robinson's and Larry Doby's signings, what was left for those who had experienced that baseball were strong memories of great times on and off the field of play. Perhaps, the most remembered of those times were those associated with the annual mid-summer East–West All-Star games in Chicago's Comiskey Park. "Jackie's writer," the great Wendell Smith, best captures the heighted excitement during the All-Star games in "There's Only One," a poem originally published in the *Pittsburgh Courier*, where he tells us we can roll into one Ziegfeld Follies and Barnum's circus, and throw in for good measure the Kentucky Derby, the Indianapolis 500, and the National Golf Open. But for this black scribe, there is only one event "that passes the crucial test". It's that stupendous, gigantic, colossal attraction when the East locks horns with the West.[27]

Smith then puts in prose what he said so well in poetry:

> CHICAGO—This is it . . . when East meets West and to hell with the "never the twain . . . !"
>
> Here in this sprawling metropolis the million-dollar gems of Negro baseball will match their brain and brawn, speed and talent Sunday afternoon in the fourteenth annual East-West classic at spacious Comiskey Park.
>
> This is the biggest and most dramatic event in the Negro sports world. Since the first game in 1933, spectators have paid out $882,000 and 434,000 have witnessed the classics. No other sporting event promoted by Negroes can equal that record. No other sports event attracts such a crowd. Not even a Joe Louis fight has more magnetism than the East-West game.[28]

THE LAST EAGLE—MONTE IRVIN

Certainly contributing to that magnetism was the great Negro and later major leaguer and National Hall of Fame member Monte Irvin. Of all those who wore proudly the emblem of the Newark Eagles of the Negro National League, Monte Irvin, along with "Red" Moore, are the "Last Eagles" we have with us today. Who better than James "Cool Papa" Bell to tell us who this baseball great was in the eyes of his fellow Negro Leaguers: "Most of the black ballplayers thought Monte Irvin should have been the first black in the Major Leagues. Monte was our best young ballplayer at the time. He could hit that long ball, he had a great arm, he could field, he could run. Yes, he could do everything."[29]

From the revolution times, Jackie is the one we remember, but there were many others as well who demand our attention. In the context of the Negro baseball road we have been traversing, among them most prominently is the "Last Eagle."

Arguably, he was the finest athlete ever to graduate from a New Jersey high school earning 16 varsity letters in four different sports at East Orange High while setting a state record for the javelin. His athletic prowess made no difference on senior prom night when he and his date, and a friend and his date, were refused service at a late night eatery in their hometown because of the color of their skin. The year was 1937.

Monte Irvin was one of the fortunate ones. An outstanding career in the Negro Leagues, interrupted by three years of service in the army during World War II, was followed by a nine-year career in the majors that saw him help lead the New York Giants to two national leagues pennants and a World Series triumph. In 1951, he had an MVP caliber season when he batted .312 with 24 homes runs and a league-leading 121 rbis, becoming the first black player to lead a major league in that later category. Given his age when he was signed by the Giants, if integration had been just a bit slower in coming, and if he hadn't been so fine a player, he might never have made it to the big leagues. Certainly, there were Negro Leaguers like his teammate and friend Ray Dandridge who may have been his equal or even his better who were left behind as the pace of integration grinded excruciatingly slow.

As we have seen, as a youngster growing up in East Orange he never dreamed that he would someday be a major leaguer. It was the Negro Leagues that were his inspiration, and where he aspired to play. And play he did. Inspired is the right word to describe his play in his beloved Negro Leagues that included six East–West All-Star Game appearances, and a 1946 season that saw him lead his Eagles to a World Series title against the Kansas City Monarchs of Satchel Paige, Hilton Smith, and Buck O'Neil. But it is his 1951 season with the New York Giants that defines his greatness as a baseball player. That was his first full season in the majors. At 32 years of age, segregation had cost him his prime. With his .312, 24 home runs, and 121 runs batted in, it is hard to imagine him not winning the MVP award where he finished third to Roy Campanella and Stan Musial. He scored 94 runs, hit 11 triples, drew 89 walks, while only striking out 44 times and went 12 for 14 in steals. In the field, he more than matched his prowess at the plate with his .996 percentage a product of only one error all season. He was 5th in batting average, 4th in On Base Percentage, 7th in slugging, tied for 10th in runs scored, 7th in hits, 9th in total bases, 3rd in triples, tied for 10th in homers, and his league-leading 121 rbi total was 12 better than his nearest competitors. It was an across-the-board outstanding season for what was essentially a rookie campaign for this veteran Negro Leaguer. Monte finished seventh in walks, tied for eighth in steals, fourth in runs created, fifth in times on base, and tied for third in times hit by a pitch. His outstanding regular season play more than carried over into the World Series where he hit .458 tying a record with his 11 hits. In game one of the Series, he gave his Giants fans the thrill of a steal of home against the redoubtable Allie Reynolds.

When he signed with the Giants in 1950, he had commented that "this should have happened to me 10 years ago. I'm not even half the ballplayer I was then."[30] Roy Campanella agreed: "Monte was the best all-round player I have ever seen. As great as he was in 1951, he was twice that good 10 years earlier in the Negro Leagues."[31]

Monte Irvin has served across the years of his retirement as an outstanding public educator as regards the history of the black leagues in which he stared. With the deaths of his teammates Max Manning and Larry Doby, he is the last of the Eagles who soared to the heights of baseball greatness on the 1946 Negro World Champion Newark club that bested the Kansas City Monarchs in one of the best and last of the great Negro League moments. He holds another important distinction, shared only with the great Martin Dihigo—membership in the halls of fame of four countries—Mexico, Cuba, Puerto Rico, and the United States. Wonderfully supportive always of the men he played with in Negro baseball, Monte Irvin has been, in every possible meaning the word can have, a champion all his life.[32]

CHAPTER 8

A History That Is Lost?
Stolen? Strayed?,
1947–Present

SETTING THE SCENE—"I WAS LOST,
AND NOW AM FOUND"

These are the years when a legacy that was lost was recovered as a band of historians, with founding fathers Bob Peterson and John Holway beginning the quest, were captured by the romance and reality of the Negro Leagues.

The Negro Leagues of the "glory years" were gone. But there remained a Negro League residue of memory and storytelling at work in black families and communities that helped to keep alive a significant interest in and presence at major league baseball in its seasonal play. Most of the heroes of the glory years were passed or living out their elder years in obscurity. But the stories of these largely unknown baseball immortals lived on in faded newspaper clippings pasted in treasured scrapbooks; on microfilm rolls that saved the national treasure of the black press; and finally in public consciousness after the pioneering work of historians Bob Peterson and John Holway; in the oral recollections the players came to share; in the histories that came to be written of their game; and in public commemorations at the National Baseball Hall of Fame in Cooperstown, in the Negro Leagues Museum in Kansas City, and at important sites such as Atlantic City, New Jersey, where they played their special brand of baseball.[1]

Although at times hidden from public view, this history never disappeared. It lived on in the love that many had for the history of America's game and all its complexities. It continued in the stories that fathers, uncles, grandfathers, mothers, and grandmothers who knew the Negro Leagues passed along to the next generation. Absent from the official baseball record, it resurged in the dedicated historians who trekked with tape recorders in hand to get the stories that mainstream newspapers had neglected to report.

Once the sporting passion of black America, baseball today no longer conveys the same sense of history, of belonging, or progress that it did in the long era in which blacks struggled for social acceptance and civil rights while excelling in the national pastime. To African Americans, the history/memory connection to baseball has been weakened by the onslaught of the competing attractions found today in popular culture and numerous sports beside the perhaps no longer "national pastime." Also the toll that time takes has increasingly removed any direct contact with the Negro Leagues generations of players and fans. The danger inherent in all of this is the loss of a sense of history that fueled the strong interest in the great game of baseball of the post-Robinson/Doby generations. This "in danger of a loss of a sense of history" is why it is so important for the future of black and white interest in the great American game of baseball that the memory and history of the Negro professional player and his era of independent and league baseball be kept alive. Curtis Granderson, Albert Pujols, and Derek Jeter and their black, and in a real sense white, counterparts are all descendants of this earlier too often forgotten chapter of Negro baseball history that so richly resonates with the story of America's identity as a nation. Preservation of this vital chapter where, through collective struggle, dreams deferred were transformed into dreams realized is something that should be of special interest to these players, for each of them stands on the shoulders of Negro League greats who, as Kansas City Monarchs first baseman James Joe Green accurately remembers, paved the way to and helped make possible the Robinson/Rickey way.

But it is important that we all be steeped in accurate and enriching ways in the history of the defeat in baseball of Jim Crow not by the courageous act of one, but through the collective struggle of many—done in this instance in one of the most visible realms of American life. It is a story that we, and most importantly they—Monte, Buck, Max, Leon, Rodolpho, Alexandro, Armando, et al.—have told in powerful and compelling ways. They have given us a history not of defeat, but of struggle—of triumph and not bitterness. It is a story of empowerment through individual and collective work. It is one that can captivate and inspire the imagination of a present-day 13-year-old potential future Derek, Alex or Mariano—or Henry, Dave or Reggie—or Max, Monte or Campy—or Cool, Satch or Josh—or Pop, Spot or Top—or Melito, Jose or Martin—or Rube, King Sol or Moses Fleetwood—or even A. Philip, Martin, or Frederick. And from that captivation may that youngster come to realize, and make his own, the wonderful strength this history offers to those who come to know what life was really like in those Negro Leagues of ancient times—in "those brave days of old":

> With a bow to Horatius, and Thomas Babington Macaulay
> And when the Goodman mends his armour,
> And trimes his helmut's plum;
> And the goodwife's shuttle merrily,
> Goes flashing through the loom;
> With weeping and with laughter,
> Still is the story told;
> How well Buck and Satch and Josh and Pop and Rube
> kept the bridge and played the game
> In the brave days of old.[2]

BIG NEWK

Don Newcombe was a Negro Leaguer for one year in the youth of his pitching prowess. If it had not been for Jackie and Mr. Rickey, he was on line for as great a career in Negro League baseball as he had as the mainstay of Brooklyn Dodger staffs in the 1950s.

His was a Dodger career interrupted by a two-year stint in the army. On his return to the club in 1954 on a trip to St. Louis to play the Cardinals, he and Jackie integrated the Chase Hotel where his white teammates had been staying while his black teammates were housed in the Adams Hotel in the black section of Missouri's principal city. The desk clerk asked the two Brooklyn Dodger teammates not to swim in the hotel pool. With tongue in cheek, Newcombe says that perhaps the clerk thought "it" was going to wash off in the pool.

He remembers another defining moment that he experienced during those years of momentous change, and treasures it as much as any moment he can recall. Sitting in his kitchen with Reverend King over a cup of coffee a few months before the assassin's bullet would take the civil rights leader from us forever, he was humbled to hear King say how much he treasured what Newcombe and Campy and Jackie had done by simply playing baseball in the way they did—a baseball that obviously counted for more than just wins and losses and Cy Young and MVP awards.*

---

*Interview with Don Newcombe for "Before You Can Say 'Jackie Robinson'" documentary.

Al White has some interesting recollections of major league baseball's first integrated clubhouse since the baseball time of Moses Fleetwood Walker, the Dodger clubhouse occupied by Don Newcombe and his teammates.

> You have to have experienced the atmosphere on a sports team dressing room, before and after a game, to fully understand and appreciate the situation—especially if the team had black players. To put it mildly, the language was pungent and racy. Consider most players, no matter what color or race, brought street talk into the dressing room. It wasn't what you'd hear in a classroom or in Sunday school. In mannerisms and actions, Preacher Roe was the one lone individual in that rowdy profane dressing room out at Ebbets Field. The closest approach to his quiet studious approach was Peewee Reese. Roe was such a fine man. In comparison to those other players you wonder how he stood the "fat." Big Don Newcombe for instance—was he a character!**

**Alvin White to Lawrence Hogan, September 14, 1981.

RECOVERING A LOST HISTORY

"Lost, Stolen and Strayed," and "now to be found," is the name we give to the historical recovery effort we write about in this chapter. So big and special a part of that effort is the finding of memories in the most serendipitous of ways. I can't remember the specifics of what led to a letter from George Olewnick of Poughkeepsie, New York, in May 1988, but what he shared with me speaks in wonderful ways to that serendipitous recovery of black baseball memories that has proved to be so rewarding a part of the historical recovery effort of which I have been privileged to be a part:

17 Monell Avenue
Poughkeepsie, N.Y. 12603

May 5, 1988

Dear Mr. Hogan:

I'm the fellow who wrote to you about the Texans/Clowns game post card. You asked about the circumstances relative to my being present at that game—so here goes.

During WW2, I was a student at Southern Methodist University (Naval V-12 Unit)—I'm white. Joe Mentesana was a grocery store owner in Dallas. He was white, Italian heritage. He wanted to enter a basketball team in a local industrial league. So he came to the campus to recruit some players (the ones who couldn't make the varsity team). I was one of the players. He sent a bus for us, with a black driver, and conveyed us to the games. Our reward was either a fried chicken dinner or ribs after the game.

Now, Joe had a grocery store in the black section of Dallas. He sponsored many black events—dances, bands, etc. He sponsored the Harlem Globetrotters for a game at the Dal-Hi (Dallas High School) Stadium in '44 or '45. The Trotters were great then. I had the good fortune to sit on their bench at that game.

Joe owned the Dallas Black baseball team. The bus he used for our basketball team was the baseball team bus. The driver was his first base-man named "Blue."

Joe called me one time and asked if I would like to see the baseball team play. So I went. The stadium was an all wood structure. The fans were all black. Joe, I, and a few other whites sat in the press box (owners' box) behind home plate on a raised platform.

During the game some V.I.P. Dallas citizens brought a guest into the press box. It was the entertainer Phil Harris—who was feeling pretty happy at that time. He watched for an inning or two, shouted some wise cracks out to the field, and then left. He was appearing at one of the downtown hotels.

Except for the "Clowns" selling the post card in the stands, I don't recall much of the game. I seem to recall the name of the Dallas team was the "Rebels." I don't recall the name of the stadium.

I'm enclosing the post card. I had hoped to sell it to a collector of black sports memorabilia. If your project has ample funds to purchase it for $5 or $10—great. If you are short of funds, consider it my contribution.

Good luck in your endeavors.

Yours truly

George Olewnick.[3]

GENTLEMAN DAVE TO GENTLEMAN BOB

Anyone who is a serious student of the history of black baseball, and of its remarkable recovery starting in the 1970s by an historical community captured by its story, acknowledges the debt he or she owes to Robert Peterson. His *Only the Ball Was White: A History of Legendary Black Players and All-Black Professional Teams,* published in 1970, would come to be recognized by *Sports Illustrated* as one of the 100 best books on sports. Its essential importance was recognized immediately by those whose history it told—especially on Dave Malarcher whose memories of the black game went back to his years with Rube Foster's outstanding 1920s Chicago American Giants teams as an outstanding third baseman, and managerial successor to the great Rube himself. In April 1970, Gentleman Bob was treated by Gentleman Dave to the best review an author could receive:

Chicago, Illinois

April 21, 1970

Mr. Robert W. Peterson
18 Lincoln Street
Ramsey N.J. 07446

Dear Bob:

When I learned from your letter of the 17th that you had been on "tenterhooks"—I, as I always say to myself when I fail to follow my mind to do a thing—"I kicked myself" for not having done what I thought and meant to do the moment I opened the package and looked at the book. I was so thrilled at just looking at it that I thought to telephone you that night to tell you how happy I was with it all. But when I began to read, there was no stopping for anything, except for meals. I stopped reading at ten thirty that night—a little past my bed-time!

When one lives alone, as I do, he speaks out aloud to himself when very pleased over a matter of great satisfaction or interest or amusement. When I first saw that gorgeous jacket, and that white ball in that black hand, I uttered out aloud to myself, "What a beautiful book!" Then "This jacket is out of this world!" And it is. It is a beautiful book, Bob. When the publishers told you last fall that they would make it a fine production, they meant it. It is all of that!

From the day I received it, I have been reading continually, between meals and other duties. I have covered every-thing from cover to cover, from the meeting of the NABBP in 1867, from John (Bud) Fowler, Ike Carter, and Fleet and Weldy Walker down to Jackie Robinson, and to the last page of the Index (406) "Zanesville, Ohio Team, 26, 27, 32."

And, Bob, it is all more than marvelous, more than wonderful, it is astoundingly magnificent!

Now to tell you why I say this and mean it; No.1. It is the first and only book—a complete one—of the history of Negro Baseball—the heretofore unknown, untold facts of what the American Negro had done in baseball through the years; of his short participation in the beginning of Organization Baseball; of his ejection and disbarment there from; and of his years of struggles, hardship, his silent joys, and unnoticed, and unheralded performance and development in our National game, while disbarred, but not stopped, not discouraged, poorly paid, meagerly traveled, outrageously segregated, yet going on, and playing the game called "The American National Pastime," and excelling in performance to the point of earning the praise of such great stars of the Major Leagues as Walter Johnson, Ted Williams, Babe Ruth, and managers as John McGraw and Connie Mack, and owners as Clark Griffith and Shibe of the Washington Senators and Philadelphia Athletics, respectively. Thus the book tells all.

No. 2. The total facts which your book portrays are astoundingly inclusive of all of the phases of our (Negro) Baseball history—the way we played, traveled, ate, slept, barnstormed, organized, managed, lived, and did our jobs as baseball players, owners and managers, and promoters and where we played, against whom we played, and how well we played as compared with white organized baseball, including the participation of white semi-pro and white independent baseball in our development and continuation to play.

It (your book) portrays photographs of the leading star players of Negro Baseball and descriptions of their individual special abilities, and of the outstanding teams and their managements and managers, from the veterans, as Bud Fowler, in 1872, to the entry of Jackie Robinson to the Major Leagues of Organized baseball.

All of the above facts were never told to the world before. Thus your book is definitely unique, and a true part of the American History, heretofore untold and unwritten.

No. 3. Of great significance, your book, the only one and only account published, gives the details of the bringing up and initiation of Jackie Robinson into the major leagues and Organized Baseball, thereby ending the long disbarment of Negro players there from. It tells the facts—heretofore not told or published—of the secret scouting of Negro players for the Majors, and especially of the work of the scouts of the Brooklyn Dodgers' Farm System—"Sisler, Matthews,

Greenwade, and Sukeforth," who therein and thereby demonstrated their spirits of true Americanism and freedom in doing their job well and unbiased in the selection of Jackie, as the best man. Also your book discloses the sordid attempts of some of the teams and players to drive Jackie Robinson out of Organized Baseball by batting and humiliating with vile remarks and castigations upon him. . . .

Your book also reveals for the first time the details of the great courage, foresight, and astute character of Branch Rickey; and the revelation of the sterling character of Ford Frick, president of the National League, in his quick and severe warning to the St. Louis Cardinals against their plan to foment a strike against Robinson, stating that they (the Cardinals) would be suspended from the league if they did. And that stopped that! There was a man, Mr. Ford Frick! I suggest a "Ford Frick Day" be incorporated in major League baseball each year.

No.4. And your book is not without its comedy and humor. I laughed aloud at Jack Marshall's recount of Rod Whitman's baseball operation in Canada and Cummings' telling of his arrival from Florida to the Bacharach Giants, and getting in politics on the side; and Judy Johnson's auto travels, and the double wreck on the road; and Buck Leonard's terrible, yet comical experiences in trying to earn a living in baseball. I found Mr. Hardy's description of the trials and triumphs of barnstorming in the Middle West most interesting and enlightening of the days in baseball in this area just before—not too many years before—I came up.

Your book is original in recording many names and places heretofore obscure, and which now, as result of your tremendous work and research, will not be forgotten through the years to come. They are in written history now to be told and retold over and over again, the family backgrounds, from Bud Fowler and Fleet Walker down to Jackie Robinson, are available to the world through "Only The Ball Was White."

For me personally, because of you and your book, future generations will know that there was a hamlet called "Whitehall," and a place known as "Union" in Louisiana; and a school teacher by the name of "William Bradley," who was a strict and harsh disciplinarian—indeed, who carried and wielded a strap, if one did not know his lesson or was naughty in school! and that there was a little boy's baseball team named "The Baby T's."

And above everything in the book, "Only The Ball Was White," are recorded the facts that my father "Was a great big strong man, tall,"—was Henry Louis Malarcher; And my mother was very fine; she loved education. And the most inspiring of all in the book is the fact that my mother's name, "Martha Malarcher," is in print, and thus recorded in American History of these United States. For this one fact—her name in history—the Malarcher clan—all of her descendants—will be eternally grateful to you and Prentice-Hall. This one fact is worth more to me than all the honor in the world; for the gratification of love is priceless.

Finally, Bob, it is my prediction that your book will win for you the "Nobel Peace Prize" and the "Pulitzer Prize"—both—the Pulitzer for the most original and best historical literature of the year; and the "Nobel Prize" for historical "literature and promotion of World Peace," because:

1. your book is the first to disclose, illustrate, and prove the fact that even an institution of sport in our country—or else where— Organized Baseball—was as heinous and cruel as war;
2. that segregation in Organized Baseball and the Major Leagues was a badge of slavery and a thief and usurpation of the opportunity, privilege and rights of Negro players to liberty, the pursuit of happiness and their well being, and the preservation of their very lives;
3. that the Negro players were kept in human and economic slavery by a "gentleman's agreement" through many years, until
4. Branch Rickey, the emancipator, moved against it, with the swift support of Ford Frick, proving, like these two, that men can abolish evil and the cruelties of hatred, war and segregation and injustice, and bring peace, understanding, and love to the hearts and affairs of men and nations; that your book reveals;
5. That Cap Adrian Constantine Anson (Cap Anson), of the old "White Stockings" baseball team of Chicago, and the others with him were as evil, hateful and tyrannical as Simon LaGree, that symbol of the slavery; But
6. As Harriet Beecher Stowe put the spotlight on slavery for the conscience of the world in 1852, your book, "Only The Ball Was White," turns the spotlight backward upon the gruesome and awful past which the Negro baseball players trod in humility, forbearance, courage and indomitable patience in his excellent performances on the diamond, that the modern world may see in sympathy, and that the conscience of modern America and the United States may recognize in regret and shame, and vow and determine that it shall not happen here again, as Ford Frick said to the Cardinals when they were planning their strike against Jackie Robinson:

"If you do this you will be suspended from the league. . . . This is the United States of America, and one citizen has as much right to play as another."

In all of this disclosure of the facts involving Negro baseball, its seg-regation and final resolve, your book points up the way to peace and understanding.

With gratitude, high esteem, and the best wishes,

Sincerely,

Dave.[4]

David J. Malarcher, known as "Gentleman Dave." Ma-larcher was third baseman and manager of the Chicago American Giants. (National Baseball Hall of Fame Library, Cooperstown, NY)

THE BUCK OF KANSAS CITY

Gentleman Dave Malarcher's peace and understanding would become the trademark watch words of the man who more than anyone else became for the historical recovery of black baseball history "Mr. Negro League History." The "Buck" indeed stopped in Kansas City as John Jordan "Buck" O'Neil became the "right on time man."

An unlikely time to be in Cooperstown—early February 2003. I had come in on Saturday in anticipation of a Monday presentation via satellite to classrooms all across the nation. When we were told that our presentation on "Baseball, Race and Ethnicity" would be viewed by over 15,000,000 youngsters, my first thought was, "Goodness, think of the damage I might do."

We gathered at 9:00 A.M. on Monday morning in the Hall of Fame Library for a final once over of the day's events. Word was about that Buck had come into town in the early hours of the morning. Not bad timing for a 92-year-old gent. I hadn't seen my friend in several years. Dapper as ever, looking not at all like a 1:00 A.M. arrivee, he strode into the room and was immediately engulfed by well-wishers. I went over, and worked my way through the wishers. We embraced, I looked at him and said, "Buck it has been too long. You look better than you ever have." Without missing a beat, and with that famous smile that seemed to embrace you with sunshine, he replied, "Larry, Good black don't crack."

Filmmaker Tom Guy and I interviewed him in Cooperstown 16 years earlier on the back porch of the grand and gracious Otesaga Hotel where he held forth with Monte Irvin in a conversation largely about their wonderful memories of the music of their baseball years with the talk running from the likes of Ben Webster and Jimmy Lunceforth to Ella and Nat and Sarah, and Hamp, the Duke and the Count. Grand and gracious he always was—and so wonderful to listen to as, in his senior years, he educated a nation about the history that he, more than anyone else, came to represent in the minds of the baseball public of his nation—an American public that in his Negro League playing time as first baseman and manager of the Kansas City Monarchs had tolerated a prejudice against his kind that he never allowed to embitter him. His was always a gospel of love and inclusion.

Those qualities were never better on display in public view than at the 2006 induction of 17 veteran Negro players and executives into the National Baseball Hall of Fame. Even more so since many of us believe that he should have been among them.

The Buck who didn't make it was chosen to speak about those of his comrades who did. And as always, speak he did in the most memorable and appropriate of ways. In his speech, the 94-year-old O'Neil, who as Negro League veteran and educator extraordinaire was one of the initial 39 that a specially convened Negro baseball panel considered for induction, "made the event a remembrance of the special world of the Negro Leaguers."[5] He told a sun-drenched crowd of thousands who had gathered on an expanse of green lawn that stretched across a former farmer's field just outside of Cooperstown and now the home of the Clark Recreational Center that "Hollywood never captured the reality of black baseball nor how much of a financial force the Negro League franchises were in the black community."[6] The world behind the color line was vibrant, O'Neil said. The world behind the color line was filled with success stories. "All you needed was a bus, and we rode in some of the best buses money could buy,"[7] O'Neil told the gathering. "A couple of sets of uniforms and you could have 20 of the best athletes that ever lived. That's who we're representing here today. The elite of black baseball."[8]

Certainly none more so than the man who recollected the greatness of inductees who played their "sundown" baseball on fields where "only the ball was white," and who had himself played a major role in the long education effort to bring forward their Hall of Fame candidacies. Inducted that day in a unique historical ceremony were Raleigh "Biz" Mackey, Ben Taylor, Andy Cooper, Jud Wilson, Ray Brown, Willard Brown, Mule Suttles, Cristobal Torriente, Frank Grant, Pete Hill, Jose Mendez, Louis Santop, executives Effa Manley, Sol White, Alex Pompez, Cum Posey, and J. L. Wilkinson.

Two years after the moving tribute, and unfortunately after Buck had gone to his eternal reward, the National Baseball Hall of Fame established the John Jordan "Buck" O'Neil Lifetime Achievement Award presented by the Hall of Fame's board of directors not more than once every three years to honor an individual whose extraordinary efforts enhanced baseball's positive impact on society, broadened the game's appeal, and whose character, integrity, and dignity are comparable to the qualities exhibited by O'Neil. The award was first given in 2008, posthumously to its first recipient, John Jordan "Buck" O'Neil.

One can't help but think that if Buck O'Neil were with us today he would say, as he did in 2006, this is a wonderful moment for the 17 inductees—but education remains to be done for there are more deserving candidates to be considered. Among those likely high on his list for consideration for Hall of Fame induction would be Cannonball Dick Redding and Richard "King" Lundy, and at the time of the 2006 election besides Buck himself, the only other living Negro League candidate, Saturnino Orestes Armas Miñoso Arrieta. Oh, and one other as well, whose candidacy he would not tout, but none the less deserving, one John Jordan "Buck" O'Neil.

ONCE AGAIN TEACHING A YOUNGSTER
TO THROW A CURVE

We began our journey into black professional baseball in the winter of 1885 in Jacksonville, Florida, with a member of the Original Cuban Giants teaching the young James Weldon Johnson how to throw a mean curveball. The clock turns. A hundred and some odd years later the scene repeats itself.

Monte Irvin is arguably the greatest of living Negro Leaguers. Along with Buck O'Neil, no one has done more to honor, preserve, extend, and pass along the legacy of Negro League baseball. Given where we started with this story, and where it has taken us, it seems only fitting that it should end as it began. The following account and accompanying photo come from your author's friend and colleague Michael Everett. Michael shares a scene that he witnessed, and took much pleasure from. At the outset of his telling, the death that he references is that of our dear friend and great Negro League player, Max Manning, who passed to his eternal reward in June 2003.

Shortly after learning the sad news of Max's death, I received a phone call from his lifelong friend and former teammate, Monte Irvin. Monte had spoken to Belinda (Max's daughter), and she suggested to him that he stay in our home during his stay for Max's funeral. Knowing of their 60 years of friendship, I was more than willing to offer our home and support to Monte. I could only imagine what must have been going though his mind when he learned the sad news of his dear friend.

During the course of the weekend, Monte, as usual, dignified and gracious, shared stories of both his time spent with Max and as a player in the Negro Leagues.

On the day after the funeral, Monte went out to our side porch looking out to the side yard. "That's an awfully green yard you have there," he exclaimed as he sat down in the wicker chair. Pausing pensively he added, "But it sure comes with a price."

At 84, having spent a career playing baseball behind the color barrier before reaching the Major Leagues, Monte Irvin knows that achieving things in life come with a price. We talked more of baseball, and before too long our 11-year-old son, Andrew, appeared with a glove and ball. Andrew is knowledgeable about Negro League baseball and knew more about scuffballs and spitballs than he did about throwing a curve ball.

Monte was eager to coach Andrew by first explaining the importance of playing often, and how as a young boy he gradually got stronger with exercise and practice. He shared some of the different kind of training techniques and how he eventually could see the stitching on the ball and knew what kind of pitch was being thrown. Taking the ball from Andrew, Monte demonstrated where the fingers should be placed and the motion of the pitcher's arm when delivering a curve. He finished the lesson with gentle encouragement and assured Andrew that he would master the technique but that it was important to keep the game of baseball fun.

I don't know if Andrew will ever have the opportunity to use the lesson taught to him. Andrew marches to his own beat and seems to enjoy the game of basketball more than baseball. He claims that he will continue to practice his "swoosh," giving hope to all short white kids who love basketball. He seems more interested in Bob Cousey than anyone in baseball. However, Andrew understands that success does come with a "price," and undoubtedly he will never forget the afternoon that Negro League and Hall of Fame great, Monte Irvin, took a moment to teach him how to throw a curve ball.[9]

Shoot for the stars Andrew. That is what Max would tell you—as does "Uncle" Stanley—and as would Josh, and Cool Papa, and Top, and the Cannonball, and our dear Pop, and Little Sol . . . and a whole baseball army of players who walk through these pages. And as would James Weldon "Lift Every Voice and Sing" Johnson. And the great Rube too . . . You have what it takes lad. And the strong shoulders to stand on.

> One thing they cannot prohibit—
> The strong men . . . coming on
> The strong men gettin' stronger
> Strong men . . .
> Stronger . . . [10]

THE GENTLE MEN OF NEGRO BASEBALL

As we ring the curtain down on the drama we have been watching, your author will exercise a prerogative and share a few personal observations about the grace and character of men who across the last 25 years have enriched his life, as well as the lives of his loved ones—and who through their generous, humorous, and serious sharing of their life experiences have taught him lessons about how to live life well that he will always cherish.

In his beautiful *The Boys of Summer,* Roger Kahn tells us that in the great Dodgers' catcher Roy Campanella there was none of (Duke) Snider's limber grace, no long-muscled fluidity to his walk. He pumped his bat toward Allie Reynolds, and then swung at a fastball, dropping his right knee so that it almost touched the earth. The mighty uppercut produced a foul tip and

Campy shook his head, indignant at the wasted exertion. Up in the press box, reporter Red Smith said quite softly, "old colored gentlemen."[11]

These were baseball men. They heard it all, and undoubtedly said it all in a baseball and larger world that was an especially tough place for their kind. It was a world where they had to stand up for themselves. The newspapers that reported their games are filled with stories of arguments on the diamond—arguments off the diamond—and at times outright personal violence. Ask, as I did, my friends Leon Day, Monte Irvin, and Max Manning to name their all-time "evil" Negro league team, and they have no hesitancy in filling out the roster with fellows you might not want as your neighbor.

But there is another side to this story as well. Let me get there by sharing a personal moment outside the realm of baseball. I interviewed then executive director of the NAACP Roy Wilkins in his New York office in the spring of 1975. His secretary had ushered me in at the outset of our meeting, and hung my coat on a hanging rack close to where we would sit and talk. With the interview finished, I got up to get my coat. Mr. Wilkins would have none of that. He came out from behind his desk, took my overcoat, and held it for me as I put my arms into its sleeves. At the time, I was a 31-year-old graduate student from the history department at Indiana University. Roy Wilkins was . . . well, Roy Wilkins. He had moved in the intimate circles of W.E.B. Du Bois, Walter White, A. Philip Randolph, and Martin Luther King. He had counseled presidents of the United States. He was the distinguished elder statesman of the modern civil rights movement. And whatever the old school was, he was one of its ranking gentlemen.

"It used to be said of Negroes," Wilkins wrote as a young reporter for the *Kansas City Call* in the mid-1920s, "they are so polite, even the poorest ones are courtly in their manners." He was upset because he had just experienced the opposite of that politeness, directed at members of his own race, and even worse, toward a race woman by Negro men. On a streetcar he was riding in Kansas City, he observed a black woman being treated curtly by the conductor. Bad as that was, what was worse was the behavior of "some young colored men" who, along with him, were the sole occupants of the car besides the woman. "Not a grumble from them, not a protest, only giggles. So-called men giggling when a streetcar conductor hands out a lot of smart talk to their women! Giggles when a word or two to the conductor would have settled the whole matter. Politeness is not for them."

And then on another occasion, he observed a "colored man scrambling onto a streetcar ahead of a young colored girl. Why not" he says, "show her a little deference? Why not be polite to her? She is a woman first, and black second, two excellent reasons for going out of one's way to show her courtesy." Then in a line as precious and definitional of an age as different from ours as one can imagine, Wilkins offered an "excuse" of sorts for the so-called men in the first instance. It might be mentioned, he says, "that they were of the 'shiek' type about twenty years old, ruined for real manhood by trick ties, balloon pants, and ukuleles."[12]

I can only tell you what I have observed and experienced time and again on my extended journey into the history that we have just traversed. On many an occasion, I have met in the veteran players of Negro League baseball the "old school" Roy Wilkinses of this world. Theirs is a gentle courtliness, a politeness that is never forced that these baseball players share with some of the most distinguished and accomplished of their generation—as well as with the "ordinary" and generally unrecognized folk. Anyone who ever met the dean of black historians, John Hope Franklin, knows what of I speak. I observed this quality of character in two elderly college professors, W. Edward Farrison and Edward Sweet, who I was privileged to have as my teachers at North Carolina Central University when, as a young high school teacher chosen to participate in a national teachers' seminar in Afro-American history and literature in the summer of 1969, I began the academic part of the journey that had brought me to where I am today. I have come to recognize this quality even in those in our story who I have not met. Today, through his son, the Reverend David Johnson, I observe it in the person of the last commissioner of the Negro National League, the pioneering Harlem minister Reverend John Howard Johnson. Clearly, this special quality of character was found in the John Henry "Pop" Lloyd who the Cuban sportswriter Pepe Conte claims "was the greatest player of all time to be produced by the national game." It was present in considerable quantity in the person of the most important historical and, on many levels, personal resource I have encountered in all my years of research in the field of black history—the *Associated Negro Press* executive correspondent and pioneering black journalist, Alvin E. White, who you have met so often on these pages.

And so I could hardly have been surprised when I found that same quality of character in the score or more of Negro League baseball men—Max, Stanley, Monte, Bill, Mahlon, Leon, Benny, the naming easily goes on—who I have been privileged to call my friends.

- Look at the way my Negro League friends all dressed when they went to ball games.
- Look at the way they still dress and carry themselves today.
- There is Al White, earthy and crusty, but polite and courtly, and so much on the mark that only he could be on.

- Listen to Leon. Goodness, he was funny tonight! How about his all-time evil team!
- Isn't Pint something else still ragging Bill 40 years later for "brushing" that umpire?
- You can't help but smile broadly when Benny tells Dave Winfield what it was like.

And on and on leaving us a bank of delightfulness to draw on when we need that the most.

The world back when they were young and in their baseball prime gave these men much reason to be impolite. As a matter of course, a big part of that world treated their kind in "impolite" ways. I have come to think that it is as if their own politeness is their answer to the coarseness and impoliteness that was directed at them. Monte Irvin speaks to this point when he addresses the meaning of the "difficulties" he and his fellow players faced in those "impolite" times:

> An incident would crop up here and there. They would call you a name or something. But being black we got used to that and we didn't let that deter us. Sometimes through adversity I think it made us better players because we would try harder. They would make us mad. And rather than fight or anything like that we would want to play so as to beat the opposition. We developed that kind of mentality. I think it was that kind of mentality that took us through.[13]

This "politeness" factor is that same Monte in his elder years, smoothly, and without missing a beat, changing topics at the get-together in the church hall after Max Manning's funeral because for him the off-color story he was telling was not appropriate to finish when Kathy Whitmore joined our conversation. It is the way Stanley Glenn carries himself all the time. It is the joy that always comes into our gathering when Mahlon Ducket, Jim Robinson, Bob Scott, Amando, and Pedro, and little 105-year-old Melito from Puerto Rico, the best dressed man I will ever meet who I swear can down more fine Scotch and be more lucid than it is humanly possible to be after doing so, start in with the storytelling. It was Leon in our *Before You Can Say Jackie Robinson* documentary simply shaking his head in disbelief with a wry look on his face 40 years after it happened at the thought of the fellow who wouldn't sell them gas on a bus trip through the South. And it is the good sadness that we feel when we think of the empty space in our lives once beautifully occupied by Max, and Leon, and Pint, and Benny, and Toots, and Buck, and so many others of our black baseball gentlemen now held dear in our memories.

What these men have given is found for me most valuably and memorably in what my family has taken from coming to know and enjoy the company of our Negro Leaguers. Ask my wife Sally what she thinks of her Negro League friends and a delightful smile comes to her face as she remembers how nice they have been to be with. And then for a father, most precious of all, the commentary that comes from my son Matthew in a "Personal Sports Biography" paper he wrote for Education 257 in the masters program at University of California–Berkeley in 2001. There is a section where he relates how he has come to understand and effectively deal with the peculiarity of his country's odd dance with its concept of race.

School was not the only setting in which I encountered race. My father is a history professor and did his dissertation on the Associated Negro Press. He has also done extensive work on the Negro leagues. This work has included a video documentary, and a photo and memorabilia exhibit that has traveled everywhere from Galveston Texas to Cooperstown, New York. As a growing boy I was able to tag along on many of the tasks that were undertaken in the production of the video and exhibit. This included many interviews with veteran Negro Leaguers, openings for the exhibit in which many Negro Leaguers were asked to attend and take part in panel discussions, and even sharing a motel room with a couple of Negro Leaguers. Throughout it all I was forced to see the humanity that is not skin deep.

Furthermore, it sends a very powerful message to a young person when an adult you greatly respect spends large amounts of time working against commonly held notions and beliefs with regard to race. While growing up I knew that race was the wrong way to categorize people because my father showed me that through his tireless work to bring awareness to a history that highlighted how wrong the ideology of racial superiority is. Within the framework of my father's undertakings, I also learned that these men were not just athletes. The men who were interviewed and who I got to know a little bit were well spoken and carried themselves with great dignity. They were old, so they were no longer competing athletes, but they were sharp and they were smart.

My father's work, the lives of these men, and the stories they told also help to highlight that sports in and of themselves were not, and are not the most important part of life. The lives of these men took place within a larger social and historical context, and it was the workings within those contexts and how things affected the lives of these men and the sport they played that was truly important. Their lives are the ones that have been the basis for social change and success for those that are out there today, and that needs to be taken note of.[14]

The Gentlemen of the Negro Leagues at Union County College in September, 1984. (Personal collection of Lawrence Hogan)

And so at the close of our journey into this long and character-filled world of black baseball that has taken us from slavery times down to the present, it seems most appropriate to say thank you to our colored gentlemen of the Negro Leagues. Thank you for giving to myself, and to my fellow researchers—and in my case to my wife and children—the wit and wisdom of your many years. Thank you for all the wonderful times we have had together as you have generously taken us back into who you were, and shared with us who you are and continue to be, "Gentlemen" all.

It is to all of them, to Max and Leon and Benny and "Pint" and "Ready" and Stanley, and Mahlon, and Monte, and Mr. Mirabal, and Buck, and old Doc Sykes, and Jim R. and Scotty—to their worthy opponents on the field of play caught no better than in their friend Gordon Ross—and to those on whose shoulders they stood, Top, and Pop, and Rube, and the Cannonball, and Smokey Joe, Gentleman Dave, and little Sol, that we dedicate, with much gratitude, *The Forgotten History of African American Baseball*. Its writing could only have been, given who it is about, a labor of love.

POSTSCRIPT

There is Bill Cash with his "nothing like baseball in those days"; Gene Benson with his "it's a fun game"; Max Manning "having no regrets"; and Buck O'Neil perhaps saying it best of all, "There is nothing like getting your body

The Unheralded. (National Baseball Hall of Fame Library, Cooperstown, NY)

to do all it has to do on a baseball field. It is as good as sex. It is as good as music. It fills you up. Waste no tears on me, I didn't come along too early. I was right on time."

We have danced on these pages to a tune of fun and awfulness. Given the racial negatives that produced our behind the veil sundown baseball world, it is customary to emphasize the unfairness of the places we have been. But again, that is not the only point, nor the most important. There is another reality, for those who played this game of apartheid baseball tell us they did not heed the awfulness. It was not a presence for them, for they were having too much fun playing the game they loved. Now that we are finished listening to Buck's, and Dandy's, and the Devil's, and El Cuchara's, and Top's and Pop's and Rube's stories hopefully it will not be said by future generations, as an echo of Dr. Du Bois's judgment of his time, that the tragedy of our age was that men knew so little of men.

Notes

INTRODUCTION

1. From dissenting opinion of John Marshall Harlan in *Plessy v. Ferguson,* 1896.

2. W. Rollo Wilson wrote a wonderful column for many years for the *Pittsburgh Courier* and the *Philadelphia Tribune* that makes him a standout among a crop of fine black sports journalists. He is one of those unsung writers who deserve much more attention than they have been given. In his columns, Wilson coined many an original phrase, among them the term "Sundown Baseball" to refer to Negro League play.

3. Robert Peterson, *Only the Ball Was White: A History of Legendary Black Players and All-Black Professional Teams* (Old Tappan, NJ: Prentice Hall, 1970).

4. Art Rust, *Get That Nigger Off the Field: A Sparkling, Informal History of the Black Man in Baseball* (New York: Delacorte Press, 1976); Lawrence Hogan et al., *Shades of Glory: The Negro Leagues and the Story of African-American Baseball* (Washington, DC: National Geographic, 2006); Jules Tygiel, *Baseball's Great Experiment: Jackie Robinson and His Legacy* (New York: Oxford University Press, 25th anniversary edition published in 2008); Arnold Rampersad, *Jackie Robinson: A Biography* (New York: Ballantine Books, 1998).

5. John Jordan O'Neil, *I Was Right on Time: My Journey from Negro Leagues to the Majors* (New York: Touchstone, 1996).

6. Clement Price interview with Lawrence Hogan for "Before You Can Say 'Jackie Robinson'" (BYCSJR) documentary.

7. Jacques Barzun, *God's Country and Mine: A Declaration of Love, Spiced with a Few Harsh Words* (New York: Praeger, 1973).

8. BYCSJR interview for Max Manning stories.

9. Lawrence Hogan, "The Gift of Alvin White," *Commonweal Magazine,* February 10, 1984.

CHAPTER 1

1. James Weldon Johnson, "Lift Every Voice and Sing," 1899. This magnificent song has come to be known as the Negro (now Black) national anthem.

2. James Weldon Johnson, *Along This Way: The Autobiography of James Weldon Johnson* (New York: Penguin Books, 1990).

3. Ibid.

4. Ibid.

5. Lawrence Hogan, *A Black National News Service: The Associated Negro Press and Claude Barnett* (Haworth, NJ: St. Johann Press, 2002).

6. Gunnar Myrdal, *An American Dilemma: The Negro Problem and American Democracy* (Piscataway, NJ: Transaction, 1944). A scholarly history of the black press cries out to be written. For scholarly studies that focus on aspects of black journalism, see Andrew Buni, *Robert Vann of the Pittsburgh Courier: Politics and Black Journalism* (Pittsburgh: University of Pittsburgh Press, 1974); Hogan, *A Black National News Service*; Roi Ottley, *The Lonely Warrior: The Life and Times of Robert S. Abbott* (Washington, DC: H. Regnery, 1955).

7. "LaForce, Veteran Trainer of Pirates Is Dead," *Kansas City Call*, February 12, 1922.

8. Ibid.

9. Ibid.

10. James Overmyer in Lawrence Hogan et al., *Shades of Glory*. The *Baltimore Afro-American* of October 29, 1920, takes the origins of baseball much further back in time, and to a place very different from where we are normally located when it comes to the telling of the origins story. In doing so, the paper takes a swipe at the integrity of the white game of baseball that at the time was beset with the "Black Sox" 1919 throwing of the World Series scandal. As the *Afro-American* has it, "Baseball first started in Africa, reports a mosaic uncovered by archeologists in Carthage. The tablet shows members of the Carthaginian '44' playing a game which is apparently the original of

baseball, but the mosaic bears no indications of an attempt by Carthage to 'throw' a world series to Rome."

11. Ric Roberts interview in Henry LaBrie Collection, Columbia University Oral History Office.

12. Ralph Ellison, *Shadow and Act* (New York: New American Library, 1964).

CHAPTER 2

1. John Hope Franklin, *From Slavery to Freedom: A History of African Americans,* 7th ed. (New York: Alfred Knopf, 2007).

2. Frank Rollin, *The Life and Public Service of Martin R. Delaney* (New York: Ayer, 1970—originally published in 1883).

3. Speech by Frederick Douglass on Dred Scott Decision, May 1857, Teaching American History.org.

4. Albert Murray, *The Omni-Americans: New Perspectives on Black Experience and American Culture* (New York: Da Capo, 1990) and *Stomping the Blues* (New York: Da Capo, 1989).

5. Mark Twain quote as found on website, *Baseball and America's Streetcars in the 19th Century,* by Robert C. Cullen.

6. All slave commentaries come from the Internet *American Memory* site at National Archives. It can be expected that a more extensive search of slave interviews will reveal more references to baseball in slavery times than were found for this study.

7. Ibid.

8. Hogan et al., *Shades of Glory.*

9. Ibid., 18.

10. George White, *Congressional Record,* 56th Congress, 2nd Session (January 29, 1901).

11. J.A. Harrison Memoirs, personal collection of Lawrence Hogan.

12. Ibid.

13. Ibid.

14. Ibid.

15. Hogan et al., *Shades of Glory;* Jerry Malloy, "The Birth of the Cuban Giants: The Origins of Black Professional Baseball," *Nine: A Journal of Baseball History and Social Perspectives* 2 (Spring 1994): 233–47.

16. R. G. Mackey, "Pop Watkins Is World's Greatest Baseball Scout," *Baltimore Afro-American,* July 13, 1923; R. G. Mackey, *Sports Mirror,* July 25, 1925. See also Agate Type website by Gary Achwell for a rich presentation of John "Pop" Watkins; "Pop Watkins Is Dead," *Pittsburgh Courier,* March 8, 1924. For Dixon and Cockrell, see James Riley, *The Biographical*

Encyclopedia of the Negro Baseball Leagues (New York: Carroll and Graf, 1994); *Cleveland Advocate*, March 29, 1919, and April 19, 1919. University archivist at Manhattan College, Amy Suark reports that "unfortunately I did not find any reference to John 'Pop' Watkins coaching the Jaspers during the 1904 season, or any season before or after. All the materials relating to the team mention only the players. Even photographs I have found of the team feature just the players. The 1904 season was one of the best in the history of the sport at the college. I am not sure if 13 members went professional, but I do know that quite a few went on to play for either major or minor teams. I counted at least nine. I am not sure which Negro teams Watkins played for, but I do know that Manhattan College did play the Cuban X Giants at that time" (c. 1902–1905). North Carolina College for Negroes is today's North Carolina Central University.

17. Ibid.

18. For Johnson obituary, see *Findlay Ohio Morning News*, October 6, 1953.

19. Riley, *The Biographical Encyclopedia*.

20. Sol White, *Sol White's History of Colored Baseball with Other Documents on the Early Black Game, 1886–1936* (Lincoln, NE: University of Nebraska Press, 1996—originally published as *Sol White's Official Base Ball Guide*, 1907).

21. "Fun with the Colored Boys," *Cleveland Leader*, May 10, 1883.

CHAPTER 3

1. Rayford Logan, *The Betrayal of the Negro from Rutherford B. Hayes to Woodrow Wilson* (New York: Da Capo Press, 1997). Logan's book has long been a standard work for the political and social sides of where black Americans stood at the turn into the 20th century. For the black baseball at this juncture, see relevant chapters in Lawrence Hogan et al., *Shades of Glory*.

2. Edwin S. Redkey, *Respect Black: The Writings and Speeches of Henry McNeal Turner* (New York: Arno Press, 1971).

3. Ibid.

4. David Zang, *Fleet Walker's Divided Heart* (Lincoln, NE: University of Nebraska Press, 1995).

5. Ibid.

6. Countee Cullen, "Heritage," in *My Soul's High Song: The Collected Writings of Countee Cullen* (New York: Anchor Books, 1994).

7. Frederick Douglass, "Colonization," *The North Star*, January 23, 1849.

8. Logan, *The Betrayal of the Negro.*

9. John Hope Franklin, *From Slavery to Freedom* (New York: Alfred Knopf, 1998).

10. Ibid.

11. Robert Brisbane, *The Negro Vanguard: Origins of the Negro Social Revolution, 1900–1960* (Valley Forge, PA: The Judson Press, 1970).

12. Ibid.

13. Ibid.

14. Walter White, *A Man Called White* (Athens, GA: University of Georgia Press, 1948).

15. Murray, *The Omni Americans.*

16. John B. Holway, *The Complete Book of Baseball's Negro Leagues: The Other Half of Baseball History* (Winter Park, FL: Hastings House, 2001).

17. Ibid.

18. Ibid.

19. Ibid.

20. Guy Johnson, *John Henry: Tracking Down a Negro Legend* (Chapel Hill, NC: University of North Carolina Press, 1929).

21. Henry Whitey Gruhler interview with Lawrence Hogan for "Before You Can Say 'Jackie Robinson'" (BYCSJR) documentary.

22. John Henry Lloyd plaque in Shrine Room of National Baseball Hall of Fame.

23. "Pop Lloyd Stadium Dedication," *Atlantic City Press,* October 3, 1949.

24. Gruhler interview with Lawrence Hogan for BYCSJR.

25. Press Release, November 6, 1929, *Associated Negro Press,* Claude Barnett Papers, Chicago Historical Society.

26. "John Lloyd Back in Town," *New York Amsterdam News,* March 28, 1928.

27. Johnson, *John Henry.*

28. Pepe Conte, "Greatest Figure of Our National Game," *New York Amsterdam News,* November 9, 1928.

29. Romeo Dougherty, *New York Amsterdam News,* November 9, 1927.

30. Johnson, *John Henry.*

31. Rollo Wilson, "Eastern Snapshots," *Pittsburgh Courier,* November 15, 1924.

32. *Baltimore Afro-American,* April 6, 1923.

33. Ibid.

34. *Chicago Defender,* March 1, 1919.

35. Ibid.

36. Henry "Whitey" Gruhler and Max Manning interviews with Lawrence Hogan for BYCSJR.

37. James Riley, *The Biographical Encyclopedia of the Negro Baseball Leagues* (New York: Carroll and Graf, 1994).

38. Ibid.

39. Ibid.

40. "Dedication of Pop Lloyd Stadium," *Atlantic City Press,* October 3, 1949.

41. Johnson, *John Henry.*

42. Ibid.

43. Ann Charters, *Nobody: The Story of Bert Williams* (London: The Macmillan Company, 1970).

44. Ernest Thayer, "Casey at the Bat," *San Francisco Examiner,* June 3, 1888.

45. *New York Age,* June 4, 1908.

46. Ibid.

47. "Nobody," music by Bert Williams, lyrics by Alex Rodgers, 1905.

48. Charters, *Nobody.*

49. Sol White, *Sol White's History of Colored Base Ball.*

50. "Nobody"; White, *Official Baseball Guide.*

51. *New York Age,* June 4, 1908.

52. Press Release, March 7, 1922, *Associated Negro Press,* Claude Barnett Papers, Chicago Historical Society.

53. *Kansas City Call,* March 18, 1922.

54. Ibid.

55. "Nobody."

56. *Kansas City Call,* March 18, 1922.

57. Ibid.

58. Ibid.

59. Ibid.

60. Ira Lewis, "The Passing Review," *Pittsburgh Courier,* March 21, 1925.

61. Bart Giblin interview with Lawrence Hogan for BYCSJR.

62. Henry "Whitey" Gruhler interview with Lawrence Hogan for BYCSJR.

63. Rollo Wilson, "Eastern Snapshots," *Pittsburgh Courier,* April 10, 1926.

64. Rollo Wilson, "Eastern Snapshots," *Pittsburgh Courier,* April 10, 1926; July 17, 1926.

65. Ibid.

66. Wilson, "Eastern Snapshots," *Pittsburgh Courier,* March 29, 1924.

67. *Baltimore Afro-American,* July 30, 1927.

68. *Chicago Defender,* June 24, 1919.

69. St. Claire Bourne, *New York Amsterdam News,* August 22, 1939.

70. Ibid.

71. *Baltimore Afro-American,* July 30, 1927.

72. Fay Young, "Fay Says," *Chicago Defender,* April 5, 1924.

73. Ibid.

74. *Pittsburgh Courier,* April 4, 1935.

75. Ibid., December 6, 1924.

76. Ibid., June 8, 1926.

77. *New York Amsterdam News,* July 7, 1927.

78. Ibid.

79. Ibid.

80. "Idol of Cuban Fans," *Baltimore Afro-American,* April, 1925.

81. W.E.B. Du Bois, "Returning Soldiers," *The Crisis* XVIII (May 1919), p. 13.

82. Ibid.

83. This poem by Andy Razaf, a takeoff of the famous poem by John McCrae, was first published in 1923 in the *New York Amsterdam News.* It reappeared in 1927 with a *News* editorial comment about the high quality and fine race focus of Razaf's writing as compared to the prominence accorded those making capital by pandering to the whims of the Greenwich Village intellectuals—an obvious swipe at the poets of the Harlem Renaissance.

84. "Rube Takes to Air," *Chicago Defender,* April 12, 1919.

85. Ibid.

86. Riley, *The Biographical Encyclopedia.*

87. W. Rollo Wilson, *The Pittsburgh Courier,* August 24, 1924.

88. Peterson, *Only the Ball Was White.*

89. Ibid.

CHAPTER 4

1. Alain Locke, "Enter the New Negro," *Survey Graphic* (March 1925 special edition), Harlem: Mecca of the New Negro, p 1–6.

2. Langston Hughes, "The Negro Artist and the Racial Mountain," *Nation Magazine,* June 23, 1926.

3. Rollin Lynde Hartt, "The New Negro. When He's Hit, He Hits Back!" *Independent,* January 15, 1921, pp. 59–60, 76.

4. Ibid.

5. "MEET WILLS—DASS ALL" by Chas Griffin, Buffalo, N.Y. in "The Sportive Spotlight," *New York Amsterdam News,* March 10, 1926. Jack

Cavanaugh, *Gene Tunney: Boxing's Brainiest Champ and His Upset of the Great Jack Dempsey* (New York: Random House, 2006). Useful individual titles for the 1920s as the Golden Age of Sport include Robert Creamer, *Babe* (New York: Simon and Schuster, 1974); Alison Danzig and Peter Brandwein, ed., *Sports Golden Age: A Close-Up of the Fabulous Twenties* (New York: Harper Brothers, 1948); Frank Deford, *Big Bill Tilden* (New York: Simon and Schuster, 1975); Roger Kahn, *A Flame of Pure Fire: Jack Dempsey and the Roaring Twenties* (New York: Harcourt Brace, 1999); and Grantland Rice, *The Tumult and the Shouting*, (New York: A. S. Barnes and Company, 1954).

6. *Pittsburgh Courier*, March 13, 1926.

7. Ibid.

8. Ibid.

9. Arthur Ashe, *A Hard Road to Glory: A History of the African-American Athlete*, with Kip Branch, Ocania Chalk, and Francis Harris (New York: Warner Books, 1988). For homing pigeon, *Pittsburgh Courier*, September 4, 1926; for Sammy Bush, *Baltimore Afro-American*, February 8, 1924; for Gardner, *Kansas City Call*, August 17, 1928; for billiards, *New York Amsterdam News*, February 16, 1927, and *Chicago Whip*, April 2, 1921; for soccer, *Amsterdam News*, March 9, 1927; for horseshoes, *Kansas City Call*, June 22, 1923; and for bowling, *Amsterdam News*, November 24, 1926. For Howard Lincoln football classic see as typical *Pittsburgh Courier*, November 17, 1923, December 1, 1923, and December15, 1925, "The Football Classic," editorial page; *Baltimore Afro-American*, November 30, 1923; *Chicago Defender*, December 8, 1923. For Robert Ball, *Chicago Defender*, August 6, 1927. Peter McDaniel, *Uneven Lies: The Heroic Story of African American in Golf* (Greenwich, CT: The American Golfer, 2000). *Courier*, September 4, 1926; *Defender*, September 13, 1925. For Harlem Renaissance Five, see Robert Peterson, *From Cages to Jump Shots: Pro Basketball's Early Years* (New York, Oxford University Press, 1990). pp. 11, 12, 95–101. For Tommy Minton, *Courier*, March 13, 1926. Arthur R. Ashe Jr., with the assistance of Kip Branch, Ocania Chalk, and Francis Harris, *A Hard Road to Glory: A History of the African American Athlete, 1919–1945* (New York: Warner Books, 1988), pp. 79–81.

10. G. L. Mackey, "Sports Mirror," *Baltimore African American*, May 23, 1925.

11. Hogan et al., *Shades of Glory*.

12. *Associated Negro Press*, April 6, 1922.

13. Hogan et al., *Shades of Glory*.

14. Ibid.

15. Ibid.

16. Ibid.

17. "Baseball Babble—The Boys Are Off," *Chicago Whip*, January 25, 1921.

18. "Palm Beach Results," *Chicago Whip*, March 5, 1921.

19. Ibid.

20. *Chicago Defender*, March 8, 1924.

21. Ibid.

22. Amiri Baraka, *The Autobiography of LeRoi Jones* (Chicago: Lawrence Hill Books, 1997).

23. Columbia University Oral History Center, Henry LaBrie Collection, interview with Eric "Ric" Roberts.

24. Ralph Ellison, *Shadow and Act* (New York: Vintage, 1995).

25. Murray, *The Omni Americans*.

26. *Preston News Service*, May 29, 1924.

27. Gene Benson to author.

28. Paul Robeson, *Scandalize My Name* (The Classics Record Library). Label: Book of the Month Club, Inc. ASIN: B000I2Z5LY.

29. James Weldon Johnson, *O Black and Unknown Bards*, Poets.org.

30. Robeson, *Scandalize*.

31. Ibid.

32. Ibid.

33. Ibid.

34. Charles Starks, *Kansas City Call*, November 3, 1922. Starks's message was echoed in commentary from the *Baltimore Afro-American Sports* editor: "The real world series baseball games have been played this fall, but the newspapers have not said much about them. Here is how they turned out. Read them Judge Landis and weep. Black Sox licked American League Stars. Bacharach Giants defeated McGraw's New York National leagues. St. Louis Negro League Stars defeated Detroit American white. Indianapolis ABC's split series with Cleveland Indians. Kansas City Negro League beat K.C. Blues, American Association, five out of six. If Jack Dunn had allowed his Orioles to come down to the Black Sox Park the Sox would have. . . . ell, what is the use of going further?"

35. Ibid.

36. Ibid.

37. Ibid.

38. Ibid.

39. Ibid.

40. Ibid.

41. Ibid.

42. Rube Currie, *Kansas City Call*, December 15, 1922.

43. Ibid.

44. Charles Starks, *Kansas City Call*, July 29, 1923.

45. Ibid.

46. Ibid.

47. Langston Hughes, *The Negro Speaks of Rivers*, Poets.org.

48. Charles Starks, *Kansas City Call*, July 29, 1923, and November 3, 1923; Rube Currie, *Kansas City Call*.

49. Roi Ottley, *The Lonely Warrior: The Life and Times of Robert Abbott* (New York: Henry Regenery, 1955). The poem is titled "Bound for the Promised Land."

50. Allan Spear, *Black Chicago: The Making of a Negro Ghetto, 1890–1920* (Chicago: University of Chicago Press, 1967).

51. John Condon, "The Great 12 Inning Game," *New York Age*, August 7, 1923.

52. Ibid.

CHAPTER 5

1. Clement Price interview with Lawrence Hogan for "Before You Can Say 'Jackie Robinson'" (BYCSJR) documentary.

2. John B. Holway, *Voices from the Great Black Baseball Leagues* (New York: Da Capo Press, 1992); David Malarcher, "Oscar Charleston," *SABR Research Journal Archive*, http://research.sabr.org/journals/oscar-charleston.

3. Hogan et al., *Shades of Glory*.

4. Ibid.

5. Malarcher, "Oscar Charleston."

6. "Charleston Has a Busy Day," *Baltimore Afro-American*, July 31, 1926.

7. Malarcher, "Oscar Charleston."

8. Alvin Moses, *Chicago Whip*, January 21, 1921.

9. Malarcher, "Oscar Charleston."

10. *Chicago Whip*, January 21, 1921.

11. Oscar Charleston plaque in Shrine Room of National Baseball Hall of Fame.

12. Ibid.

13. "Ruth Gets Home Run Off of Redding," *Baltimore Afro-American*, October 8, 1920.

14. "Babe Ruth of Eastern League," *Pittsburgh Courier*, September 14, 1924,.

15. "A Colored Babe Ruth," *Chicago Whip*, March 20, 1920; Jorge S. Figueredo, "November 4, 1920: The Day Torriente Outclassed Ruth,"

SABR Research Journals Archives, http://research.sabr.org/journals/ day-torriente-outclassed-ruth.

16. Ibid.

17. Babe Ruth, "Home Run King Gives Pointers," *Baltimore Afro-American,* June 10, 1921. Ruth's instruction piece appears to be a syndicated article reprint from the *Washington Herald,* and is found in the *Chicago Defender,* April 18, 1921.

18. The best account of Babe Ruth's relationship with African American baseball and its players is Bill Jenkinson's fine study *The Year Babe Ruth Hit 104 Home Runs* (New York: Da Capo, 2007). Supplementing and extending Jenkinson's account is his fine analysis of Ruth's relationship with African Americans and Negro Leaguers in the essay "Babe Ruth and Race" found on Jenkinson's Internet site, *Bill Jenkinson, Baseball.*

19. *Kansas City Call,* October 20, 1922.

20. *Kansas City Call,* October 27, 1922.

21. *Chicago Defender,* April 18, 1931.

22. W.E.B. Du Bois, "Foreword," in *Bronze: A Book of Verse,* ed. Georgia Douglas Johnson (Boston: B.J. Brimmer Co., 1922). "Those who know what it means to be a colored woman in 1922—and know it not so much in fact as in feeling, apprehension, unrest and delicate yet strong thought—must read Georgia Douglas Johnson's *Bronze.* Much of it will not touch this reader and that, and some of it will mystify and puzzle them as a sort of reiteration and over-emphasis. But none can fail to be caught here and there by a word—a phrase—a period that tells a life history or even paints the history of a generation. Can you not see that marching of the mantled with voices strange to ecstasy? Have you ever looked on the 'twilight faces' of their throngs, or seen the black mother with her son when her heart is sandaling his feet? Or can you not conceive that infinite sorrow of a dark child wandering the world seeking the breast of an unknown face! I hope Mrs. Johnson will have wide reading. Her word is simple, sometimes trite, but it is singularly sincere and true, and as a revelation of the soul struggle of the women of a race it is invaluable."

23. Ibid. Georgia Douglas Johnson, "Black Woman," *Poets.org,* http://www.poets.org/viewmedia.php/prmMID/19686.

24. Ibid.

25. *New York Age,* July 18, 1925.

26. Curiously enough the Alfred Lawson identified in numerous black newspaper reportage on the Continental League story as the proposer of this league appears not to be the actual Lawson who attempted to organize the

interracial Continental League. That "honor" belongs to his brother George, who often went by the nickname "Andy." Historian Jerry Kuntz, who has done the definitive research on this story, reports in a letter to the author that "many sportswriters confused the two brothers, thinking that they were the same man. And who can blame them? What are the odds that two brothers would gain infamy as egotistical con-men specializing in minor league scams? George Lawson also frequently used nicknames and aliases, which added confusion. In baseball he frequently used his nickname Andy Lawson. George/Andy's brother Al Lawson (who the Black press mistakenly identifies as the organizer of the Continental League) left baseball for good by 1916. By 1921 he was deeply involved in trying to launch the first national airline. In our narrative I leave stand the Black press' identification of Al Lawson as the organizer of the Continental League as that is the way this story would have come to readers of Black newspapers."

27. *Baltimore Afro-American,* May 6, 1921.

28. Dave Wyatt, *Chicago Whip,* January 22, 1921.

29. Ibid.

30. Ibid.

31. Dave Wyatt, "The Continental League," *Chicago Whip,* March 12, 1921.

32. Ibid.

33. Ibid.

34. *The Sporting News,* December 6, 1923, reprinted in the *Chicago Defender,* December 29, 1923.

35. Ibid.

36. Ibid.

37. Ibid. Rollo Wilson commented interestingly on the flogging charge: "And now a big league ball player is alleged to be a woman-beater and member of the K.K.K. Last week there was indicted in Georgia, Bob Hasty, one of Connie Mack's pitchers, along with several others on the charge of flogging a man and a woman. Of course Bob denies the charge, and for the good of the game, we hope he is innocent. At the close of the season Hasty lost a hot pitching duel to Phil Cockrell of Hilldale. If he is a Ku Kluxer we can imagine how he appreciated that licking at the hands of the colored guy." Rollo Wilson, "Eastern Snapshots," *Pittsburgh Courier,* December 1, 1923.

38. Underlying the enmity between Eastern and Western baseball lords was the "sinister" figure of white booking agent Nat Strong. In the *Baltimore Afro-American* of January 12, 1923, Rube Foster, as angry author, went public in an extraordinary piece of accusatory writing linking Ed Bolden to Strong, the later painted as a monopolistic greedy book agent. Also for this story, see *Kansas City Call,* January 19, 1923. Ed Bolden replied to

Foster's charges in *Baltimore Afro-American*, January 23, 1923. In a February 21, 1923, letter to the *New York Amsterdam News* respected sports editor, Romeo Dougherty, Foster condemned Bolden as a "teller of deliberate lies. I know the facts, and the kind of man he really is, and how little he meant to advance the Negro in his profession." The quarrel continued to take up considerable print through the 1923 season, up into the fall, and well into 1924. See Rollo Wilson, "The Sportive Realm," *Pittsburgh Courier*, September 1, 1923; "No Peace in Baseball Says Rube Foster," *Baltimore Afro-American*, February 8, 1924, with accompanying cartoon; *Chicago Defender*, August 3, 1924.

39. For agitation for Word Series, see *Pittsburgh Courier*, August 2, 1924; "Word Series between East and West Seems Possible," *Chicago Defender*, August 30, 1924; "Judge Landis Offers to Arbitrate," *Chicago Defender*, September 6, 1924; "World Series October 3," *Chicago Defender*, September 13, 1924. For John Lloyd on Rube Foster, see "John Lloyd Back from Cuba," *Baltimore Afro-American*, April 6, 1923.

40. *Chicago Defender*, September 27, 1924.

41. *Chicago Defender*, September 14, 1924.

42. *Chicago Defender*, September 27, 1924.

43. *Chicago Defender*, October 1, 1924.

44. *Kansas City Call*, October 14, 1924.

45. *Kansas City Call*, October 24, 1924.

46. Ibid.

47. *Chicago Defender*, September 27, 1924; October 1, 1924; October 25, 1924;, November 15, 1924.

48. *Pittsburgh Courier*, November 24, 1924.

49. *Pittsburgh Courier*, October 11, 1924; *Kansas City Call*, October 14, 1924 and October 24, 1924.

50. *Chicago Defender*, October 18, 1924.

51. Ibid.

52. *Kansas City Call*, April 3, 1925.

53. *Chicago Defender*, April 3, 1926.

54. *Chicago Defender*, October 18, 1924.

55. Sterling Brown, "Strong Men," *National Humanities Center* (2007), nationalhumanitiescenter.org/pds/. Originally published in *The Book of American Negro Poetry*, ed. James Weldon Johnson (New York: Harcourt, Brace, 1931); later published in *Southern Road* (New York: Harcourt, Brace, 1932), Brown's first book of poems; reprinted in *The Collected Poems of Sterling A. Brown* (New York: Harper & Row, 1980).

56. *Pittsburgh Courier*, July 31, 1926.

57. *Baltimore Afro-American,* August 5, 1933.

58. Ibid.

59. *Kansas City Call,* September 21, 1922.

60. *Baltimore Afro-American,* October 19, 1921.

61. Sterling Brown, "Strong Men."

62. *Baltimore Afro-American,* October 21, 1921.

63. *Baltimore Afro-American,* July 13, 1923.

64. Ibid.

65. *Baltimore Afro-American,* August 3, 1933.

66. Ibid.

67. *Pittsburgh Courier,* July 31, 1926; *Baltimore Afro-American,* October 19, 1921; July 13, 1923; and August 5, 1933.

68. Fay Young, "Fay Says," *Chicago Defender,* July 2, 1927.

69. "An If for Girls," *Baltimore Afro-American,* November 11, 1923.

70. White, "Eastern Sporting World," *Chicago Defender,* June 1, 1919.

71. "Pop Ups from Mr. Wiselogy," "Girl Ushers for Monarchs," *Kansas City Call,* March 25, 1922.

72. "Female Pitching Ace Is Mainstay of Southern Club," *Pittsburgh Courier,* July 18, 1925.

73. *Chicago Defender,* March 26, 1927.

74. "Bloomer Girls Play Saturday," *Baltimore Afro-American,* April 18, 1922.

75. "N.Y. Bloomer Girls Swamp BSB Birls," *Baltimore Afro-American,* April 25, 1922.

76. Ibid.

77. Ibid.

78. Ibid.

79. "Girls Games Is Attracting Much Attention," *Pittsburgh Courier,* August 14, 1926.

80. Ibid.

81. Ibid.

82. Henry "Whitey" Gruhler interview with Lawrence Hogan for BYCSJR.

83. Robert Queen interview with Lawrence Hogan for BYCSJR.

84. Leonard Wilkerson interview with Lawrence Hogan for BYCSJR.

85. "Shortstop Moore, The Fried Pie Man," *Chicago Defender,* July 8, 1922.

86. "Near Riot Stops Game," *Chicago Defender,* May 13, 1922.

87. "Rowdyism May Case Monarchs to Lose Park," *Kansas City Call,* June 2, 1922.

88. Rollo Wilson, "Eastern Snapshots," *Pittsburgh Courier,* April 22, 1925.

89. Ibid.

90. Ibid.

91. "Poet's Corner, The Negro National Anthem," *New York Amsterdam News,* July 25, 1923.

92. Ibid.

93. Robert Brisbane, *The Black Vanguard: Origins of the Negro Social Revolution, 1900–1960* (Valley Forge, PA: Judson Press, 1970).

94. John Gray to Editor, *Chicago Defender,* December 3, 1927.

95. J.A. Jackson, "Rival Organizations Select Colored Umpire for Big Sports Event," *Baltimore Afro-American,* January 25, 1924.

96. Hogan, *A Black National News Service.*

97. Juli Jones, *Chicago Defender,* December 16, 1922.

98. Philip Brown letter to Ray Schalk, *Chicago Defender,* June 10, 1928.

99. "Monarchs Trainer," *Kansas City Call,* November 17, 1926; "Monarchs Will Be in Perfect Condition," *Kansas City Call,* March 2, 1928.

100. Ibid.

101. Rollo Wilson, "Eastern Snapshots," *Pittsburgh Courier,* July 11, 1926.

102. *Pittsburgh Courier,* July 11, 1926; *Chicago Whip,* February 25, 1922; and *Chicago Defender,* February 16, 1924.

103. Homer, *The Illiad.*

104. "Rube" Foster, Black Mathewson of National Game, A Great Ball Player Despite His Resemblance to a Barr'l", author not legible, *Albany Times Union,* September 5, 1912.

105. *Pittsburgh Courier,* February 28, 1925 and January 16, 1926; "Netty George Speedy, My Scrapbook of Doers," *Chicago Defender,* October 19, 1925.

106. Ira Lewis, *Pittsburgh Courier,* February 28, 1925.

107. "Faith's Reward," *Chicago Whip,* March 12, 1921.

108. *Pittsburgh Courier,* January 23, 1926, for Ed Lamar commentary. One report has it that Foster's first exposure to the national side of the game came on the white side of the baseball ledger when Connie Mack discovered him during the Philadelphia Athletics' spring training in 1901. He found employment there in warming up young Athletics' pitchers, and pitching to Mack's backstops, and was sent North by the redoubtable Mack himself. The *Chicago Whip* has him coming to Chicago, or at least to the North in 1902 from the Arlington baseball team of Hot Springs, Arkansas, that also gave to black baseball Eugene "Gabbie" Miller reported to be the fastest man whoever trod in baseball shoes. If we accept what Foster himself tells us in an article he wrote for the black press in 1921, his association with the game,

whatever it consisted of, began in 1897. See Dave Wyatt, "Rube Foster as I Knew Him," *Pittsburgh Courier,* January 10, 1931, for an account that differs slightly from the previous one.

109. *Pittsburgh Courier,* January 23, 1926.

110. Ira Lewis, "National Baseball League Formed," *The Competitor,* March 1920.

111. Ibid. While it is clear that Rube Foster played the key role in the establishment of Negro league baseball, the role of Indianapolis ABCs owner C. I. Taylor is often slighted. The sportswriter and black baseball insider Dave Wyatt says about Taylor that "he can rightly be called the father of the idea of organized baseball among colored players. Taylor and Foster almost had a court battle through Taylor's insistency for organized baseball." Taylor himself lays out the case for his influence in citing an extraordinary letter he wrote to Rube Foster in 1916 arguing strongly that the time was now for the organization of a colored baseball league. See "The Future of Colored Baseball," *The Competitor,* February 1920.

112. Rollo Wilson, "Eastern Snapshots," *Pittsburgh Courier,* January 16, 1926.

113. Lewis, "National Baseball League Formed."

114. Rollo Wilson, "Eastern Snapshots," *Pittsburgh Courier,* January 16, 1926.

115. *Chicago Defender,* December 1, 1921; December 19, 1921; December 21, 1921; and December 31, 1921. Andrew Foster was a reporter's dream. He learned early in his career the value of the press, and used it with great effectiveness. He was always a good source for good copy, whether written by the press, or produced by himself. Witness what the *Baltimore Afro-American* did in composing attention-getting headlines for his 1921 series of articles on the state of black baseball. "College Players Ruining Baseball— Greatest Whiskey Drinkers, Greatest Liars, and Biggest Contract Jumpers Are College Players Who Have Turned Professional" reads the banner headline over what Foster had titled "Colored Baseball Players as I Have Known Them." His last piece in the series, which had simply been titled "Colored Umpires," easily becomes in the hands of the *Afro* editor, "Colored Umpires Are Incompetent—Colored Baseball Magnate Says They Don't Know Rules and Are Not Fair and Square." *Baltimore Afro-American,* December 30, 1921 and January 2, 1922.

116. Ibid.

117. Ibid.

118. Ibid.

119. Ibid.

120. Ibid.

121. *Chicago Whip,* March 12, 1921.

122. Dave Wyatt, "Rube Foster as I Knew Him," *Pittsburgh Courier,* December 10, 1930.

123. Homer, *The Illiad.*

124. Carl Beckwith, "End of a Great Career," *Kansas City Call,* September 10, 1926.

125. Dave Wyatt, "Rube Foster as I Knew Him," *Pittsburgh Courier,* December 10, 1930.

126. "Loss of Rube Foster a Hard Blow," *New York Age,* September 11, 1926.

127. Robert Brisbane, *The Black Vanguard: Origins of the Negro Social Revolution, 1900–1960* (Valley Forge, PA: Judson Press, 1970).

128. Ibid.

129. Press Release, July 1929, *Associated Negro Press,* Claude Barnett Papers, Chicago Historical Society, "Present Bill to Repay Slave Owners for Slaves Freed."

CHAPTER 6

1. Leslie Fishel, Jr., "The Negro in the New Deal Era," in *America's Black Past,* ed. Eric Foner (New York: Harper and Row, 1970).

2. The phrase "one third of a nation, ill housed, ill clad, ill fed" was used by Franklin D. Roosevelt during his campaign for the Presidency in 1932.

3. James Weldon Johnson, *Black Manhattan* (New York: Da Capo, 1991); David Levering Lewis, *The Portable Harlem Renaissance Reader* (New York: Penguin, 1995).

4. Lewis, *Portable Harlem Renaissance.*

5. Ibid. "Talented Tenth" references a well-known phrase used by W.E.B. Du Bois to refer to the best and the brightest among his race who bore the responsibility of being race leaders and uplifting their fellow blacks.

6. Ibid.

7. Andrew Buni, *Robert L. Vann of the Pittsburgh Courier: Politics and Black Journalism* (Pittsburgh: University of Pittsburgh Press, 1974).

8. Fishel, "The Negro in the New Deal Era"; Harvard Sitkoff, *A New Deal for Blacks: The Emergence of Civil Rights as a National Issue, Volume I: The Depression Decade* (New York: Oxford University Press, 1981); and T. H. Watkins, *The Great Depression* (New York: Back Bay Books, 1993).

9. Hogan et al., *Shades of Glory.*

10. Ibid.

11. See Rob Ruck in Hogan et al., *Shades of Glory*, "Revival, Recovery, Demise" for a fine account of black baseball in Pittsburgh.

12. *New York Amsterdam News*, September 15, 1934.

13. *Providence Journal*, September 25, 1932, and October 1, 1932.

14. Lawrence Hogan, "Baseball and the Sound of Music," *Memories and Dreams: National Baseball Hall of Fame Magazine* (Spring 2008).

15. Ibid.

16. Amiri Baraka, *The Autobiography of LeRoi Jones* (Chicago: Lawrence Hill and Company, 1995).

17. Albert Murray, *Stomping the Blues* (New York: Da Capo, 1989).

18. Interview with Monte Irvin by Lawrence Hogan.

19. St. Louis Browns Official Roster, 1953.

20. Leon Ruppert, *Inside Baseball*, January 1953.

21. Larry Tye, *Satchel Paige, the Life and Times of an American Legend* (New York: Random House, 2009).

22. Ibid.

23. Ibid.

24. Ned Garvey, *Touching All the Bases* (Pepperpot Production, 2003).

25. Max Manning interview with Lawrence Hogan for "Before You Can Say 'Jackie Robinson'" (BYCSJR) documentary.

26. James Riley, *The Biographical Encyclopedia of the Negro Leagues*.

27. Mal Goode interview with Lawrence Hogan for BYCSJR.

28. Tye, *Satchel Paige*.

29. Bill Cash interview with Lawrence Hogan for BYCSJR.

30. Holway, *The Complete Book of Baseball's Negro Leagues*.

31. "Bill to Reimburse Slave Owners," *Associated Negro Press*, June 25, 1930.

32. Charles Biot interview with Lawrence Hogan for BYCSJR.

33. Ibid.

34. Holway, *The Complete Book of Baseball's Negro Leagues*.

35. Mal Good interview with Lawrence Hogan for BYCSJR.

36. John Craig, *Chappie and Me* (New York: Dodd Meade, 1979).

37. Riley, *Biographical Encyclopedia*.

38. Ibid.

39. Holway, *The Complete Book of Baseball's Negro Leagues*.

40. Riley, *Biographical Encyclopedia*.

41. Holway, *The Complete Book of Baseball's Negro Leagues*.

42. Ibid.

43. Ibid.

44. Ibid.; Riley, *Biographical Encyclopedia*; Clarance Israel interview with Lawrence Hogan for BYCSJR.

45. Clarance Israel interview with Lawrence Hogan for BYCSJR.

46. Ibid.

47. Gene Benson interview with Lawrence Hogan for BYCSJR.

48. Max Manning interview with Lawrence Hogan for BYCSJR; transcript of Geraldine Day induction speech, July 30, 1995, National Baseball Hall of Fame Library.

49. Bill Cash interview with Lawrence Hogan for BYCSJR.

50. Charles Biot interview with Lawrence Hogan for BYCSJR.

51. Robert Luke, *The Baltimore Elite Giants: Sports and Society in the Age of the Negro Leagues* (Baltimore: Johns Hopkins University Press, 2007).

CHAPTER 7

1. Langston Hughes, "Dear Dr. Butts." This is one of a series of essays that Hughes wrote that originally appeared in the *Chicago Defender* during the 1940s and 1950s that were supposedly written by a character named Jesse B. Semple. Satirical in their substance, they were a powerful critique of the way blacks had to live in the United States.

2. Ibid.

3. Richard M. Dalfiume, "The 'Forgotten Years' of the Negro Revolution," *Journal of American History* 55, no. 1 (June 1968): 90–106.

4. Gunnar Myrdal, *An American Dilemma: The Negro and the Problem of Democracy* (Piscataway, NJ: Transaction Publishers, 1995, new edition).

5. Dalfiume, "Forgotten Years."

6. Ibid.

7. Charles Osgood reference in letter from Dr. Peter Curtis to author.

8. Account by June Fiefield, National Baseball Hall of Fame Library. A copy of this letter came to the author from James Gates, Librarian, National Baseball Hall of Fame.

9. Monte Irvin interview with Lawrence Hogan for "Before You Can Say 'Jackie Robinson'" (BYCSJR) documentary.

10. *Sporting News,* December 28, 1945.

11. Gene Benson interview with Lawrence Hogan for BYCSJR.

12. *Pittsburgh Courier,* December 29, 1945.

13. David Malarcher to Robert Peterson, April 21, 1970.

14. Amiri Baraka, *The Autobiography of LeRoi Jones* (Chicago: Lawrence Hill Books, 1997).

15. Ibid.

16. Ibid.

17. Ibid.

18. Ibid.

19. David Malarcher to Robert Peterson, April 21, 1970.

20. John Holway, "James 'Joe' Green," essay in possession of author.

21. Jerry Izenberg, *Through My Eyes: A Sports Writer's 58 Year Journey* (Haworth, NJ: St. Johann Press, 2009).

22. Ibid.

23. Ibid.

24. Ibid.

25. Fay Vincent, *We Would Have Played for Nothing* (New York: Simon and Schuster, 2008).

26. Lawrence Eugene Doby interview for BYCSJR.

27. Wendell Smith, *Pittsburgh Courier,* July 25, 1946.

28. Ibid.

29. James Riley, *Nice Guys Finish First: The Autobiography of Monte Irvin* (New York: Carroll and Graf, 1996).

30. Ibid.

31. Ibid.

32. Ibid.

CHAPTER 8

1. This section has benefited from the work of Adrian Burgos for *Shades of Glory.*

2. Thomas Babington Macaulay, "Horatius at the Bridge," From the Lays of *Ancient Rome. Lays of Ancient Rome* is a collection of narrative poems, or lays, by Thomas Babington Macaulay. Four of these recount heroic episodes from early Roman history with strong dramatic and tragic themes, giving the collection its name. The *Lays* were composed by Lord Macaulay during his spare time, while he was the "legal member" of the Governor-General of India's Supreme Council from 1834 to 1838.

The Roman ballads are preceded by brief introductions, discussing the legends from a scholarly perspective. Macaulay explains that his intention was to write poems resembling those that might have been sung in ancient times. The *Lays* were first published by Longman in 1842, at the beginning of the Victorian Era. They became immensely popular, and were a regular subject of recitation, then a common pastime. The *Lays* were standard reading in British public schools for more than a century. Winston Churchill memorized them while at Harrow School, in order to show that he was capable of mental prodigies, notwithstanding his lackluster academic performance.

3. George Olewnick to Lawrence Hogan, May 5, 1988.

4. David Malarcher to Robert Peterson, April 21, 1970.

5. John Jordan "Buck" O'Neil induction keynote speech, National Baseball Hall of Fame, July 2006.

6. Ibid.

7. Ibid.

8. Ibid.

9. Michael Everett to Lawrence Hogan, April 9, 2008.

10. Sterling Brown, *Strong Men The Book of American Negro Poetry*, ed. James Weldon Johnson (New York: Harcourt, Brace, 1931).

11. Roger Kahn, *The Boys of Summer* (New York: Harper Collins, 1972).

12. Roy Wilkens, *Kansas City Call*, February 3, 1929.

13. Monte Irvin interview with Lawrence Hogan for BYCSJR.

14. Matthew Hogan, seminar paper in possession of his father. "Personal Sports Biography" paper, Education 257, Master's Program at University of California–Berkeley, spring semester, 2001.

Selected Bibliography*

Before You Can Say Jackie Robinson: Black Baseball in America in the Era of the Color Line (BYCSJR). (One-hour video documentary by Lawrence D. Hogan, Thomas C. Guy, Clement Alexander Price, Monte Irvin, and Ray Dandridge. Available from National Baseball Hall of Fame and *Black Enterprise Magazine*.)

Brunson, James. *The Early Image of Black Baseball: Race and Representation in the Popular Press, 1871–1890.* Jefferson, NC: McFarland & Company, Inc., 2009.

Chadwick, Bruce. *When the Game Was Black and White: The Illustrated History of Baseball's Negro Leagues.* New York: Abbeville Press, 1992.

Clark, Dick, and Larry Lester. *The Negro Leagues Book.* Cleveland, OH: Society for American Baseball Research, 1994.

Cvornyek, Robert L., editor, Manley, Effa, and Leon Herbert Hardwick. *Negro Baseball . . . Before Integration.* Haworth, NJ: St. Johann Press, 2006.

Dixon, Phil S., and Patrick Hannigan. *The Negro Baseball Leagues: A Photographic History, 1867–1955.* Mattituck, NY: Amereon House, 1992.

---

* It is not possible to include here the works that explore the areas of the African American experience that go beyond the baseball story and present the larger story of which baseball was a part. This "beyond the baseball literature" selection of works can be accessed at **www.facebook.com/Dr.LawrenceD.Hogan.** Also at that site, to complement and extend *The Forgotten History of African American Baseball*, are a photographic essay, a list of Negro Baseball Stories Still to Be Told, and a section on children's books.

Gay, Timothy M. *Satch, Dizzy & Rapid Robert: The Wild Saga of Interracial Baseball before Jackie Robinson*. New York: Simon and Schuster, 2011.

Hauser, Christopher. *The Negro Leaguers Chronology: Events in Organized Black Baseball, 1920–1948*. Jefferson, NC: McFarland & Company, Inc., 2006.

Heaphy, Leslie A., ed. *Black Baseball and Chicago: Essays on the Players, Teams and Games of the Negro Leagues Most Important City*. Jefferson, NC: McFarland & Company, Inc., 2006.

Heaphy, Leslie A. *The Negro Leagues, 1869–1960*. Jefferson, NC: McFarland & Company, 2002.

Heaphy, Leslie A., ed. *Satchel Paige and Company: Essays on the Kansas City Monarchs, Their Greatest Star, and the Negro Leagues*. Jefferson, NC: McFarland & Company, Inc., 2007.

Hoffbeck, Steven R. *Swinging for the Fences: Black Baseball in Minnesota*. St. Paul: Minnesota Historical Society Press, 2005.

Hogan, Lawrence. "Blackball and the Sound of Music." "Memories and Dreams." Cooperstown, NY: National Baseball Hall of Fame, April–May, 2008.

Holway, John B. *Blackball Stars: Negro League Pioneers*. Westport, CT: Meckler Books, 1988. Reprint, New York: Carroll & Graf Publishers, 1992.

Holway, John B. *Black Ball Tales: Rollicking, All New, True Adventures of the Negro Leagues by the Men Who Lived and Loved Them*. Springfield, VA: Scorpio Books, 2008.

Holway, John B. *Black Diamonds: Life in the Negro Leagues from the Men Who Lived It*. Westport, CT: Meckler Books, 1989. Reprint, New York: Stadium Books, 1991.

Holway, John B. *The Complete Book of Baseball's Negro Leagues: The Other Half of Baseball History*. Fern Park, FL: Hastings House, 2001.

Holway, John B. *Voices from the Great Black Baseball Leagues*. New York: Dodd, Mead Company, 1975. Reprint, New York: DeCapo Press, 1993.

Kelley, Brent. *I Will Never Forget: Interviews with 39 Former Negro League Players*. Jefferson, NC: McFarland & Company, Inc. 2003.

Kelley, Brent. *The Negro Leagues Revisited: Conversations with 66 More Baseball Heroes*. Jefferson, NC: McFarland & Company, Inc. 2000.

Kelley, Brent. *Voices from the Negro Leagues: Conversations with 52 Baseball Standouts*. Jefferson, NC: McFarland & Company, Inc., 1998.

Kirwin, Bill, ed. *Out of the Shadows: African American Baseball from the Cuban Giants to Jackie Robinson*. Lincoln: University of Nebraska Press, 2005.

Lanctot, Neil. *Fair Dealing and Clean Playing: The Hilldale Club and the Development of Black Professional Baseball, 1910–1932*. Jefferson, NC: McFarland & Company, 1994.

Lanctot, Neil. *Negro League Baseball: The Rise and Ruin of a Black Institution*. Philadelphia: University of Pennsylvania Press, 2004.

Lester, Larry. *Baseball's First Colored World Series: The 1924 Meeting of the Hilldale Giants and the Kansas City Monarchs*. Jefferson, NC: McFarland & Company, Inc., 2006.

Lester, Larry. *Black Baseball's National Showcase: The East-West All-Star Games, 1933–1953*. Lincoln: University of Nebraska Press, 2002.

Lomax, Michael E. *Black Baseball Entrepreneurs, 1860–1901: Operating by Any Means Necessary*. Syracuse: Syracuse University Press, 2002.

Luke, Bob. *The Baltimore Elite Giants: Sports & Society in the Age of Negro League Baseball*. Baltimore, MD: Johns Hopkins University Press, 2009.

McNary, Kyle. *Black Baseball: A History of African Americans & the National Game*. New York: Sterling Publishing Co., 2003.

McNary, Kyle. *Black Baseball Out of Season: Pay for Play Outside the Negro Leagues*. Jefferson, NC: McFarland & Company, Inc., 2007.

McNary, Kyle. *The California Winter League*. Jefferson, NC: McFarland & Company, Inc., 2002.

McNeil, William F. *Cool Papas and Double Duties: The All-Time Greats of the Negro Leagues*. Jefferson, NC. McFarland & Company, Inc., 2002.

Motley, Bob, with Bryon Motley. *Ruling over Monarchs, Giants and Stars: Umpiring in the Negro Leagues and Beyond*. Champaign, IL: Sports Publishing, L.L.C, 2007.

Peterson, Robert. *Only the Ball Was White: A History of Legendary Black Players and All-Black Professional Teams*. New York: Oxford University Press, 1992.

Peterson, Todd. *Early Black Baseball in Minnesota: The St. Paul Gophers, Minneapolis Keystones and Other Barnstorming Teams of the Deadball Era*. Jefferson, NC: McFarland & Company, Inc., 2010.

Riley, James. *The Biographical Encyclopedia of the Negro Leagues*. New York: Carroll and Graf, 2002.

Rogosin, Donn. *Invisible Men: Life in the Negro Leagues*. Lincoln: University of Nebraska Press, 2007.

Ruck, Rob. *Sandlot Seasons: Black Sport in Pittsburgh*. Urbana: University of Illinois Press, 1986.

Rust, Arthur George, Jr. *Get That Nigger Off the Field*. New York: Delacorte Press, 1976.

Swanton, Barry. *The Mandak League: Haven for Former Negro League Ballplayers, 1950–1957*. Jefferson, NC: McFarland & Company, Inc., 2006.

White, Sol. *Sol White's History of Colored Base Ball: With Other Documents of the Early Black Game, 1886–1936,* with introduction by Jerry Malloy. Lincoln: University of Nebraska Press, 1995.

Wiggins, David K. *Glory Bound: Black Athletes in a White America*. Syracuse: Syracuse University Press, 1997.

Wiggins, David K., ed. *Out of the Shadows: A Biographical History of African American Athletes*. Fayetteville: University of Arkansas Press, 2006.

Wiggins, David K., and Patrick B. Miller. *Sports and the Color Line: Black Athletes and Race Relations in Twentieth-Century America*. New York: Routledge, 2004.

Wiggins, David K., and Patrick B. Miller. *The Unlevel Playing Field: A Documentary History of the African American Experience in Sport*. Chicago: University of Illinois, Urbana, 2003.

Index

About the Author

LAWRENCE D. HOGAN, PhD, is professor of history emeritus at Union County College in Cranford, New Jersey. He has authored *A Black National News Service: The Associated Negro Press and Claude Barnett,* and is the author and coordinating editor of *Shades of Glory: The Negro Leagues and the Story of African American Baseball.* In 2012 his *So Many Seasons in the Sun: A Century and More of Conversations with Baseball's Greatest Clubhouse Managers* was published by St. Johann Press. He is presently researching and writing *Harlem's First Citizen,* a biography of Reverend John Howard Johnson, who was rector of St. Martin's Episcopal Church throughout most of the 20th century.

For much more on the men and women you've met in *The Forgotten History of African American Baseball,* including a wonderful photographic essay, a section on children's books, and an extended bibliography, please visit the author on Facebook at: www.facebook.com/Dr.LawrenceD.Hogan.